Yc

Withdrawn/ABCL

W9-CSI-902

JAN 0 5 2016

National Security and
Double Government

Praise for *National Security and Double Government*

"Shrewdly updating Walter Bagehot's theory of 'double government,' Michael Glennon shows how present-day Washington really works. In our faux democracy, those we elect to govern serve largely ornamental purposes, while those who actually wield power, especially in the realm of national security, do so chiefly with an eye toward preserving their status and prerogatives. Read this incisive and richly documented book, and you'll understand why."

Andrew J. Bacevich
Professor of History and International Relations
Boston University

"Taking a leaf from Walter Bagehot's thesis of dual government in Britain, Michael Glennon has transported the concept of 'double government' to the United States analyzing the constitutional institutions, or what he calls the 'Madisonian' side; and a cohort of several hundred senior military, diplomatic, and intelligence officials who run the daily business of national security, or what he calls the 'Trumanite' side. This explains the relatively little difference between the Bush 43 and the Obama presidencies. In this brilliant, deeply researched book, Glennon spells out the relation of his overall thesis to contemporary issues such as the Snowden revelations."

Charles G. Cogan
Associate, International Security Program
Belfer Center for Science and International Affairs
Harvard Kennedy School

"*National Security and Double Government* is an important and insightful book. It should be read by anyone concerned that Obama's national security policies differ so little from those of the Bush Administration, and by every in-coming President and her staff."

Morton H. Halperin
Senior Advisor
Open Society Foundations

"In this timely book Michael Glennon provides a compelling argument that America's national security policy is growing outside the bounds of existing government institutions. This is at once a constitutional challenge, but is also a case study in how national security can change government institutions, create new ones, and, in effect, stand-up a parallel state. This is a well-argued book of academic import and policy relevance. It is recommended reading for an informed debate on an issue of great significance."

Vali Nasr
Dean of Johns Hopkins University's School of
Advanced International Studies

"Michael Glennon's *National Security and Double Government* explains why U.S. foreign policy is prone to recurring failure and resistant to genuine reform. Instead of being responsive to citizens or subject to effective checks and balances, U.S. national security policy is in fact conducted by a shadow government of bureaucrats and a supporting network of think tanks, media insiders, and ambitious policy wonks. Presidents may come and go, but the permanent national security establishment inevitably defeats their efforts to chart a new course. Gracefully written and extensively researched, this book is the most penetrating analysis of U.S. foreign policy that I have read in years."

Stephen M. Walt
Robert and Renee Belfer Professor of International Affairs
Harvard Kennedy School

Yours to Keep
Withdrawn/ABCL

National Security and Double Government

Michael J. Glennon

3 9075 05001986 5

OXFORD
UNIVERSITY PRESS

OXFORD
UNIVERSITY PRESS

Oxford University Press is a department of the University of Oxford. It furthers the University's objective of excellence in research, scholarship, and education by publishing worldwide.

Oxford   New York

Auckland   Cape Town   Dar es Salaam   Hong Kong   Karachi   Kuala Lumpur   Madrid
Melbourne   Mexico City   Nairobi   New Delhi   Shanghai   Taipei   Toronto

With offices in

Argentina   Austria   Brazil   Chile   Czech Republic   France   Greece   Guatemala
Hungary   Italy   Japan   Poland   Portugal   Singapore   South Korea
Switzerland   Thailand   Turkey   Ukraine   Vietnam

Oxford is a registered trademark of Oxford University Press in the UK and certain
other countries.

Published in the United States of America by
Oxford University Press
198 Madison Avenue, New York, NY 10016

© Oxford University Press 2015

All rights reserved. No part of this publication may be reproduced, stored in a retrieval
system, or transmitted, in any form or by any means, without the prior permission in
writing of Oxford University Press, or as expressly permitted by law, by license, or under
terms agreed with the appropriate reproduction rights organization. Inquiries concerning
reproduction outside the scope of the above should be sent to the Rights Department,
Oxford University Press, at the address above.

You must not circulate this work in any other form
and you must impose this same condition on any acquirer.

Library of Congress Cataloging-in-Publication Data
Glennon, Michael J., 1947- , author.
National security and double government / Michael J. Glennon.
pages cm
Includes bibliographical references and index.
ISBN 978-0-19-020644-4 ((hardback) : alk. paper)
1. National security—United States—Management. 2. National security—United States—
Decision making. 3. Legislative oversight—United States. 4. Judicial review—
United States. 5. Government accountability—United States. I. Title.
UA23.G643 2015
353.10973—dc23

2014012991

3 5 7 9 8 6 4

Printed in the United States of America on acid-free paper

Note to Readers

This publication is designed to provide accurate and authoritative information in regard to
the subject matter covered. It is based upon sources believed to be accurate and reliable
and is intended to be current as of the time it was written. It is sold with the understanding
that the publisher is not engaged in rendering legal, accounting, or other professional
services. If legal advice or other expert assistance is required, the services of a competent
professional person should be sought. Also, to confirm that the information has not been
affected or changed by recent developments, traditional legal research techniques should be
used, including checking primary sources where appropriate.

*(Based on the Declaration of Principles jointly adopted by a Committee of the
American Bar Association and a Committee of Publishers and Associations.)*

**You may order this or any other Oxford University Press publication
by visiting the Oxford University Press website at www.oup.com**

For J. Norvill Jones

In framing a government which is to be administered by men over men, the great difficulty lies in this: you must first enable the government to control the governed; and in the next place oblige it to control itself.

—*James Madison*, THE FEDERALIST NO. 51

CONTENTS

ACKNOWLEDGMENTS

This book would not have been possible without the generosity of many people. I am grateful to Artin Afkhami, Ashley Belyea, Mike Eckel, Ian Johnstone, Robert Hillman, William Martel, John Perry, Luca Urech, and Fletcher political science workshop participants for insightful comments on an earlier draft. Beaudre Barnes, Julia Brooks, Claudio Guler, Amy Tan, and Cecilia Vogel provided cheerful and indefatigable research assistance. The book expands an article, "National Security and Double Government," that initially appeared at page 1, volume 5 of the *Harvard National Security Journal* (copyright 2014 by the Presidents and Fellows of Harvard College and Michael J. Glennon). The staff of the *Journal* contributed considerably in form and substance as the article evolved; Heather Alpino, Catherine Arney, Aaron Blacksberg, Michael Dziuban, Brian Kelly, Samuel Beswick, and the rest of the *Journal* article team deserve special thanks. Innumerable Trumanites and Madisonians, past and present, with whom I have thought, talked, and worked over the years, shaped the ideas expressed in this book. My debt to Joanna Glennon is vast and inexpressible.

CHAPTER 1

✦

Introduction

Few who follow world events can doubt that the Obama administration's approach to multiple national security issues has been essentially the same as that of the Bush administration.[1] The Obama administration, like its predecessor, has sent terrorism suspects overseas for detention and interrogation;[2] claimed the power to hold, without trial, American citizens who are accused of terrorism in military confinement;[3] insisted that it is for the President to decide whether an accused terrorist will be tried by a civilian court or a military tribunal;[4] kept the military prison at Guantánamo Bay open,[5] argued that detainees cannot challenge the conditions of their confinement,[6] and restricted detainees' access to legal counsel;[7] resisted efforts to extend the right of habeas corpus to other offshore prisons;[8] argued that detainees cannot invoke the Geneva Conventions in habeas proceedings;[9] denied detainees access to the International Committee of the Red Cross for weeks at a time;[10] engaged the United States in a military attack against Libya without congressional approval, in the face of no actual or imminent threat to the nation;[11] and continued, and in some respects expanded, the Bush administration's ballistic missile defense program.[12]

The Obama administration, beyond ending torture, has changed "virtually none" of the Bush administration's Central Intelligence Agency (CIA) programs and operations,[13] except that in continuing targeted killings, the Obama adminis- tration has increased the number of covert drone strikes in Pakistan to six times the number launched during the Bush administration.[14] The Obama administration has declined to prosecute those who committed torture (after the President himself concluded that waterboarding is torture);[15] approved the targeted killing of American citizens (Anwar al-Awlaqi and a compatriot[16]) without judicial warrant;[17] rejected efforts by the press and Congress to release legal opinions justifying those killings or describing the breadth of the claimed power;[18] and opposed legislative proposals to expand intelligence oversight notification requirements.[19] His administration has increased the role of covert special operations,[20] continuing each of the covert action programs that President Bush handed down.[21] The Obama administration has continued the Bush administra- tion's cyberwar against Iran (code-named "Olympic Games")[22] and sought to block lawsuits challenging the legality of other national security measures,[23] often claiming the state secrets privilege.[24]

The Obama administration has also continued, and in some ways expanded, Bush-era surveillance policies. For example, the Obama administration continued to intercept the communica- tions of foreign leaders;[25] further insisted that GPS devices may be used to keep track of certain citizens without probable cause or judicial review[26] (until the Supreme Court disapproved[27]); continued to investigate individuals and groups under Justice Department guidelines rewritten in 2008 to permit "assess- ments" that require no "factual basis" for FBI agents to conduct secret interviews, plant informants, and search government and commercial databases;[28] stepped up the prosecution of gov- ernment whistleblowers who uncovered illegal actions,[29] using the 1917 Espionage Act eight times during his first administration to prosecute leakers (it had been so used only three times in the previous ninety-two years);[30] demanded that businesses turn over personal information about customers in response to "national security letters" that require no probable cause and cannot legally be disclosed;[31] continued broad National Security Agency (NSA) homeland surveillance;[32] seized two months of phone records of reporters and editors of the Associated Press for more than twenty telephone lines of its offices and journalists, including their home phones and cellphones, without notice;[33] through the NSA, collected the telephone records of millions of Verizon customers, within the United States and between the United States and other countries, on an "ongoing, daily basis" under an order that prohibited Verizon from revealing the operation;[34] and tapped into the central servers of nine leading U.S. Internet companies, extracting audio and video chats, photographs, emails, documents, and connection logs that enable analysts to track foreign targets and U.S. citizens.[35] At least one significant NSA surveillance program, involving the collection of data on the social connections of U.S. citizens and others located within the United States, was initiated after the Bush administration left office.[36]

These and related policies were formulated and carried out by numerous high- and mid-level national security officials who served in the Bush administration and continued to serve in the Obama administration.[37]

Given Senator Obama's powerful criticism of such policies before he took office as President, the question,[38] then, is this: Why does national security policy remain constant even when one President is replaced by another, who as a candidate repeatedly, forcefully, and eloquently promised fundamental changes in that policy?[39]

Various hypotheses have been suggested. One asserts the substantive correctness of the Bush/Obama policies as a response to perceived security threats. The continuity of national security policy under politically differing presidents, according to this view, demonstrates the essential rightness of those policies and President Obama's open-mindedness.[40] With greater knowledge and responsibility have come understanding and consensus. A second set of answers emphasizes domestic politics and personality. These relate to Obama personally, suggesting that he was never sincere, or that he has no core beliefs, or that he was well-intentioned but ineffectual, or that he simply sold out. The political context, it is suggested, has reinforced these personality traits: only a leader able to act out-of-type can realistically be expected to effect fundamental policy change, as did, for example, Franklin Roosevelt with Wall Street, Richard Nixon with China, and Bill Clinton with welfare. According to this approach, a hairpin turn in U.S. national security policy cannot be pulled off by a black liberal academic with the middle name of Hussein.

The scholarly literature offers two broad, conflicting models that embrace and elaborate these popular explanations.[41] On the one hand, the "rational actor" model predicts that, regardless of the identity of the decision maker, policy will be chosen rationally based on an objective assessment of threats and the relative costs and benefits of competing options to address those threats. The "government politics" model, on the other hand, has it that decisions result from bargaining among individual governmental actors, focusing on characteristics such as their perceptions, preferences, position, and "clout."

Neither of these two conjectures can be dismissed out of hand. For reasons that I spell out later,[42] however, neither is satisfactory. I present what seems a better though disquieting explanation. It borrows from the approach suggested in 1867 by Walter Bagehot to explain the evolution of the English Constitution.[43] Bagehot brought *The Economist* magazine to prominence; his own eminence became such that the middle years of nineteenth-century England were sometimes referred to as the "Age of Bagehot."[44] While not without critics, his theory has been widely acclaimed and has generated significant commentary.[45] Indeed, it is something of a classic on the subject of institutional change, and it foreshadowed modern organizational theory, discussed in chapter 5.[46] In brief, Bagehot's notion was as follows.

Power in Britain reposed initially in the monarch alone. Over the decades, however, a dual set of institutions emerged.[47] One set comprises the monarchy and the House of Lords.[48] These Bagehot called the "dignified" institutions—dignified in the sense that they provide a link to the past and excite the public imagination.[49] Through theatrical show, pomp, and historical symbolism, they exercise an emotional hold on the public mind by evoking the grandeur of ages past.[50] They embody memories of greatness. Yet it is a second, newer set of institutions— Britain's "efficient" institutions—that do the real work of governing.[51] These are the House of Commons, the Cabinet, and the Prime Minister.[52] As Bagehot put it: "[I]ts dignified parts are very complicated and somewhat imposing, very old and rather venerable; while its efficient part ... is decidedly simple and rather modern.... Its essence is strong with the strength of modern simplicity; its exterior is august with the Gothic grandeur of a more imposing age."[53]

Together these institutions make up a "disguised republic"[54] that obscures the massive shift in power that has occurred, which if widely understood would create a crisis of public confidence.[55] This crisis has been averted because the efficient institutions have been careful to hide where they begin and where the dignified institutions end.[56] They do this by ensuring that the dignified institutions continue to partake in at least some real governance and also by ensuring that the efficient institutions partake in at least some inspiring public ceremony and ritual.[57] This promotes continued public deference to the efficient institutions' decisions and continued belief that the dignified institutions retain real power.[58] These dual institutions, one for show and the other for real, afford Britain expertise and experience in the actual art of governing while at the same time providing a façade that generates public acceptance of the experts' decisions. Bagehot called this Britain's "double government."⁵⁹ The structural duality, some have suggested, is a modern reification of the "Noble Lie" that, two millennia before, Plato had thought necessary to insulate a state from the fatal excesses of democracy and to ensure deference to the golden class of efficient guardians.⁶⁰

Bagehot's theory may have overstated the naiveté of Britain's citizenry. When he wrote, probably few Britons believed that Queen Victoria actually governed. Nor is it likely that Prime Minister Lord Palmerston, let alone 658 members of the House of Commons, could or did consciously and intentionally conceal from the British public that it was really they who governed. Big groups keep big secrets poorly. Nonetheless, Bagehot's enduring insight—that dual institutions of governance, one public and the other concealed, evolve side by side to maximize both legitimacy and efficiency—is worth pondering as one possible explanation of why the Obama and Bush national security policies have been essentially the same. There is no reason in principle why the institutions of Britain's juridical offspring, the United States, ought to be immune from the broader bifurcating forces that have driven British institutional evolution.

As it did in the early days of Britain's monarchy, power in the United States lay initially in one set of institutions—the presidency, Congress, and the courts. These are America's "dignified" institutions. Later, however, a second institution emerged to safeguard the nation's security. This, America's "efficient" institution (actually, as will be seen, more a network than an institution), consists of the several hundred executive officials who sit atop the military, intelligence, diplomatic, and law enforcement departments and agencies that have as their mission the protection of America's international and internal security. Large segments of the public continue to believe that America's constitutionally established, dignified institutions are the locus of governmental power. By promoting that impression, both sets of institutions maintain public support. But when it comes to defining and protecting national security, the public's impression is mistaken. America's efficient institution makes most of the key decisions concerning national security, removed from public view and from the constitutional restrictions that check America's dignified institutions. The United States has, in short, moved beyond a mere imperial presidency to a bifurcated system—a structure of double government—in which even the President now exercises little substantive control over the overall direction of U.S. national security policy. Whereas Britain's dual institutions evolved toward a concealed republic, America's have evolved in the opposite direction, toward greater centralization, less accountability, and emergent autocracy.

The parallels between U.S. and British constitutionalism are, of course, inexact. In the United States, the transfer of power has not been purposeful, as Bagehot implied it was in Britain.[61] Members of America's efficient institutions have not secretly colluded in some dark plot aimed at wresting control over national security from its dignified institutions. What may appear in these institutions' collective motivation as conscious parallelism has in fact been a wholly open and, indeed, unabashed response to incentives deeply rooted in the legal and political structures in which they operate.

Some of the evolutionary drivers, on the other hand, have been similar in both countries. Electoral incapacity, for example, has been key. Organized deception would be unnecessary, Bagehot suggested, and the trappings of monarchy could be dispensed with, if Britain's population had been generally well-educated, well-off, and politically intelligent.[62] But he believed it was not.[63] The lower and middle classes were "narrow-minded, unintelligent, incurious";[64] they found educated discourse "unintelligible, confused and erroneous."[65] Bagehot wrote: "A life of labour, an incomplete education, a monotonous occupation, a career in which the hands are used much and the judgment is used little"[66] had produced "the last people in the world to whom...an immense nation would ever give" controlling authority.[67] No one will ever tell them that, of course: "A people *never* hears censure of itself,"[68] least of all from political candidates. The road to public respect (and re-election) lies in ingratiation. So long as their awe and imaginations remain engaged, however, the public could be counted upon to defer—if not to their real rulers, then to what Bagehot referred to as "the theatrical show" that accompanied the apparent rulers.[69] The "wonderful spectacle" of monarchical pomp and pageantry captured the public's imagination, convinced the public that they were not equal to the greatness governance demanded, and induced them to obey.[70]

America's population today is of course far removed from the Dickensian conditions of Victorian England. Yet the economic and educational realities remain stark.[71] Nearly fifty million Americans—more than 16 percent of the population and almost 20 percent of American children—live in poverty.[72] A majority of students in public schools throughout the American South and West meet federal low-income requirements for free and reduced-price meals.[73] A 2009 federal study estimated that thirty-two million American adults, about one in seven, are unable to read anything more challenging than a children's picture book and are unable to understand the side effects of medication listed on a pill bottle.[74] The Council on Foreign Relations reported that the United States has "slipped ten spots in both high school and college graduation rates over the past three decades."[75] One poll found that nearly 25 percent of Americans do not know that the United States declared its independence from Great Britain.[76] A 2011 *Newsweek* survey disclosed that 80 percent did not know who was president during World War I; 40 percent did not know who the United States fought in World War II; 29 percent could not identify the current vice president of the United States; 70 percent did not know that the Constitution is the supreme law of the land; 65 percent did not know what happened at the constitutional convention; 88 percent could not identify any of the writers of the *Federalist Papers;* 27 percent did not know that the President is in charge of the executive branch; 61 percent did not know the length of a Senate term; 81 percent could not name one power conferred on the federal government by the Constitution; 59 percent could not name the Speaker of the House; and 63 percent did not know how many Justices are on the Supreme Court.[77] Far more Americans can name the Three Stooges than any member of the Supreme Court.[78] Other polls have found that 71 percent of Americans believe that Iran already has nuclear weapons[79] and that 33 percent believed in 2007 that Saddam Hussein was personally involved in the 9/11 attacks.[80] In 2006, at the height of U.S. military involvement in the region, 88 percent of American 18- to 24-year-olds could not find Afghanistan on a map of Asia, and 63 percent could not find Iraq or Saudi Arabia on a map of the Middle East.[81] Three-quarters could not find Iran or Israel,[82] and 70 percent could not find North Korea.[83] In 1998—after nearly three decades of often heated debate about the Anti-Ballistic Missile (ABM) Treaty and arguments over related issues such as the proposed Strategic Defense Initiative—two-thirds of Americans mistakenly believed that a missile defense system was already in place.[84] The "over-vote" ballots of several thousand voters—greater in number than the margin of difference between George W. Bush and Al Gore—were rejected in Florida in the 2000 presidential election because voters did not understand that they could vote for only one candidate.[85]

There is, accordingly, little need for purposeful deception to induce generalized deference; in contemporary America as in Bagehot's Britain, a healthy dose of theatrical show goes a long way.

CHAPTER 2

၈၀

The Trumanite Network

"The trained official," Bagehot wrote, "hates the rude, untrained public."[1] "He thinks that they are stupid, ignorant, restless...."[2] President Harry Truman's Secretary of State Dean Acheson, not renowned for bluntness, let slip his own similar assessment of America's electorate. "If you truly had a democracy and did what the people wanted," he said, "you'd go wrong every time."[3] Acheson's views were shared by other influential foreign policy experts,[4] as well as government officials;[5] thus emerged America's "efficient" national security institution.[6]

Before examining its origins and contemporary operation, let us adopt more neutral terms that better describe its historical roots. The terms "efficient" and "dignified" have taken on somewhat different implications over the years and, to put it delicately, imply qualities that not all contemporary American institutions fully embody.

James Madison was perhaps the principal architect of the American constitutional design.[7] Honoring Madison's founding role, let us substitute "Madisonian" for "dignified," referring to the three branches of the federal government formally established by the Constitution to serve as checks on the instruments of state security. Under the Madisonian system, Congress was given power to "raise and support Armies";[8] to "provide and maintain a Navy";[9] to "make Rules for the Government and Regulation of the land and naval Forces";[10] to "provide for calling forth the Militia to execute the laws of the Union, suppress Insurrections and repel Invasions";[11] and to "provide for organizing, arming, and disciplining, the Militia, and for governing such Part of them as may be employed in the Service of the United States, reserving to the States respectively, the Appointment of the Officers, and the Authority of training the Militia according to the discipline prescribed by Congress."[12] The commander-in-chief of the armed forces was to be a civilian, the President.[13] The President was authorized to make treaties, but only with the advice and consent of two-thirds of the Senate.[14] No special immunities were carved out for the military from judicial process, to be exercised by courts with jurisdiction over "all Cases, in Law and Equity, arising under this Constitution, the Laws of the United States, and Treaties...."[15]

These constitutional provisions thus divide power over national security. Animating the separation of powers is a well-known theory. Madison believed that dividing authority among the three branches of government would cause the members of each of the three branches to seek to expand their power but also to rebuff encroachments on their power.[16] An equilibrium would result, and this balance would forestall the rise of centralized, despotic power. But more than mere institutional design was required; the government Madison envisioned was not a machine that would check itself.[17] Essential to the effectiveness of these checks and the maintenance of balance was civic virtue—an informed and engaged electorate.[18] The virtue of the people who held office would rest on the intelligence and public-mindedness of the people who put them there. Absent civic virtue, the governmental equilibrium of power would face collapse.[19] This is the Madisonian model.

President Harry S Truman, more than any other President, is responsible for creating the nation's "efficient" national security apparatus.[20] Under him, Congress enacted the National Security Act of 1947, which unified the military under a new secretary of defense, set up the CIA, created the modern Joint Chiefs of Staff, and established the National Security Council (NSC).[21] Truman also set up the National Security Agency, which was intended at the time to monitor communications abroad.[22] Friends as well as detractors viewed Truman's role as decisive.[23] Honoring Truman's founding role, let us substitute "Trumanite" for "efficient," referring to the network of several hundred high-level military, intelligence, diplomatic, and law enforcement officials within the executive branch who are responsible for national security policymaking.

ORIGINS

President Truman's national security initiatives were controversial, with liberal and conservative positions in the debate curiously inverted from those prevalent in current times. In the late 1940s and early 1950s, congressional liberals generally supported Truman's efforts to create more centralized national security institutions on the theory, held by many and summarized by Michael Hogan, that "peace and freedom were indivisible, that American power had to be mobilized on behalf of democracy 'everywhere,' and that tradition had to give ground to this new responsibility."[24] Senator Hubert Humphrey of Minnesota, for example, dismissed objections to the constitutionality of the new arrangements: "It is one thing to have legalistic arguments about where the power rests," he said, but another to straitjacket a President in trying to deal with a totalitarian state capable of swift action.[25] Stalin could strike a deathblow at any time, he argued; "[t]hose days of all the niceties and formalities of declarations of war are past...."[26] Under these conditions, "it is hard to tell... where war begins or where it ends."[27] Senator Paul Douglas of Illinois insisted that U.S. military power should support democracy "everywhere."[28]

Unanswered aggression would lead only to further aggression, he suggested, requiring the United States to move to a posture of permanent military preparedness.[29]

Conservatives in Congress, on the other hand, feared that Truman's ballooning national security payrolls, reliance upon military solutions to tackle international problems, and efforts to centralize national security decision-making posed a threat to democratic institutions and the principle of civilian leadership. Republican Senator Edward V. Robertson of Wyoming, for example, worried that Truman's military consolidations could amount to the creation of an "embryonic" general staff similar to that of Germany's Wehrmacht.[30] A new national intelligence agency, he said, could grow into an American "gestapo."[31] Republican Senator William Langer of North Dakota and his allies believed that the Soviet threat was exaggerated; in their eyes, the real enemy was the Pentagon, where "military leaders had an insatiable appetite for more money, more men, and more power, whatever the cost to democracy."[32] The conservatives invoked the specter of a "garrison state," a "police state," and a "slave state" run by "power-grabbing bureaucrats."[33] They saw peacetime military conscription as "aping the military clique of Hitler" and leading to a "complete militarization of the country," creating a "permanent military caste."[34] Republican Congresswoman Katherine St. George of New York, recalling Washington's Farewell Address, foresaw the possibility of military domination of the nation's civilian leadership.[35] Republican Senators John Bricker and Robert Taft of Ohio and Homer Capehart of Indiana voted to cap the size of active U.S. military forces in part to halt what they regarded as "a drift from 'congressional responsibility' to 'administrative policymaking'...which would destroy the 'liberty of the people.'"[36] "The truth is that we are slowly losing our freedoms as we move toward the garrison state," said the Republican leader of the House of Representatives, Joseph W. Martin of Massachusetts.[37]

Truman himself appeared to share these concerns, at least to an extent. He was "very strongly anti-FBI," according to his aide Clark Clifford.[38] Truman was "afraid of a 'Gestapo'" and wanted to "hold [the] FBI down," which he regarded as "dangerous."[39] Although a military officer would be permitted to head the CIA, Truman accepted an amendment to the National Security Act under which the Agency would be prohibited from performing any "police, subpoena, law enforcement powers, or internal security functions."[40] As for the military, while wasteful duplication had to be eliminated and better coordination established, Truman feared that collective deliberation could force the President to share responsibility and decision-making power, resulting in a diminution in presidential authority and a weakening of civilian control over the military.[41] With half of the members of the new National Security Council coming from the military, Truman believed it would be difficult for the President to ignore their recommendations, even though their counsel was only advisory.[42] Truman was particularly annoyed by interservice rivalries and pressure from military lobbyists to increase their services' budgets.[43] "We must be very careful that the military does not overstep the bounds from an economic standpoint domestically," he wrote.[44] He also believed that "[m]ost of them would like to go back to a war footing."[45] But he considered the new national security apparatus necessary to rein in the military as well as to improve the United States' ability to respond to the looming (though exaggerated[46]) Soviet threat. The Hoover Commission had warned in 1949 that the Joint Chiefs had come to act as "virtually a law unto themselves"[47] and that "centralized civilian control scarcely exists" in certain military departments.[48] Internecine warfare among the services had come to undermine the nation's defense. Truman believed that his new national security architecture was the best bet to bolster the capacity of the nation to meet security threats while safeguarding the democratic institutions that the newly empowered military and intelligence organizations were expected to protect.[49]

OPERATION

Sixty years later, sitting atop its national security institutions, an intragovernmental network that has descended from what Truman created now manages the real work of preventing the country from, in Acheson's phrase, "go[ing] wrong."[50] The *Washington Post*'s landmark 2011 study of Truman's modern handiwork, "Top Secret America," identified forty-six federal departments and agencies engaged in classified national security work.[51] Their missions range from intelligence gathering and analysis to war-fighting, cyberoperations, and weapons development. Almost 2,000 private companies support this work, which occurs at over 10,000 locations across America.[52] The size of their budgets and workforces are mostly classified, but it is clear that those numbers are enormous—a total annual outlay of around $1 trillion and millions of employees.[53] "The nightmare of the modern state," Henry Kissinger has written, "is the hugeness of the bureaucracy, and the problem is how to get coherence and design in it."[54]

Coherence and design, however, must come largely from the bureaucracy itself. Presidents can appoint only between 3,000 and 4,000 individuals (including domestic policy officials).[55] Of the 668,000 civilian employees in the Department of Defense and related agencies in 2004, only 247 were political appointees.[56] Several hundred policymakers, therefore, must be drawn from the national security bureaucracy to oversee and direct it. They include, but are not limited to, the President's personal assistants, the top professional staff members of the National Security Council[57]—"the single most powerful staff in Washington."[58] As recently as the 1990s the NSC professional staff numbered about 50; by 2014 it numbered more than 350.[59] Among this larger group of national security policymakers that make up the National Security Council are careerists as well as "in-and-outers"—political appointees, academics, analysts from think tanks, military officers, and other officials seconded from executive agencies.

These several hundred officials constitute America's Trumanite network. They sit at the pinnacle of what Jack Goldsmith has called "Washington's tight-knit national security culture."[60] After spending their professional lives writing what they did not sign, finally they sign what they did not write. They are not yet driven to work in the morning by a black car but are one step away. They are more likely to have been to Kabul than Tulsa. They visit the hinterlands of fly-over America on holidays, if then. They seldom appear on television and seek neither celebrity nor wealth. High school class trips do not visit their offices. Awake at night they think about the implications of the next Stuxnet,[61] not ten-year treasury yields. Success lies in being in the big meeting, reading the key memo—being part of the big decision. The Trumanites draw little overt attention but wield immense, unnoticed power.

Unlike "the best and the brightest" of earlier times, the Trumanites are not part of big decisions because of wealth, family connections, or an elite education. Most have no assured financial or social safety net to save them should they slip. They are "in" because they are smart, hard-working, and reliable, which among other things means unlikely to embarrass their superiors. What they may lack in subtlety of mind or force of intellect they make up in judgment.[62] Love of country draws the Trumanites to their work but so also does the adrenaline rush of urgent top-secret news flashes, hurried hallway briefings, emergency teleconferences, intense confrontation, knowing the confidential subplot, and, more broadly, their authority. The decisions they secretly shape are the government's most crucial. They are Trollope's Tom Towers: "It is true he wore no ermine, bore no outward marks of a world's respect; but with what a load of inward importance was he charged! It is true his name appeared in no large capitals...but what member of Parliament had half his power?"[63]

The Trumanites are, above all, efficient, or at least efficient relative to the Madisonians. They can move quickly. They are concise summarizers; they know their superiors have as little time as they do and need predigested ideas. They face no need for hearings or markups or floor debates and afford no occasion for briefs, oral arguments, or appeals. True, the interagency process does take time; papers do have to be cleared and disagreements resolved. But, again—relative to the Madisonian institutions—the Trumanite network is the paragon of efficiency. "The decisive reason for the advance of bureaucratic organization," Max Weber noted, "has always been its purely technical superiority over any other form of organization."[64]

The Trumanites share the public's faith in American exceptionalism, but they are not ideologues. As Bagehot said of Britain's analogous institution, "[it] is permanently efficient, because it is not composed of warm partisans."[65] Trumanites are, above all, rationalists. They appear at all costs sound, responsible, serious, and disinterested, never extreme or sentimental, never too far ahead of policy or too far behind it, creative but not too creative, never boringly predictable, and, above all, never naïve. They are, in Bagehot's words, "in contact with reality."[66] They go only "where [they] think[] ... the nation will follow."[67] "[T]he way to lead them—the best and acknowledged way—is to affect a studied and illogical moderation."[68] Their objective is to be *uncategorizable*—neither predictably hard-line nor predictably soft-line, weighing options on their merits but remaining always—for it is, after all, national security that is at stake—tough.[69]

"[T]his cast of mind," C. Wright Mills concluded, "defines international reality as basically military."[70] John Kenneth Galbraith recalled the friendly counsel of McGeorge Bundy, National Security Advisor to Presidents John F. Kennedy and Lyndon Johnson: "Ken," Bundy told him, "you always advise against the use of force—do you realize that?" The result of being typecast, Galbraith said, was that on security issues he found himself always like an Indian, "firing occasional arrows into the campsite from the outside."[71] Les Gelb, former president of the Council on Foreign Relations and an assistant secretary of state in the Carter administration, later explained his initial support of the Iraq War as "symptomatic of unfortunate tendencies within the foreign policy community, namely the disposition and incentives to support wars to retain political and professional credibility."[72] One must always retain credibility, which counsels against fighting losing battles at high credibility costs, particularly for a policy option that would play in Peoria as a weak one. Whether the policy is in reality the most effective is beside the point. It is the appearance that matters, and in appearance, the policy must seem hard-hitting. That reality permeates national security policymaking. "[T]he White House [was] ever afraid," Vali Nasr has written, "that the young Democratic President would be seen as 'soft.'"[73] To have gone against the military on Afghanistan would have made the President look weak. "Mr. President," advised an NSC staff member, "I don't see how you can defy your military chain" on Afghanistan force levels.[74] "No Democratic president can go against military advice, especially if he asked for it," said CIA Director Leon Panetta.[75]

THREAT EXAGGERATION

The Trumanites thus define security in military and intelligence terms rather than political and diplomatic ones. This propensity reinforces a powerful structural dynamic. That dynamic can be succinctly stated: *Overprotection of national security creates costs that the Trumanite network can externalize; underprotection creates costs that the network must internalize.* The resulting incentive structure encourages the exaggeration of existing threats and the creation of imaginary ones. The security programs that emerge are, in economic terms, "sticky down"—easier to grow than to shrink.

The Trumanites sacrifice little when disproportionate money or manpower is devoted to security. The operatives that they direct do not incur trade-off costs.[76] The Trumanites do, however, reap the benefits of that disproportionality—a larger payroll, more personnel, broader authority, and an even lower risk that they will be blamed in the event of a successful attack.[77] Yet Madisonian institutions incur the costs of excessive resources that flow to the Trumanites. The President must submit a budget that includes the needed taxes. Members of Congress must vote for those taxes. A federal agency must collect the taxes. When it comes to picking up the tab, Trumanites are nowhere to be seen.

If national security protection is inadequate, on the other hand, the Trumanites are held accountable. They are the experts on whom the Madisonian institutions rely to keep the nation safe. They are the recipients of Madisonian largesse, doled out to ensure that no blame will be cast by voters seeking retribution for a job poorly done. In the event of a catastrophic attack, the buck stops with the Trumanites. No Trumanite craves to be the target of a 9/11 commission following a catastrophic failure. Thus they have, as Jeffrey Rosen put it, an "incentive to exaggerate risks and pander to public fears"[78]—"an incentive to pass along vague and unconfirmed threats of future violence, in order to protect themselves from criticism"[79] should another attack occur. Seymour Hersh recalls the comment of a senior FBI counterterrorism official concerning dire public warnings of increased terrorism threats. "Is there some C.Y.A.—cover your ass—involved when officials talk about threats to power supplies, or banks, or malls? Of course there is."[80]

Indeed, a purely "rational" actor in the Trumanite network might hardly be expected to do anything other than inflate threats. In this way, the domestic political dynamic reinforces the security dilemma familiar to international relations students, the quandary that a nation confronts when, in taking steps to enhance its security, it unintentionally threatens the security of another nation and thus finds its own security threatened when the other nation takes compensatory action.[81] An inexorable and destabilizing arms race is thereby fueled by seemingly rational domestic actors responding to seemingly reasonable threats—threats that they unwittingly helped create.

The budget figures, compiled by David Sanger,[82] reflect the incentive structure within which the Trumanite network has emerged and thrives. Over the last decade the defense budget has grown 67 percent in real terms.[83] It is now 50 percent higher than it was for an average year during the Cold War[84]—greater than the spending of the next twenty largest military powers combined.[85] During the decade following the 9/11 attacks, the United States spent at least $3.3 trillion in response.[86] This represents $6.6 million for every dollar al Qaeda spent to stage the attacks.[87]

It is unclear the extent to which the specific threats at which the Obama national security policy is directed have been inflated; that information is classified, and the handful of Trumanites in a position to know the truth of the matter can hardly be expected to disclose it.[88] No reliable outside threat assessment is available. Although it is the Madisonians, not the Trumanites, who are expert in assessing the preferences of the public, including public risk tolerance—the Madisonians are the ones who hear out constituents, litigants, and lobbyists—the only way to know whether more insurance is needed is to ask the same Trumanite network that will gladly provide it. If the precise nature of the threatened harm is uncertain, what is not uncertain is the fear of threats, which is essential to the maintenance of the Trumanite network's power—for the fundamental driver of Trumanite power has been emergency, the appearance of threats that must be addressed immediately, without bringing in the Madisonian institutions.[89] The network thus has little incentive to identify or eliminate the ultimate source of threats (e.g., unwanted intervention in the internal affairs of other nations[90]), for its vitality depends upon the continuation of those threats. Lessened accountability, which some regard as a cost of meeting those threats, is experienced by Trumanites as a benefit. "[A]n entire era of crisis in which urgent decisions have been required again and again,"[91] in the words of Senator J. William Fulbright, has given rise to the Trumanites' power. Speedy decisions are required that the Madisonian institutions are ill-equipped to make; the Trumanites have the means at their disposal to act quickly. The perception of threat, crisis, and emergency has been the seminal phenomenon that has created and nurtures America's double government.

SECRECY

What has held the Trumanites together during this era is what Bagehot believed held Britain's efficient institutions together: loyalty, collective responsibility, and—most important—secrecy.[92] "Secrecy, once accepted, becomes an addiction," Edward Teller said.[93] The Trumanite network is not alone in accepting the need for secrecy in national security matters—the Madisonian institutions do as well—but in breadth and depth, the Trumanites' opaqueness is striking. Trumanites can have no real discussions with family or friends about work because nearly all of their work is classified. They hold multiple compartmented clearances. Their offices are located in the buildings' expensive real estate—the Pentagon's E-Ring, the CIA's Seventh Floor, the State Department's Seventh Floor. Keypads lock their doors. Next to their desks are a safe and two computers, one unclassified and the other classified. Down the hall is a SCIF[94] where the most sensitive briefings take place. They speak in acronyms and code words that the public has never heard and, God (and the FBI) willing, never will hear. The experts they consult are their colleagues. Outside expertise, when needed, is difficult to tap. The Trumanites sign nondisclosure agreements under which they promise to submit for prepublication review anything they write on the subject of their work. Outside experts have signed nothing; normally they do not even hold a security clearance. Outside experts can thus provide insights but are not in the flow of intelligence and have little sense of the internal, organizational decision-making context in which issues arise. Nor have they any particular loyalty to the group, not being a part of it.

The Trumanites have additional incentives to keep information to themselves. Knowing that information in Washington is power, they are, in the words of Jack Balkin, both information gluttons and information misers.[95] They are information gluttons in that they "grab as much information as possible"; they are information misers in that they try to keep it from the public and the Madisonian institutions that represent it. Potential critics, power competitors, and adversaries are starved for information concerning the Trumanite network while it feasts on information concerning them. Potential power competitors include congressional overseers. Power competitors can also include the White House itself; during the ostensibly friendly Nixon administration, a spy for the Pentagon stole highly classified NSC documents and passed them to the Joint Chiefs of Staff.[96] The secrecy of Trumanite activities thus grows as the privacy of the general public and power of the Madisonians diminishes, while the Trumanites' shared "secret[s] of convenience"[97] bind them ever more tightly together.

The Trumanites' ability to mask the identity of "the decider" is another factor that accounts for the network's durability and resilience. Efforts by the press and congressional oversight committees to pinpoint exactly who is responsible for a given policy are easily deflected by the shield of secrecy provided by the network structure.[98] The most sensitive decisions frequently are not reduced to writing.[99] Because everyone—the entire "national security team"—is accountable, no one is accountable.[100] The network's success in evading questions concerning the continuation of military assistance to Egypt following the removal from office of President Mohamed Morsi in 2013—despite a clear statutory prohibition against the continuation of such aid following a military coup[101]—is illustrative. Below is an excerpt from the State Department spokeswoman, Jen Psaki, answering questions from the press on July 26, 2013:

QUESTION: And who ultimately made the decision not to make a determination?

MS. PSAKI: Well, obviously, there's a factor as it relates to the legal component, which our legal office here played a significant role in, and certainly this was discussed and agreed to through the interagency process.

QUESTION: But who decided? I mean, the buck stops somewhere. As Harry Truman said, it stopped with him. Does the buck stop with the President in this case, or with the Secretary, or with the acting legal advisor of the State Department, or who? Who made the decision?

MS. PSAKI: Well, I'm not going to read out who was where on what and all the players involved in this.

QUESTION: I'm not asking that. I'm asking who made the decision.

MS. PSAKI: This was agreed to by the national security team. Beyond that, I'm not going to—I don't have anything.

QUESTION: Why are you afraid to say who made the decision?

MS. PSAKI: I'm not afraid of anything, Arshad. I'm just not— I'm not getting into more specifics than that for you.[102]

Its cohesion notwithstanding, the Trumanite network is curiously amorphous. It has no leader. It is not monolithic. It has no formal structure.[103] Its actual membership blurs at the margins. Its ranks reflect the same organizational, philosophical, and personal rivalries and fissures common to all bureaucracies. Blame avoidance ranks high among its priorities.[104] But while Trumanites' view of the world differs at the margins, it does not differ at the core. It has been said that there is no such thing as a military mind,[105] but this is not true. Mills captured the military mindset; in the military, he wrote, there is an "intensified desire, too deeply rooted to examine, to conform to type, to be indistinguishable, not to reveal loss of composure to inferiors, and above all, not to presume the right to upset the arrangements of the chain of command."[106] Operating as it does under the long shadow of the military, the range of internal disagreement within the Trumanite network is tiny, like differences over appropriate necktie width. The conformist mentality percolates upward. Bob Woodward reported on the response to President Obama's question as he sat down with eighteen top advisers for the second meeting of the Afghanistan-Pakistan strategy review. "'Is there anybody who thinks we ought to leave Afghanistan,' the President asked? Everyone in the room was quiet. They looked at him. No one said anything."[107] The incident was unexceptional. "The dirty little secret here," a former associate counsel in the Bush White House, Brad Berenson, explained, "is that the United States government has enduring institutional interests that carry over from administration to administration and almost always dictate the position the government takes."[108]

CONFORMISM

The Trumanite network is as little inclined to stake out new policies as it is to abandon old ones. The Trumanites' *grundnorm* is stability, and their ultimate objective is preservation of the status quo. The status quo embraces not only American power but the Trumanites' own careers, which are steadily elevated by the conveyer belt on which they sit. Preoccupied as they are with cascading crises, swamped with memos and email and overwhelmed with meetings, Trumanites have no time to re-examine the cosmological premises on which policy is based.[109] Their business is reacting, day and night. Working weekends and evenings is routine; theirs are 24/7 jobs[110] that leave no time for pondering big pictures. They are caught up in tactics;[111] larger ends are for memoirs. Reflecting on the "fail[ure] to take an orderly, rational approach" to Vietnam decision-making, Robert McNamara wrote that "we faced a blizzard of problems, there were only twenty-four hours a day, and we often did not have time to think straight."[112] His successors encountered an equally frenetic environment.[113] With the anger, frustration, emotion, and the mental and physical exhaustion induced in working long hours under crisis conditions, a pernicious but existing policy gradually comes to be seen as the least bad choice. The status quo is preserved by minimizing risks, which means no bold departure from the settled long-term policy trajectory. "Men who have participated in a decision," as James Thomson succinctly put it, "develop a stake in that decision."[114] Slow is therefore best. The risk of embarrassment is lower in continuing a policy someone else initiated than in sponsoring one's own new one. If the policy fails, the embarrassment is someone else's. This is particularly true in the context of crisis and emergency.[115]

Trumanites are therefore, above all, team players. They are disinclined to disagree openly. "The further up you go," one prominent organization theorist put it, "the less you can afford to stick out in any one place."[116] As one seasoned adviser said, because "there is a real team concept and where money disputes are not usually the core, radically different views of the direction to be taken by an administration can cause serious trouble."[117] He advises that a "new president should take care that his key officials in foreign policy all have a roughly similar outlook on the world and America's place in it."[118] Accordingly, once a policy is final, Trumanites rally readily round it, however much they might once have disagreed. Dissent shades into disloyalty and risks marginalization, particularly in a policy group with high *esprit de corps*. As Kissinger put it, "[s]erving the machine becomes a more absorbing occupation than defining its purpose."[119] Little credit is gained by advocating for an option that has earlier been rejected. Credit lies in building upon and expanding the insight and programs of one's superiors. Likelier than not, one's superior, or his superior, was present at the creation of the policy and takes pride in its authorship.[120] "In government it is always easier to go forward with a program that does not work," David Halberstam wrote, "than to stop it altogether and admit failure."[121] Even those immersed in the policymaking process are often bewildered by its outcome. The Army chief of staff, Harold Johnson, could think of "no logical rationale" to explain the military's continuing recommendations for incremental escalation of the U.S. war effort in Vietnam—even though the military had difficulty devising any persuasive strategy to produce victory.[122] The Trumanites' commitment is therefore to process rather than outcome. "It is an inevitable defect," Bagehot wrote, that "bureaucrats will care more for routine than for results; or, as Edmund Burke put it, 'that they will think the substance of business not to be much more important than the forms of it.'"[123] "Men so trained," he believed, "must come to think the routine of business not a means but an end—to imagine the elaborate machinery of which they form a part, and from which they derive their dignity, to be a grand and achieved result, not a working and changeable instrument."[124] At a certain point, policy within such a system reaches critical mass, and its gravitational pull is too strong to escape even for political appointees, who are easily co-opted.[125] "The vast bureaucratic mechanisms that emerge develop a momentum and a vested interest of their own," Kissinger wrote.[126] "There is a trend toward autarky."[127] There thus emerges, as Goldsmith put it, a "persistence in the interests and outlook of the national security leadership and especially of the national security bureaucracy."[128] The upshot is a form of what social scientists have called "path dependence"—the tendency of a future policy trajectory to align with a past policy trajectory, even though the decisions that comprised the past trajectory were ill-considered or were taken in response to different conditions.[129]

As in all government bureaucracies, the tendency is to "*get along* with others and *go along* with the system...."[130] The safe course for an ambitious Trumanite is to propose the continuation of existing policy before the decision is made to do so; one will then be on the winning side.[131] Changing a big policy requires changing lots of little policies as well; small details, inconveniences perhaps, which together create major headaches for innovators.[132] Suggesting some limiting principle is dangerous; the facts may unexpectedly turn out to fall beyond that limit, and the author of a limit that seemed so innocuous when it was proposed would then be blamed. Trite but true, the perfect is the enemy of the good, the Trumanites know; good wheels ought not be reinvented. Thus a policy takes on a life of its own, feeding on caution, living off the bureaucratic land, resistant to the changing preferences of elected officials who come and go[133]—a "self-generating enterprise," as Senator Frank Church described it.[134] The careerists, as President Truman himself said, "look upon the elected officials as just temporary occupants," particularly in the realm of national security.[135] The careerists can always wait them out. "It has often happened in the War and Navy Departments that the generals and the admirals, instead of working for and under the Secretaries, succeeded in having the Secretaries act for and under them. And it has happened in the Department of State."[136] Truman expected that his newly elected successor, Dwight Eisenhower, would be surprised by the bureaucratic inertia. "He'll sit here, and he'll say, 'Do this! Do that!'" Truman said. "*And nothing will happen.* Poor Ike—it won't be a bit like the Army. He'll find it very frustrating."[137]

Neil Sheehan[138] reflected on why nothing would happen. Sheehan's *Times* colleague Halberstam recalled that Sheehan came away with one impression: that "the government of the United States was not what he had thought it was; it was as if there were an inner U.S. government, what he called 'a centralized state, far more powerful than anything else....It had survived and perpetuated itself....[I]t does not function necessarily for the benefit of the Republic but rather for its own ends, its own perpetuation; it has its own codes which are quite different from public codes.'"[139]

The Trumanite network has achieved, in a word, *autonomy*.[140] The maintenance of Trumanite autonomy has depended upon two conditions. The first is that the Madisonian institutions appear to be in charge of the nation's security. The second is that the Madisonian institutions not actually be in charge.

CHAPTER 3

❧

The Sources of Madisonian Illusion

For double government to work, the Madisonian institutions must seem in charge, for the Trumanites' power flows from the legitimacy of those institutions. Occasionally slip-ups occur,[1] but the Trumanite members generally maintain the appearance of Madisonian control. Without public deference to the President, Congress, and the courts, the Trumanite network could never command obedience. Behind the scenes, the Madisonians defer to them; technocratic expertise and years of experience are useful resources for any policymaker to draw upon. Madisonian complaisance is not only inevitable but useful in promoting informed and knowledgeable decisions.

Expertise, efficiency, and experience are not, however, sufficient in and of themselves to induce the Madisonians' general acquiescence in measures needed for effective governance. For all its proficiency, the Trumanite network is still too "artificial," too unfamiliar to generate public reverence.[2] Like Britain's real rulers, the Trumanites bring up the rear in Bagehot's "splendid procession"[3] of governance. They are "secreted in second-rate carriages; no one cares for them or asks about them, but they are obeyed implicitly and unconsciously by reason of the splendour of those who eclipsed and preceded them."[4] Those who preceded them are the apparent rulers, the "imposing personages" for "whom the spectators cheer"; "it is by them the mob are influenced."[5] The Trumanite network survives by living in the Madisonian institutions' glow. Because the Trumanites could never by themselves generate the requisite public veneration, evolution toward double government was necessarily slow. Quick alteration would have been seen, Bagehot theorized, as a "catastrophic change" that would have "killed the State."[6]

The Trumanites thus operate under a strong incentive to ensure that Madisonian institutions shine brightly. That is also in the interests of the Madisonian institutions themselves; its members wish to be seen by the public as in charge, for their own sake as well as the nation's. Members of Congress are loath to exhibit any lack of authority that would make them look weak and undermine their legitimacy or re-election chances. Likewise, the illusion persists that the President is the "decider" on Trumanite proposals. The Trumanites and their operational enterprises are, after all, "his." Announcements are made regularly that "he" has ordered "his" secretary of state to do this and that "he" has ordered "his" secretary of defense to do that. The judiciary, too, continues to appear to be the ultimate arbiter of legality, for its own power as well as that of the Trumanites. At the level of appearances—and it is above all appearances that count—interests are aligned, fed by the need simultaneously to maximize both expertise and legitimacy.[7]

Maintaining the appearance of control and thus the ability to generate deference, Bagehot suggests, requires five attributes: historical pedigree, ritual, intelligibility, mystery, and harmony.[8] Together, these elements inspire a sense of duty, a felt obligation on the part of the public to obey.[9]

Pedigree is the Madisonian institutions' strong suit. Congress, the President, and the courts, unlike the Trumanites, trace their lineage directly to the Framers, whom Americans (mostly) still appear to revere. Biographies of the Founding Fathers and accounts of their virtuosity appear regularly on best-seller lists and television documentaries. Whatever else they lack, the three constitutional branches present an impressive pedigree. They owe their position to the design of individuals whom many have come to regard as demi-gods—Washington, Madison, Hamilton, Franklin, and others. Many still view that design as almost divinely inspired. The public may not be directly aware of the veneration the Constitution has generated over the ages.[10] But the public partakes in the process of filling offices the Constitution established, and it thus has a derivative emotional tie to current occupants of offices that are revered through the mists of memory. And at least some part of the public knows that the earlier holders of those offices also included quasi-mystical figures—Lincoln and Roosevelt, Webster and Calhoun, Marshall and Holmes. To varying extents, their images still shimmer in the public imagination and still stir the millions of tourists who flock to Washington every year, watch the History Channel, and read David McCullough.

Pedigree is reinforced by solemn ritual, which also traces to the earliest days of the Republic. The high-church ceremony of presidential inauguration indicates to American voters that the identity of the President and his policies are their choice. The State of the Union address suggests that it is the peoples' representatives in Congress who will approve or disapprove the President's proposals. An occult jargon of Latin and legalese conjures an oracular Supreme Court, sitting on high in its Greek temple, solomonically deciding cases based upon timeless principles, esoteric doctrine, and precedents that limit every institution, Madisonian and Trumanite alike. From "Hail to the Chief" to intonations of "Oyez, Oyez, Oyez" on the first Monday in October, the illusion is perpetuated that nothing has changed since the Founding. All is right with the world, and the Madisonian institutions are still on their thrones.

One reason that the public assumed that a President like Eisenhower could simply snap his fingers and change course—that the Madisonian institutions are what they seem—is that these institutions are intelligible. It requires no canniness to understand that three branches exist to make, execute, and interpret the laws. These are "easy ideas"; in Bagehot's words, "anybody can make them out, and no one can ever forget them."[11] A fourth-grade civics book can make Madisonians' jobs comprehensible. By contrast, the Trumanite network is anything but simple. Try explaining the frustrations of the interagency process to a general public that cannot identify the National Security Council, let alone its relationship to the intelligence and defense communities or the congressional oversight committees. Even to the extent that it is transparent, the Trumanite network is too amorphous, too byzantine, its missions and relationships too convoluted, and its powers and limits too obscure for ready public understanding.

Mystery is the fourth prerequisite of institutions that generate public obeisance. They must spark the public imagination. They must convince the public that they are not like us, that in native capacity, education, or access to secrets, they are a breed apart. "Most men...are encouraged to assume that, in general, the most powerful and the wealthiest are also the most knowledgeable or, as they might say, 'the smartest.'"[12] This is particularly true if "superiors'" manner of presentation is superior. The people defer to "theatrical show," Bagehot wrote.[13] "Their imagination is bowed down; they feel they are not equal to the life which is revealed to them."[14] This requires that the Madisonian officials operate at something of a remove from the general public, "aloof"[15] as Bagehot writes. How they do what they do must be "hidden like a mystery."[16] And to an extent it still is. What exactly happens in meetings in the Oval Office, in the Supreme Court conference where cases are decided, or in hearings of the Senate Intelligence Committee is shrouded in mystery.

Finally, to all appearances, harmony prevails between the Trumanite network and Madisonian institutions. This is not because the Trumanites click their heels and salute the Madisonians. Trumanites believe that the Madisonian institutions, in Bagehot's phrase, "tend to diminish simple efficiency."[17] They know that needless bellicosity toward other nations often originates on Capitol Hill.[18] They can tick off multiple military (mis)adventures pushed by "the civilians" that Pentagon planners prudently opposed. They know from history how Joe McCarthy and his merry band savaged the State Department,[19] petrified sensible policymakers, and made the CIA a veritable political safehouse for enlightened "China hands."[20] They know how, before the Trumanite network arrived on the scene, Madisonian institutions bungled American membership in the League of Nations and toyed dangerously with indifference and isolationism[21] while Hitler's shadow lengthened.[22] To the Trumanites, "[t]he nation [has] outgrown its institutions, and [is] cramped by them."[23] With Acheson, they regard the Madisonian institutions as lacking the requisite expertise, experience, and seriousness of purpose needed to safeguard the nation's security. Rather, the Trumanites are not seen publicly to resist the policies set by the Madisonians because the Madisonian institutions must always be perceived as the authors of the Trumanites' projects. For the Trumanite network to be identified as the authors of initiatives such as warrantless National Security Agency (NSA) surveillance, the mining of Nicaragua's harbors,[24] or the Bay of Pigs invasion[25] would risk delegitimizing the Madisonian institutions—and thus undermining the ultimate power source on which the Trumanites themselves must rely, electoral assent. Ostensible harmony is therefore imperative.

Creating and maintaining this illusion is not difficult. The Madisonian institutions go along with policymaking by the Trumanites so long as it is popular, and if it is popular, their incentive is to be seen as its sponsor. Thus with the 2001 Authorization for Use of Military Force,[26] hastily enacted following the September 11 attacks, Congress positioned itself to take credit for the retaliatory actions all knew, at least in general terms, the Trumanites were preparing. It is in the interests of neither to clash publicly with the other. Open confrontation calls into question both the expertise of the Trumanites as well as the seeming authority of the Madisonians. For the Madisonian institutions to challenge the Trumanite network publicly would entail an uncertain outcome and risk a loss of credibility for both, as occurred when Truman fired MacArthur, when Obama fired McChrystal, when the Supreme Court gave the press the go-ahead to publish the top-secret Pentagon Papers, or when the Church Committee roughed up the CIA. The Madisonian challenge to the CIA's enhanced interrogation program ended, unsurprisingly, with a Madisonian decision to absolve the Trumanites of all responsibility.[27] In clashes such as these, both sets of institutions lose a degree of public respect, albeit among different constituencies. Members of Congress, similarly, do have policy preferences, but their first objective is to stay in office. Falling out of sync with the Trumanites is not a wise strategy for career longevity. Buried in the *New York Times'* reportage on the Benghazi controversy was the tip-of-the-iceberg revelation that the House Intelligence Committee, whose members needed talking points to use with reporters in discussing the attacks, asked that they be prepared by then-Director of the CIA David Petraeus.[28] Far safer is for Congress to "approve" initiatives that, if not its own, at least appear to be.

The press reinforces the illusion of Madisonian control. This is particularly true with respect to presidential decision-making, as Hugh Heclo has pointed out:

> The modern media industry has a vested interest in the illusion of presidential government. Its technology is far from neutral for our understanding of government. The media need simple "shots" and clean lines of conflict to communicate a "story." The most compelling image of a situation is a person, and the president is the most easily communicated person. Thus the media amplify what we know to be a predisposition in the general public, namely, an impulse to understand public affairs mainly through a prominent political actor's behavior and not in terms of more complex, situational factors.[29]

Together, then, these five elements—historical pedigree, ritual, intelligibility, mystery, and harmony—foster the appearance that "The People" rule through constitutionally established institutions; they "cling to the idea that the government is a sort of automatic machine, regulated by the balancing of competing interests."[30] Accordingly, they are wont to believe that the purpose of a presidential election is to determine whether to continue existing policy and that when a new President takes office he begins with a blank slate.[31] The rhetoric of presidential campaigns reinforces this belief; it is no accident that "change" has been the recurring theme in recent elections. Congress, too, and its stance on national security policy are seen to be wholly a function of public will. If only the right person were elected and if only these right officials were to approve the right judges, policy would change. Public attention is thus deflected from networks and institutions to the individuals who hold office. Those individuals are the Madisonians, the Trumanites being all but invisible.

More sophisticated public opinion polling highlights this key distinction.[32] It asks respondents whether they approve of Congress, the presidency, and the Supreme Court as *institutions*—explaining that "institutions have their own buildings, historical traditions, and purposes laid out in the Constitution"—and then it asks whether they approve of the officeholders—"the people currently in office" within each institution. The results are striking. When this bifurcated polling was done in the 1990s, only 24 percent of respondents approved of the members of Congress, 46 percent approved of the President (George H. W. Bush), and 73 percent approved of the members of the Supreme Court.[33] But approval of the three institutions was overwhelming: 88 percent approved of Congress, 96 percent of the presidency, and 94 percent of the Supreme Court.[34] Policy is thus seen as a function of personnel rather than of institutional structure, and policy change requires merely placing different people in office. If policy does not change, the personnel—not the system—are to blame. The possibility that the *system* might somehow select the *individuals* who are within it eludes the public. The public seems not to notice that numerous senior national security offices remain vacant for months with no perceptible effect on policy.[35] In the public understanding, if the Trumanites do not act quickly enough, it is because the President is not forceful enough (even though, in Eisenhower's case, he was the Supreme Allied Commander in Europe who led the Normandy invasion). Presidents simply need to issue commands more forcefully. The details and operation of double government thus remain veiled.

Nonetheless, in the United States today, as in Bagehot's Britain, "[m]ost do indeed vaguely know that there are some other institutions"[36] involved in governance besides those established by the Constitution. But the popular conception of an "invisible government," "state within," or "national security state" is off the mark.[37] The existence of the Trumanite network is no secret. The network's emergence has not been the result of an enormous, nefarious conspiracy conceived to displace constitutional government.[38] The emergence of the Trumanite network has not been purposeful. America's dual national security framework has evolved gradually in response to incentives woven into the system's structure as that structure has reacted to society's felt needs. Yet, as a whole, Americans still do not recognize the extent to which Madisonian institutions have come to formulate national security policy in form more than in substance.

One reason that they do not is that the double government system has exceptions. For the dual institutional structure to work, it is crucial, Bagehot believed, to "hide where the one begins and where the other ends."[39] Overlap is required. Enough counterexamples must exist to persuade an optimistic public that the reason for policy continuity is human, not systemic. Thus, the counterexamples must be sufficient for the public to believe that if they elect different people then policy will change, giving credence to the idea that the real institutions have not lost all power in making national security policy. Similarly, the Trumanites often include some quasi-Madisonian officers, such as the secretaries of state and defense, who themselves generate deference through the same theatrical show common to the Madisonian institutions. Congress, the President, and the courts do sometimes say no to the Trumanites. But they do not do so often enough to endanger double government. The Trumanite network makes American national security policy; it is occasional exceptions to that policy that are made by the Madisonian institutions.

CHAPTER 4

✿

The Reality of Madisonian
Weakness

Although the Madisonian institutions seem to be in charge
and, indeed, to be possessed of power broad enough to remedy their own deficiencies, a close look at each branch of government reveals why they are not. A more accurate description
would be that those institutions are in a state of entropy[1] and
have become, in Bagehot's words, "a disguise"—"the fountain
of honour" but not the "spring of business."[2] The presidency,
Congress, and the courts appear to set national security policy,
but in reality their role is minimal. They exercise decisional
authority more in form than in substance. This is the principal
reason that the system has not, as advertised, self-corrected.[3]

THE JUDICIARY

The courts, which Hamilton called the "least dangerous"
branch,[4] pose the least danger to the silent transfer of power
from the nation's Madisonian institutions to the Trumanite

network.[5] Federal judicial appointees are selected, and vetted along the way, by those whose cases they will later hear: the Trumanites and their associates in the White House and Justice Department. Before an individual is named to the federal bench, a careful investigation takes place to ensure that that individual is dependable. What this means, in practice, is that appointees end up as trusted friends of the Trumanites in matters touching upon national security. Presidents do not appoint individuals who are hostile to the Trumanites, nor does the Senate confirm them. The deck is stacked from the start against challenges to Trumanite policies.

Judicial nominees often come from the ranks of prosecutors, law enforcement, and national security officials, and they have often participated in the same sorts of activities the lawfulness of which they will later be asked to adjudicate.[6] A prominent example was former Chief Justice William Rehnquist.[7] Before his 1971 appointment to the Supreme Court by President Richard Nixon, Justice Rehnquist served as Assistant Attorney General for the Office of Legal Counsel (OLC) under Attorney General John Mitchell.[8] In that capacity, Rehnquist participated directly in military surveillance of domestic political groups, including the preparation of a memorandum for Mitchell in 1969 dealing with the Army's role in the collection of intelligence on civilians in the United States.[9] He also "played a critical role in drafting the 1969 presidential order that established the division of responsibility between the military and the Justice Department for gathering of intelligence concerning civil disturbances."[10] He testified before the Senate Judiciary Committee's Subcommittee on Constitutional Rights in March 1971 that there were no serious constitutional problems with respect to collecting data or keeping under surveillance persons who are merely exercising their right of a peaceful assembly or petition to redress a grievance.[11] After his confirmation hearings to become Chief Justice, however, he wrote in August 1986 in response to written questions from Senator Mathias that he could not recall participating in the formulation of policy concerning the military surveillance of civilian activities.[12] The Senate confirmed his appointment by a vote of sixty-eight to twenty-six on December 10, 1971.[13] Shortly thereafter, the Court began considering *Laird v. Tatum*,[14] a case involving the lawfulness of Army surveillance of civilians who were engaged in political activities critical of the government.[15] Justice Rehnquist declined to recuse himself, and the case was decided five to four.[16] The result was that the case was not sent back to the trial court to determine, as the Court of Appeals had ordered, the nature and extent of military surveillance of civilian groups.[17] Instead, Justice Rehnquist's vote most likely prevented the discovery of his own prior role and that of his Justice Department colleagues in developing the Nixon administration's military surveillance policy.[18]

Justice Rehnquist's case is but one example of the symbiosis that binds the courts to the Trumanite network. Justice Rehnquist was not the only member of the judiciary with Trumanite links. Other potential appointees had ample opportunity to prove their reliability. Justice Antonin Scalia, before his appointment to the Supreme Court, also served as Assistant Attorney General for OLC and also was appointed initially by President Nixon.[19] During his tenure from 1974 to 1977 at OLC, Scalia later recalled, it fell to him to pass upon the legality of proposed covert operations by the intelligence community: "believe it or not, for a brief period of time, all covert actions had to be approved by me."[20] He attended daily meetings in the White House Situation Room with Director of Central Intelligence William Colby and other top intelligence officials and decided which classified documents should be made available to Congress.[21] He was the legal point-person in dealing with congressional requests for information on intelligence matters; on behalf of the Ford administration he asserted executive privilege before a House investigating committee when it recommended that Henry Kissinger be cited for contempt of Congress for failing to produce classified documents concerning U.S. covert operations abroad.[22]

Justice Samuel Alito is a former captain in the Army Signal Corps, which manages classified communication systems for the military. He later became an Assistant U.S. Attorney, prosecuting drug and organized crime cases, and then an assistant to Attorney General Ed Meese before moving to OLC. There he worked, as he put it, to "increase the power of the executive to shape the law."[23] He was nominated to be a federal court of appeals judge in 1990 by President (and former Director of Central Intelligence) George H. W. Bush. Once confirmed, Judge Alito established his reliability by voting against the daughters of civilians killed in a military plane crash to uphold the government's refusal to show a federal judge the official accident report, on grounds of the state secrets privilege.[24]

Chief Justice John Roberts was a law clerk for Justice Rehnquist.[25] In that capacity he reportedly[26] contributed significantly to the preparation of Rehnquist's opinion in *Dames & Moore v. Regan*,[27] in which the Court upheld the executive's power to extinguish pending law suits by Americans seeking compensation from Iran for property seized by the Iranian government.[28] He moved on to the Justice Department and then President Reagan's White House Office of General Counsel, where he drafted a letter for the President responding to retired Justice Arthur Goldberg, who had written Reagan that the U.S. invasion of Grenada was of doubtful constitutionality.[29] Roberts wrote in the reply that the President had "inherent authority in international affairs to defend American lives and interests and, as Commander-in-Chief, to use the military when necessary in discharging these responsibilities."[30] Roberts's memos, Charlie Savage has reported, "regularly took more extreme positions on presidential power than many of his colleagues."[31] Appointed to the U.S. Court of Appeals for the District of Columbia in 2003,[32] Roberts, like Alito, further confirmed his reliability. He voted to uphold the system of military tribunals established by the Bush administration[33] (which the Supreme Court overturned in *Hamdan v. Rumsfeld*,[34] a decision in which Roberts recused himself)[35] and to uphold the power of the President, pursuant to statute, to prevent the courts from hearing certain lawsuits (in that case, brought by members of the U.S. military who had been captured and tortured during the Gulf War).[36]

It might be thought that these and other similarly inclined judges who adhere to views congenial to the Trumanite network have been appointed not because of Trumanite links but because of their judicial philosophy and particular interpretation of the Constitution—because they simply believe in a strong executive branch, a viewpoint that appointing Presidents have found attractive. Justice Scalia seemingly falls into this category.[37] As Assistant Attorney General he testified twice before Congress in opposition to legislation that would have limited the President's power to enter into sole executive agreements.[38] In judicial opinions and speeches before his appointment to the Supreme Court he frequently expressed opposition to judicial involvement in national security disputes. "[J]udges know little"[39] about such issues, as he wrote in one such case decided while he was a member of the U.S. Court of Appeals for the District of Columbia.[40] He argued again for deference in another national security case that came before that court that raised claims of "summary execution, murder, abduction, torture, rape, wounding, and the destruction of private property and public facilities."[41] It was brought by plaintiffs that included twelve members of Congress, who argued violations of the Constitution, War Powers Resolution,[42] and the Boland Amendments[43] (which cut off funds for the activities at issue).[44] Judge Scalia refused to hear arguments on the merits; where a policy had been approved by "the President, the Secretary of State, the Secretary of Defense, and the Director of the CIA," he wrote, discretionary relief is inappropriate.[45] After his appointment to the Supreme Court, Justice Scalia supported the executive-oriented approach to treaty interpretation that the Reagan administration relied upon in arguing that deployment of a space-based anti-ballistic missile (ABM) system would not violate the ABM treaty (referring in his opinion to various

Washington Post articles on the controversy).[46] Later, in *Rasul v. Bush*,[47] the Court's majority held that federal district courts may exercise jurisdiction under the federal habeas statute to hear claims by foreign nationals detained by the United States. Justice Scalia dissented, denouncing the majority for "judicial adventurism of the worst sort."[48] In *Hamdan v. Rumsfeld*,[49] the majority held that a military commission established by the executive lacked power to try the defendant; Justice Scalia dissented again, insisting that that conclusion was "patently erroneous."[50] In *Boumediene v. Bush*,[51] the majority held that the defendant, a foreign national, had a constitutional privilege of habeas corpus; again Justice Scalia dissented. It came as no surprise when Justice Scalia expressed concern in a 2013 speech that the lawfulness of National Security Agency (NSA) surveillance could ultimately be decided by the courts—"the branch of government that knows the least about the issues in question, the branch that knows the least about the extent of the threat against which the wiretapping is directed."[52] When the Trumanites' actions are at issue, submissiveness, not second-guessing, is the appropriate judicial posture.

It is of course true that Justice Scalia and other such judges were and are appointed because of their judicial philosophy. The *cause* of their beliefs, however, is as irrelevant as it is unknowable; whatever the cause, the effect is the same—they are reliable supporters of the Trumanites. People tend to end up in organizations with missions compatible with their larger worldview, just as people once in an organization tend to adopt a worldview supportive of their organization's mission. Position and judicial philosophy *both* are indicia of reliability. The question is not *why* a potential judicial appointee will come down the right way. The question is *whether* the appointee might reasonably be expected to do so.

It might also be argued that these justices were not sufficient in number ever to constitute a majority on the Supreme Court. In an era of increasingly close decisions, however, one or two votes can be decisive, and it must be remembered that this cursory review embraces only the Supreme Court; numerous district and appellate court judges with ties to the Trumanite network also adjudicate national security cases. This group includes, most prominently, the closest that the nation has to a national security court[53]—the eleven members of the Foreign Intelligence Surveillance Court.

The court, or FISC as it is commonly called, was established in 1978 to grant warrants for the electronic surveillance of suspected foreign intelligence agents operating in the United States.[54] Each judge is selected by the Chief Justice of the Supreme Court from the pool of sitting federal judges.[55] They are appointed for a maximum term of seven years; no further confirmation proceedings take place, either in the Senate or the executive branch.[56] The Chief Justice also selects a chief judge from among the court's eleven judges.[57] All eleven of the sitting judges on the FISC were selected by Chief Justice John Roberts; ten of the eleven were initially appointed to the federal bench by Republican presidents.[58] A study by the *New York Times* concluded that since Roberts began making appointments to the court, 50 percent have been former executive branch officials.[59]

Normally, of course, courts proceed in public, hear arguments from opposing counsel, and issue opinions that are available for public scrutiny. Not so with the FISC. All of its proceedings are closed to the public.[60] The adversarial system integral to American jurisprudence is absent. Only government lawyers appear as counsel, unanswered by any real or potential adverse party.[61] The FISC has pioneered a two-tiered legal system, one made up of public law, the other of secret law.[62] FISC opinions— even redacted portions of opinions that address only the FISC's interpretation of the constitutional rights of privacy, due process, or protection against unreasonable search or seizure—are rarely available to the public.[63] Nancy Gertner, a former federal judge in Massachusetts, summed up the court: "The judges that are assigned to this court are judges that are not likely to rock the boat....All of the structural pressures that keep a judge independent are missing there. It's one-sided, secret, and the judges are chosen in a selection process by one man."[64] The chief judge of the FISC candidly described its fecklessness. "The FISC is forced to rely upon the accuracy of the information that is provided to the Court," said Chief Judge Reggie B. Walton. "The FISC does not have the capacity to investigate issues of non-compliance, and in that respect the FISC is in the same position as any other court when it comes to enforcing [government] compliance with its orders."[65] The NSA's own record proved him correct; an internal NSA audit revealed that it had broken privacy rules or overstepped its legal authority thousands of times since 2008.[66]

The judiciary, in short, does not have the foremost predicate needed for Madisonian equilibrium: "a will of its own."[67] Whatever the court, judges normally are able to find what appear to the unschooled to be sensible, settled grounds for tossing out challenges to the Trumanites' projects. Dismissal of those challenges is couched in arcane doctrine that harks back to early precedent, invoking implicitly the courts' mystical pedigree and an aura of politics-transcending impartiality. But challenges to the Trumanites' projects regularly get dismissed before the plaintiff ever has a chance to argue the merits either before the courts or, sometimes more important, the court of public opinion. Try challenging the Trumanites' refusal to make public their budget[68] on the theory that the Constitution does, after all, require "a regular statement and account of the receipts and expenditures of all public money";[69] or the membership of members of Congress in the military reserve[70] on the theory that the Constitution does, after all, prohibit Senators and Representatives from holding "any office under the United States";[71] or the collection of phone records of the sort given by Verizon to the NSA on the theory that the law authorizing the collection is unconstitutional.[72] Sorry, no standing, case dismissed.[73] Try challenging the domestic surveillance of civilians by the U.S. Army[74] on the theory that it chills the constitutionally protected right to free assembly,[75] or the President's claim that he can go to war without congressional approval[76] on the theory that it is for Congress to declare war.[77] Sorry, not ripe for review, case dismissed.[78] Try challenging the introduction of the armed forces into hostilities in violation of the War Powers Resolution.[79] Sorry, political question, nonjusticiable, case dismissed.[80] Try challenging the Trumanites' refusal to turn over relevant and material evidence about an Air Force plane accident that killed three crew members through negligence,[81] or about racial discrimination against CIA employees,[82] or about an "extraordinary rendition" involving unlawful detention and torture.[83] Sorry, state secrets privilege, case dismissed.[84]

Sometimes the courts have no plausible way of avoiding the merits of national security challenges. Still, the Trumanites win. The courts eighty years ago devised a doctrine—the "non-delegation doctrine"—that forbids the delegation of legislative power by Congress to administrative agencies.[85] Since that time it has rarely been enforced, and never has the Court struck down any delegation of national security authority to the Trumanite apparatus.[86] Rather, judges stretch to find "implied" congressional approval of Trumanite initiatives. Congressional silence, as construed by the courts, constitutes acquiescence.[87] Even if that hurdle can be overcome, the evidence necessary to succeed is difficult to get; as noted earlier,[88] the most expert and informed witnesses all have signed nondisclosure agreements, which prohibit any discussion of "classifiable" information without prepublication review by the Trumanites. As early as 1988, over three million present and former federal employees had been required to sign such agreements as a condition of employment.[89] Millions more have since become bound to submit their writings for editing and redaction before going to press. And as the ultimate trump card, the Trumanites are cloaked in, as the Supreme Court put it, "the very delicate, plenary and exclusive power of the President as the sole organ of the federal government in the field of international relations—a power which does not require as a basis for its exercise an act of Congress."[90] The basis of their power, the Court found, is, indeed, not even the Constitution itself; the basis of Trumanite power is external sovereignty—the membership of the United States in the community of nations, which confers extraconstitutional authority upon those charged with exercising it.[91]

As is true with respect to the other Madisonian institutions, there are, of course, instances in which the judiciary has poached on the Trumanites' domain. The courts rebuffed an assertion of the commander-in-chief power in ordering President Truman to relinquish control of the steel mills following their seizure during the Korean War.[92] Over the Trumanites' objections, the courts rejected specious claims of security threats[93] and permitted publication of the Pentagon Papers that revealed duplicity, bad faith, and ineptitude in the conduct of the Vietnam War.[94] The Supreme Court did overturn military commissions set up to try enemy combatants for war crimes,[95] and two years later found that Guantánamo detainees had unlawfully been denied habeas corpus rights.[96] Personnel *does* sometimes matter. A federal district court did find that the NSA's "almost Orwellian" telephony metadata collection program was "almost certainly" unconstitutional.[97] Enough apparent counterexamples exist to preserve the façade.

Yet the larger picture remains valid. Through the long list of military conflicts initiated without congressional approval—Grenada, Panama, Kosovo, and, most recently, Libya—the courts have never stopped a war, with one minor (and temporary) exception. In 1973, Justice William O. Douglas did issue an order to halt the bombing of Cambodia[98]—which lasted a full nine hours, until the full Supreme Court overturned it.[99] The Court's "lawless" reversal was effected through an extraordinary telephone poll of its members conducted by Justice Thurgood Marshall. "[S]ome Nixon men," Douglas believed, "put the pressure on Marshall to cut the corners."[100] Seldom do judges call out even large-scale constitutional violations that could risk getting on the wrong side of an angry public, as American citizens of Japanese ethnicity discovered during World War II.[101] Whatever the cosmetic effect, the four cases representing the Supreme Court's supposed "push-back" against the War on

Terror during the Bush administration freed, at best, a tiny handful of detainees.[102] As of 2010 fewer than 4 percent of releases from Guantánamo followed a judicial release order.[103] A still-unknown number of individuals, numbering at least in the dozens, fared no better.[104] These individuals were detained indefinitely—without charges, based on secret evidence, sometimes without counsel—as "material witnesses" following 9/11.[105] One can barely find a case in which anyone claiming to have suffered even the gravest injury as the result of the Bush-Obama counterterrorism policies has been permitted to litigate that claim on the merits—let alone to recover damages. The Justice Department's seizure of Associated Press (AP) records was carried out pursuant to judicially approved subpoenas, in secret, without any chance for the AP to be heard.[106] The FISC[107] has barely pretended to engage in real judicial review. Between 1979 and 2013, the court received 35,333 requests for surveillance warrants. It granted 35,311 of those requests, and it turned down twelve.[108] This is the "robust legal regime" that unnamed executive branch officials claimed, following the disclosure of NSA collection of Verizon's phone records, to be "in place governing all activities conducted pursuant to the Foreign Intelligence Surveillance Act."[109] The occasional counterexample notwithstanding, the courts cannot seriously be considered a check on America's Trumanite network.

THE CONGRESS

Like the courts, Congress's apparent power also vastly outstrips its real power over national security. Similar to the Trumanites, its members face a blistering work load. Unlike the Trumanites, their work is not concentrated on the one subject of national security. On the tips of members' tongues must be a ready and reasonably informed answer not only to whether the United States should arm Syrian rebels but also whether the medical device tax should be repealed, whether and how global warming should be addressed, and myriad other issues. The pressure on legislators to be generalists creates a need to defer to national security experts. To a degree congressional staff fulfill this need. But few can match the Trumanites' informational base, drawing as they do on intelligence and even legal analysis that agencies often withhold from Congress. As David Gergen put it, "[p]eople . . . simply do not trust the Congress with sensitive and covert programs."[110]

The Trumanites' threat assessments,[111] as well as the steps they take to meet those threats, are therefore seen as presumptively correct whether the issue is the threat posed by the targets of drone strikes, by weapons of mass destruction in Iraq, or by torpedo attacks on U.S. destroyers in the Gulf of Tonkin. Looming in the backs of members' minds is the perpetual fear of casting a career-endangering vote. No vote would be more fatal than one that might be tied causally to a cataclysmic national security breakdown. While the public may not care strongly or even know about many of the Bush policies that Obama has continued, the public could and would likely know all about any policy change—and who voted for and against it—in the event Congress bungled the protection of the nation. No member wishes to confront the "if only" argument: the argument that a devastating attack would not have occurred if only a national security letter had been sent, if only the state secrets privilege had been invoked, if only that detainee had not been released. Better safe than sorry, from the congressional perspective. Safe means strong. Strong means supporting the Trumanites. Accordingly, Congress often enacts authorizing legislation without knowing what it is approving.[112] The Senate Armed Services Committee, for example, "seemed generally clueless and surprised about the legal standard"[113] that was applied by the executive in construing the scope of its authority under the AUMF.[114] On other occasions the oversight committees acquiesce in semantic stratagems to make activities appear less significant than they are.[115]

Because members of Congress are chosen by an electorate that is disengaged and uninformed, Madison's grand scheme of an equilibrating separation of powers has failed, and a different dynamic has arisen.[116] His design, as noted earlier,[117] anticipated that ambition counteracting ambition would lead to an equilibrium of power and that an ongoing power struggle would result among the three branches that would leave room for no perilous concentration of power.[118] The government's "several constituent parts" would be "the means of keeping each other in their proper places."[119] But the overriding ambition of legislators chosen by a disengaged and uninformed electorate is not to accumulate power by prescribing policy for the Trumanites, as Madison's model would otherwise have predicted. Their overriding ambition is to win re-election,[120] an ambition often inconsistent with the need to resist encroachments on congressional power. All members of Congress know that they cannot vote to prescribe—or proscribe—any policy for anyone if they lose re-election. It is not that Madison was wrong; it is that the predicate needed for the Madisonian system to function as intended—civic virtue—is missing.

As a result, Trumanite influence permeates the legislative process, often eclipsing even professional committee staff. Trumanites draft national security bills that members introduce. They endorse or oppose measures at hearings and markups. They lobby members, collectively and one-on-one. Their positions appear on the comparative prints that guide members through key conference committee deliberations. Sometimes Trumanites draft the actual language of conference reports. They wait outside the chambers of the House and Senate during floor debates, ready on-the-spot to provide members with instant arguments and data to back them up. Opponents frequently are blindsided. Much of this activity is removed from the public eye, leading to the impression that the civics-book lesson is correct; Congress makes the laws. But the reality is that virtually everything important on which national security legislation is based originates with or is shaped by the Trumanite network.[121]

Conversely, congressional influence in the Trumanites' decision-making processes is all but nil. The courts have, indeed, told Congress to keep out. In 1983, the Supreme Court invalidated a procedure, called the "legislative veto," which empowered Congress to disapprove of Trumanite arms sales to foreign nations, military initiatives, and other national security projects.[122] The problem with the concept, the Court said, was that it permitted Congress to disapprove of executive action without the possibility of a presidential veto.[123] A legislative proposal thereafter to give the Senate Intelligence Committee the power to approve or disapprove covert actions was rejected, on the grounds that the Court had ruled out such legislative controls.[124]

The executive is required by law to keep Congress (through the two intelligence oversight committees) "fully and currently informed of all intelligence activities…including any significant anticipated intelligence activity."[125] Defenders of the oversight process often claim that congressional oversight works.[126] How they can know this they do not say.[127] Information concerning the oversight committees' efficacy remains tightly held and is seldom available even to members of Congress, let alone the general public.

Often the failure of congressional oversight has been the result of resistance or outright opposition by the departments and agencies that are supposed to be overseen. This has been true since the beginning. "The business of Congress," CIA director William Casey said in 1984, "is to stay out of my business."[128] He and many successors treated Congress accordingly. "We are like mushrooms," Representative Norman Mineta, a senior member of the House Intelligence Committee, said in 1983. "They [the CIA] keep us in the dark and feed us a lot of manure."[129] In fact, when it comes to some of its most controversial programs, the CIA may not feed the oversight committees anything.[130] Senator Dianne Feinstein recounted that the

CIA's detention and interrogation program began operations in 2002, though it was not until September 2006, that Members of the Intelligence Committee, other than the Chairman and Vice

Chairman, were briefed. In fact, we were briefed by then-CIA Director Hayden only hours before President Bush disclosed the program to the public.[131]

Senator Martin Heinrich expressed his displeasure with the CIA's tactics to John Brennan, the Director of Central Intelligence. He said that he wanted

> to publicly note my continued disappointment with how the CIA, under your leadership, has chosen to engage and interact with this committee, especially as it relates to the committee's study of the CIA's detention and interrogation program. Recent efforts undertaken by the CIA, including but not limited to inaccurate public statements about the committee's study, are meant to intimidate, deflect and thwart legitimate oversight.[132]

Sometimes the agencies' obstruction takes the form of outright deception. Senator Ron Wyden, speaking in January 2014, complained of "years of misleading and deceptive statements that senior officials made to the American people."[133] Even when intelligence activities such as the NSA surveillance are truthfully reported, meaningful scrutiny is generally absent.[134] The information conveyed to the oversight committees often is "wildly over-classified" (in Senator Sheldon Whitehouse's words) and vague, making it difficult for members to ask questions about programs of which they are unaware[135]—particularly when denied access to the expertise of their staff, which is common.[136] Staff members seen by the CIA as pressing too hard can find themselves improperly monitored by the Agency, according to senators whose complaints resulted in an investigation by the CIA's inspector general.[137] In one case, according to Feinstein, "the acting general counsel of the CIA filed a crimes report with the Department of Justice concerning the committee staff's action."[138] The multiyear failure of the two intelligence oversight committees to agree upon what were supposed to be annual authorization bills has caused them to "cede having a formal say on any intelligence issue."[139] Members of the committees typically are precluded from making available to nonmember colleagues classified information that is transmitted to the committees.[140] This is true even if the activities in question are unlawful. Following the NSA surveillance leaks, for example, Senator Wyden said that he "and colleagues" believed that additional, unnamed "secret surveillance programs...go far beyond the intent of the statute."[141] But the few committee members who wish to speak out publicly are precluded from doing so by secrecy rules. It was no surprise that the oversight committees were "largely mum" on many of the controversial policies that the Bush administration pursued, including warrantless wiretapping, torture and interrogation, and rendition and the CIA's secret prisons.[142]

The norm, however, is not members who want to speak out, but members who have been co-opted or who have never believed in the concept of congressional oversight. When CIA officials destroyed videotapes that were made of the waterboarding sessions, no one in the CIA ever told anyone in Congress that they had done so.[143]

> None of the four [intelligence committee] leaders would ever ask to look at the tapes. None of them ever inquired about their status, even though the CIA had put them on notice more than a year earlier that the Agency intended to destroy the tapes at some point. None of them ever asked anything about the tapes.[144]

One of the early chairmen of the Senate committee no doubt spoke for more than one future chairman (and chairwoman). "I don't even like to have an intelligence committee," Goldwater said. "I don't think it's any of our business."[145]

Goldwater was the classic illustration of the type of intelligence overseer referred to by Loch Johnson as an "ostrich."[146] Another, Representative (and later President) Gerald R. Ford, served on a predecessor intelligence oversight committee "and never heard anything about the CIA's domestic spying or assassination plots."[147] Others come to the process intent upon demonstrating their loyalty to the overseen agencies with unswerving devotion. George Tenet (then deputy director of the CIA) recounted that after Anthony Lake's nomination was announced, the chairman of the Senate committee, Senator Richard Shelby, told him, "George, if you have any dirt on Tony Lake, I'd sure like to have it."[148] Shelby, Dianne Feinstein, and other "cheerleaders," to use Johnson's term, come to the task of oversight for the purpose of cheering more loudly on behalf of the intelligence agencies.[149] These two groups have in recent years come to outnumber the overseers that Johnson describes as "skeptics," like Senator Daniel Patrick Moynihan (who called for the CIA's abolition), or "guardians," like Senator Frank Church and Representative Lee Hamilton, who see the oversight role as not simply responding to crises but actively preventing spy scandals and intelligence failures.[150]

Even the committees' flimsy structural backstop has been regularly circumvented by the agencies' increasing resort to a new, pseudostructure, the "Gang of Eight," which consists of the leadership of each chamber and the two committees. "[N]o staff can attend and members are precluded from taking notes or disclosing the information to anyone, including other members of the committees or legal counsel."[151] Normally no advance notice is given, so no preparation is possible. Nor is discussion or deliberation feasible, because the briefings, such as they are, often are given individually.[152] The net result, in the words of former Senate committee chairman Bob Graham, is that members are "very restricted in their ability to understand and question" what they are briefed on.[153] More recently, the agencies have moved increasingly to a "Gang of Four"—which even a former CIA head, Leon Panetta, acknowledged to be "overused...and abused."[154]

Other oversight committees have fared no better. U.S. and foreign intelligence services enter into international agreements concerning a variety of significant foreign policy questions including, for example, the sharing of surveillance information, jointly conducted paramilitary operations, and the rendition of detainees.[155] These arrangements bear directly upon the legislative responsibilities of the foreign affairs, judiciary, and armed services committees of both houses of Congress. They too have oversight obligations. When the Senate Foreign Relations Committee attempted to make clear, however, that existing reporting requirements (contained in the "Case Act"[156]) extended to such agreements, the CIA objected[157] and the executive threatened to veto the legislation unless the clarification was removed.[158] Information from the CIA, NSA, and other intelligence agencies has been regularly denied to such committees with the claim that only the co-opted intelligence committees have jurisdiction—even though the measures that initially established the intelligence committees anticipated precisely such a contention and made clear that other committees' jurisdiction was not narrowed by the intelligence committees' establishment.[159]

Why has Congress not insisted upon more rigorous oversight? Robust oversight in any policy realm requires an "electoral connection"—that is, members' all-important interest in maximizing their chances for re-election must reinforce, or at least align with, their interest in holding bureaucrats' feet to the fire. In contrast to other policy areas, however, intelligence presents what Amy Zegart and Julie Quinn have described as "an extreme case of electoral disconnection."[160] They identify three principal reasons. First, few voters cast votes based upon intelligence issues. As the House Permanent Select Committee on Intelligence noted in 1996,

> [i]ntelligence, unlike virtually all other functions of government, has no natural advocates in the public at large. Its direct effect on the lives of most citizens is largely unfelt or unseen; its industrial base is too rarefied to build a large constituency in many areas; it is largely an "inside the Beltway" phenomenon in terms of location, logistics, budget and concern.[161]

Second, voters who do care deeply about intelligence are geographically dispersed across congressional districts.[162] No concentrated natural constituency therefore emerges of the sort that characterizes, for example, farming or various industrial sectors. Third, compared with other policy areas, intelligence interest groups are few and feeble. One obvious reason is that they are blinded by secrecy and classification restrictions; the Trumanites resist accountability. "These electoral disconnections provide entrenched barriers to robust oversight."[163]

Knowledgeable assessments of the performance of Congress's oversight apparatus have therefore been bleak. Zegart and Quinn conclude that the "House and Senate intelligence committees have been dramatically less active in their oversight duties compared to other committees."[164] Johnson, perhaps the most experienced scholar/practicioner of intelligence oversight, summarizes the existing literature by noting that "[m]ost observers agree that members of Congress are performing far below their potential when it comes to supervision of secret agencies."[165] James Bamford, among the most informed outside critics, has written that "[t]oday the intelligence committees are more dedicated to protecting the agencies from budget cuts than safeguarding the public from their transgressions."[166] Even a former director of the CIA found oversight lacking. "I would say with all candor that in my four years when I think we had a very cooperative relationship, I believe the committees of Congress could have been more rigorous with me..." said Admiral Stansfield Turner. "[I]t would be more helpful if you are probing and rigorous."[167] The 9/11 Commission was unambiguous in its own conclusions concerning the reliability of congressional intelligence oversight; the word the Commission used to describe it was "dysfunctional."[168] The oversight committees' performance from the Iranian Revolution through the mining of Nicaraguan harbors,[169] the Iran-Contra affair,[170] NSA surveillance,[171] and other similar episodes[172] provides scant evidence to contradict the Commission's conclusion.

THE PRESIDENCY

One might suppose, at this point, that what is at issue is not the emergence of double government so much as something else that has been widely discussed in recent decades: the emergence of an imperial presidency.[173] After all, the Trumanites work for the President. Can't he simply "stand tall" and order them to do what he directs, even though they disagree?

The answer is complex. It is not that the Trumanites would not obey;[174] it is that such orders would rarely be given. *Could not* shades into *would not*, and improbability into near impossibility: President Obama *could* give an order wholly reversing U.S. national security policy, but he *would not*, because the likely adverse consequences would be prohibitive.

Put differently, the question of whether the President *could* institute a complete about-face supposes a top-down policy-making model. The illusion that presidents issue orders and that subordinates simply carry them out is nurtured in the public imagination by media reports of "Obama's" policies or decisions or initiatives, by the President's own frequent references to "my" directives or personnel, and by the Trumanites own reports that the President himself has "ordered" them to do something. But true top-down decisions that order fundamental policy shifts are rare.[175] As Acheson put it, "One fact...is clear to anyone with experience in government: The springs of policy bubble up; they do not trickle down."[176] The reality is that when the President issues an "order" to the Trumanites, the Trumanites themselves normally formulate the order.[177] The Trumanites "cannot be thought of as men who are merely doing their duty. They are the ones who determine their duty, as well as the duties of those beneath them. They are not merely following orders: they give the orders."[178] They do that by "entangling"[179] the President, who repeatedly finds himself negotiating with the military.[180] This dynamic is an aspect of what one scholar has called the "deep structure" of the presidency.[181] As Theodore Sorensen put it, "Presidents rarely, if ever, make decisions—particularly in foreign affairs—in the sense of writing their conclusions on a clean slate. . . . [T]he basic decisions, which confine their choices, have all too often been previously made."[182] When it comes to national security, the President is less decider than presider.

Justice Douglas, a family friend of the Kennedys, saw the Trumanites' influence first hand: "In reflecting on Jack's relation to the generals, I slowly realized that the military were so strong in our society that probably no President could stand against them."[183] The CIA, too, plays a greater role than many realize, particularly in what seems to be the realm of diplomacy.[184] As the roles of the generals and CIA have converged, the CIA's influence has expanded—aided in part by a willingness to shade the facts, even with sympathetic Madisonian sponsors. A classified, 6,000-word report by the Senate Intelligence Committee reportedly concluded that the CIA was "so intent on justifying extreme interrogation techniques that it blatantly misled President George W. Bush, the White House, the Justice Department and the Congressional intelligence committees about the efficacy of its methods."[185] "The CIA gets what it wants," President Obama told his advisers when the CIA asked for authority to expand its drone program and launch new paramilitary operations.[186]

Sometimes, however, the Trumanites proceed without presidential approval. In 1975, a White House aide testified that the White House "didn't know half the things" intelligence agencies did that might be legally questionable.[187] "If you have got a program going and you are perfectly happy with its results, why take the risk that it might be turned off if the president of the United States decides he does not want to do it," he asked.[188] The CIA's former general counsel acknowledged that the Agency never told anyone in the White House about the existence of videotapes of detainees being waterboarded. "[W]e didn't think the White House had a 'need to know,' the classic litmus test in the intelligence business."[189] Sometimes they proceed with White House approval but leave the congressional oversight committees in the dark, as with the CIA's secret prison system and waterboarding.[190] Other occasions arise when Trumanites in the CIA and elsewhere originate presidential "directives"—directed to themselves.[191] Presidents then ratify such Trumanite policy initiatives after the fact.[192] To avoid looking like a bystander or mere commentator, the President embraces these Trumanite policies, as does Congress, with the pretense that they are their own.[193] To maintain legitimacy, the President must appear to be in charge. In a narrow sense, of course, Trumanite policies are the President's own; after all, he did formally approve them.[194] But the policies ordinarily are formulated by Trumanites—who prudently, in Bagehot's words, prevent "the party in power" from going "all the lengths their orators propose[]."[195] The place for presidential oratory, to the Trumanites, is in the heat of a campaign, not in the councils of government where cooler heads prevail.[196] Even presidents broadly sympathetic to Trumanite policies are taken aback. In the summer of 2008, an aide asked Bush what one thing had surprised him most about the presidency. "Bush answered without hesitation. 'How little authority I have,' he said with a laugh."[197]

The idea that presidential backbone is all that is needed further presupposes a model in which the Trumanites share few of the legitimacy-conferring features of the constitutional branches and will easily submit to the President. But that supposition is erroneous. Mass entertainment glorifies the military, intelligence, and law enforcement operatives that the Trumanites direct. The public is emotionally taken with the aura of mystery surrounding the drone war, Seal Team Six, and cyberweapons. Trumanites, aided by Madisonian leaks, embellish their operatives' very real achievements with fictitious details,[198] such as the events surrounding the killing of Osama bin Laden[199] or the daring rescue of a female soldier from Iraqi troops.[200] They cooperate with the making of movies that praise their projects, like *Zero Dark Thirty* and *Top Gun*, but not movies that lampoon them, such as *Dr. Strangelove* (an authentic F-14 beats a plastic B-52 every time).[201] Friendly fire incidents are downplayed or covered up.[202] The public is further impressed with operatives' valor as they are lauded with presidential and congressional commendations, in the hope of establishing Madisonian affiliation.[203] Their simple mission—find bad guys and get them before they get us—is powerfully intelligible.[204] Soldiers, commandos, spies, and FBI agents occupy an honored pedestal in the pantheon of America's heroes. Their secret rituals of rigorous training and preparation mesmerize the public and fortify its respect. To the extent that they are discernible, the Trumanites, linked as they are to the dazzling operatives they direct, command a measure of admiration and legitimacy that the Madisonian institutions can only envy.[205] Public opinion is, accordingly, a flimsy check on the Trumanites; it is a manipulable tool of power enhancement. It is therefore rarely possible for any occupant of the Oval Office to prevail against strong, unified Trumanite opposition, for the same reasons that members of Congress and the judiciary cannot; a nonexpert president, like a nonexpert senator and a nonexpert judge, is intimidated by expert Trumanites and does not want to place himself (or a colleague or a potential political successor) at risk by looking weak and gambling that the Trumanites are mistaken. So presidents wisely "choose" to go along.

The drone policy has been a case in point. Vali Nasr has described how the Trumanite network not only prevailed upon President Obama to continue its drone policy but succeeded in curtailing discussion of the policy's broader ramifications:

> When it came to drones there were four formidable unanimous voices in the Situation Room: the CIA, the Office of the Director of National Intelligence, the Pentagon, and the White House's counterterrorism adviser, John Brennan. Defense Secretary Robert Gates…was fully supportive of more drone attacks. Together, Brennan, Gates, and the others convinced Obama of

both the urgency of counterterrorism and the imperative of viewing America's engagement with the Middle East and South Asia through that prism. Their bloc by and large discouraged debate over the full implications of this strategy in national security meetings.[206]

What Nasr does not mention is that, for significant periods, all four voices were hold-overs from the Bush administration; two Bush administration officials, Michael J. Morell and David Petraeus, headed the CIA from July 1, 2011 to March 8, 2013.[207] The Director of National Intelligence, Dennis C. Blair, had served in the Bush administration as Commander-in-Chief of the U.S. Pacific Command and earlier as Director of the Joint Staff in the Office of the Chairman of Joint Chiefs of Staff;[208] Brennan had been Bush's Director of the National Counterterrorism Center;[209] and Gates had served as Bush's secretary of defense.[210]

Gates's own staying power illuminates the enduring grip of the Trumanite network.[211] Gates was recruited by the CIA at Indiana University in 1965 after spending two years in the Air Force, briefing ICBM missile crews.[212] He went on to become an adviser on arms control during the SALT talks in Vienna.[213] He then served on the National Security Council staff under President Nixon, and then under President Ford, and again under the first President Bush.[214] During the 1980s, Gates held positions of increasing importance under Director of Central Intelligence William Casey; a colleague described Casey's reaction to Gates as "love at first sight."[215] Casey made Gates his chief of staff in 1981.[216] When Casey died of a brain tumor, President Reagan floated Gates's name for director, but questions about his role in the Iran-Contra scandal blocked his nomination.[217] Gates continued to brief Reagan regularly, however, often using movies and slides (though Nancy Reagan was annoyed because he "ate all the popcorn"[218]). Fellow CIA officers almost succeeded in blocking his nomination when it was revived by President Bush, recalling again his role in the

Iran-Contra affair.[219] Gates nonetheless got the job and escaped indictment, though Independent Counsel Lawrence E. Walsh reported that his statements during the investigation "often seemed scripted and less than candid."[220] He took office as President Bush's secretary of defense in 2006, overseeing the aftermath of the Iraq War, and continued in that position in the Obama administration until July 2011.[221]

It is, of course, possible to reject the advice of a Gates, a Brennan, or other prominent Trumanites.[222] But battle-proven survivors normally get their way, and their way is not different from one administration to the next, for they were the ones who formulated the national security policies that are up for renewal. A simple thought experiment reveals why presidents tend to acquiesce in the face of strong Trumanite pressure to keep their policies intact. Imagine that President Obama announced within days of taking office that he would immediately reverse the policies that I detailed at the outset. The outcry would have been deafening—not simply from the expected pundits, bloggers, cable networks, and congressional critics but from the Trumanites themselves. When Obama considered lowering the military's proposed force levels for Afghanistan, a member of his National Security Council staff who was an Iraq combat veteran suggested that, if the President did so, the Commander of U.S. and International Security Assistance Forces (ISAF) in Afghanistan (General Stanley McChrystal), the Commander of U.S. Central Command (General David Petraeus), the Chairman of the Joint Chiefs of Staff (Admiral Michael Mullen), and even Secretary of Defense Gates all might resign.[223] Tom Donilon, Obama's National Security Advisor and hardly a political ingénue, was "stunned by the political power" of the military, according to Bob Woodward.[224] Recall the uproar in the military and Congress when President Bill Clinton moved to end only one Trumanite policy shortly after taking office—the ban on gays in the military.[225] Clinton was quickly forced to retreat, ultimately accepting the policy of "Don't Ask, Don't Tell."[226] A president must choose his battles carefully, Clinton discovered; he has limited political capital and must spend it judiciously. Staff morale is an enduring issue.[227] No president has reserves deep enough to support a frontal assault on the Trumanite network. Under the best of circumstances, he can only attack its policies one by one, in flanking actions, and even then with no certainty of victory. Like other presidents in similar situations, Obama thus "had little choice but to accede to the Pentagon's longstanding requests for more troops" in Afghanistan.[228]

Presidential choice is further circumscribed by the Trumanites' ability to frame the set of options from which the President may choose—even when the President is personally involved in the decision-making process to an unusual degree, as occurred when President Obama determined the number of troops to be deployed to Afghanistan.[229] Richard Holbrooke, the President's Special Representative for Afghanistan and Pakistan, predicted that the military would offer the usual three options—the option they wanted, bracketed by two unreasonable alternatives that could garner no support.[230] "And that is exactly what happened,"[231] Nasr recalled. It was, as Secretary Gates said, "the classic Henry Kissinger model.... You have three options, two of which are ridiculous, so you accept the one in the middle."[232] The military later expanded the options—but still provided no choice. "You guys just presented me [with] four options, two of which are not realistic." The other two were practically indistinguishable. "So what's my option?" President Obama asked. "You have essentially given me one option."[233] The military was "really cooking the thing in the direction that they wanted," he complained. "They are not going to give me a choice."[234] "Obama and his advisers," Robert Gates has written, "were incensed that the Department of Defense—specifically the military—had taken control of the policy process from them and threatened to run away with it."[235] But Afghanistan is not the only realm of civilian-military relations in which presidential control of the military has weakened. Richard Kohn has cited "repeated efforts on the part of the military to frustrate or evade civilian authority when the opposition seems likely to preclude outcomes the military dislikes."[236]

This is, again, hardly to suggest that the President is without power. Exceptions to the rule occur with enough regularity to create the impression of overall presidential control. "As long as we keep up a double set of institutions—one dignified and intended to impress the many, the other efficient and intended to govern the many—we should take care that the two match nicely," Bagehot wrote.[237] He noted that "[t]his is in part effected by conceding some subordinate power to the august part of our polity...."[238] Leadership does matter, or at least it can matter. President Obama's decision to approve the operation against Osama bin Laden against the advice of his top military advisers is a prominent example.[239] Presidents are sometimes involved in the decisional loops, as Bagehot's theory would predict. Overlap between Madisonians and Trumanites preserves the necessary atmospherics. Sometimes even members of Congress are brought into the loop.[240] But seldom do presidents participate personally and directly, let alone the Madisonian institutions *in toto*. The range of presidential choice is tightly hemmed in.[241] As Sorensen wrote in 1981, "[e]ven within the executive branch, the president's word is no longer final...."[242] When the red lights flash and the sirens wail, it is the Trumanites' secure phones that ring.

A CASE STUDY: NSA SURVEILLANCE

Among the principal national security initiatives that the Bush administration began and the Obama administration continued were several surveillance programs carried out by the NSA. The inception, operation, and oversight of these programs illuminate a number of the elements responsible for policy continuity: the symbiotic relationship between Madisonian institutions and the Trumanite network; the Trumanites' crucial role as authors, initiators, and executors of policy; the subservience of the courts; the fecklessness of congressional oversight; the secretiveness and disingenuousness of the executive; and the incentive that all share to ensure that enough overlap exists between the Trumanite network and the Madisonian institutions to maintain a veneer of Madisonian endorsement. Thus long before serious reform efforts were underway, a former director of national intelligence, John Negroponte, could understandably feel confident in predicting the outcome of efforts to curb the NSA's surveillance programs. Any changes, he knew, would be relatively minor: at most, the programs would be, in his word, "tweaked."[243]

The NSA was established in 1952 not by statute but by President Truman's top secret executive order.[244] Its very existence remained unacknowledged until it received unwanted public attention in the 1970s, when a report by the Senate Select Committee to Study Governmental Operations with Respect to Intelligence Activities disclosed that the NSA had kept tabs on Vietnam War opponents, assembling a "watch list" of individuals and organizations involved in the civil rights and anti-war movements.[245] The report further revealed that, between 1945 and May 1975, "[the] NSA received copies of millions of international telegrams sent to, from, or transiting the United States."[246] Following the committee's investigation into domestic spying by the U.S. intelligence community, Committee Chairman Frank Church made a prophetic statement: "[The NSA's] capability at any time could be turned around on the American people, and no American would have any privacy left, such [is] the capability to monitor everything: telephone conversations, telegrams, it doesn't matter."[247] There is, Church said, "tremendous potential for abuse" should the NSA "turn its awesome technology against domestic communications."[248] He added:

> I don't want to see this country ever go across the bridge. I know the capacity that is there to make tyranny total in America, and we must see to it that this agency and all agencies that possess this

technology operate within the law and under proper supervision, so that we never cross over that abyss. That is the abyss from which there is no return.[249]

Church, it turns out, was one of the individuals whose overseas phone calls were tapped by the NSA in the 1970s.[250]

In response to such concerns, Congress in 1978 enacted the Foreign Intelligence Surveillance Act (FISA).[251] A principal purpose of the law was to prohibit the government from monitoring Americans' electronic communications without a judicially granted warrant.[252] FISA set up a special court, the FISC, described above,[253] to review requests for such warrants.[254]

Even before 9/11, NSA Director Michael Hayden had proposed more expansive collection programs in a transition report to the incoming Bush administration.[255] Following 9/11, Hayden quickly sought approval of a program to monitor the communications of Americans living within the United States.[256] The program "sucked up the contents of telephone calls and e-mails, as well as their 'metadata' logs."[257] The Bush administration concluded that aspects of the proposed program probably were illegal[258] and therefore considered seeking a change in the law that would permit the expanded program.[259] It decided against such a request, however, because it concluded that Congress would not approve.[260] Instead, President Bush authorized the NSA to proceed with the program on the basis of the President's supposed independent constitutional power as commander-in-chief, spelled out in a still-classified memorandum written by John Yoo, an attorney in the Office of Legal Counsel (OLC).[261] The program went into operation on October 4, 2001.[262] A change in OLC's leadership brought a different interpretation of the law, with the result that, in March 2004, Attorney General John Ashcroft declined to re-authorize those aspects of the program (reportedly concerning Internet metadata) that OLC now considered illegal, with the result that President Bush rescinded his approval to the NSA to collect Internet data.[263]

The illegal program remained nonoperational for only four months, however; during that period, Justice Department lawyers joined with NSA officials and "immediately began efforts to recreate this authority," an authority to which they believed the FISC would be "amenable."[264] The chief judge of the FISC, Coleen Kollar-Kotelly, quickly obliged, issuing an ex parte order on July 14, 2004.[265] Kollar-Kotelly's order permitted bulk collection of Internet data, with no warrant requirement;[266] it "essentially gave NSA the same authority to collect bulk internet metadata that it had under the [earlier program]."[267] None of the other judges on the FISC was apparently told about the NSA's secret surveillance programs.[268] Nor were they told about Kollar-Kotelly's secret order.[269] This was the first time the surveillance court had exercised any authority over the two-and-a-half-year-old surveillance program.[270]

The program came to public attention when the *New York Times* disclosed it on December 16, 2005.[271] The *Times*, by its own admission, had "held that story for more than a year at the urging of the Bush administration, which claimed it would hurt national security."[272] When it was finally published, Judge James Robertson resigned his seat on the FISC "in apparent protest of the program."[273]

When President Obama took office, as noted earlier,[274] he continued two particularly controversial NSA surveillance programs. One was a program under which the NSA secretly collected the telephone records of tens of millions of Americans who are customers of Verizon and also collected Internet communications.[275] The phone records were collected under an order issued by the FISC, also described earlier.[276] The order, issued under section 215 of the PATRIOT Act,[277] included phone numbers of both parties to every call, their locations, the time the call was made, and the length of the call.[278] The order prohibited its recipient from discussing its existence.[279] The second program Obama continued, PRISM, allowed the NSA to obtain private information about users of Google, Facebook, Yahoo, and other Internet companies.[280] The government claimed authority for this program under section 702 of the FISA Amendments Act of 2008.[281]

When the first program, concerning telephone records, was reported by the British newspaper *The Guardian*,[282] criticism in Congress was muted,[283] and "senior government officials" in the United States were quick to release talking points that did not deny the report but reminded everyone that "all three branches of government are involved" in these sorts of activities.[284] The NSA refused, however, to release its classified interpretation of the applicable statutory authorities.[285] One member of the Senate Intelligence Committee familiar with that interpretation—but prohibited from discussing it publicly—said that the government's theory under the PATRIOT Act to collect records about people from third parties was "essentially limitless."[286] The *New York Times* had filed a Freedom of Information Act suit in 2011 asking for the government's interpretation of the law, but the Obama administration refused to say, and the courts dismissed the suit.[287] The upshot was that neither Congress nor the public had any knowledge that surveillance of this magnitude was permitted or whether any checks were working. As Senator Chris Coons put it: "The problem is: we here in the Senate and the citizens we represent don't know how well any of these safeguards actually work."[288]

Members of Congress were unaware of more than simply the administration's interpretation of the law, however. They had no knowledge about how the administration actually used the phone records that the NSA collected. The chairman of the Senate Intelligence Committee, Dianne Feinstein, confirmed this.[289] But, she added, it was important to collect phone records of the American public in case someone might become a terrorist in the future[290] (a rationale the *New York Times* called "absurd"[291]). Feinstein's coziness with the intelligence community[292] was not without precedent; an earlier chairman of the committee, Senator Barry Goldwater, claimed to know nothing about the CIA's mining of Nicaraguan harbors—even though Director of Central Intelligence William Casey had earlier told the committee.[293] By contrast, the NSA did not inform the committee about warrantless surveillance during the Bush administration, which the committee, of course, never discovered on its own.[294] Senators not on the Intelligence Committee seemed equally uninterested. Normally only the senior congressional leadership is kept fully abreast of intelligence activities, said the Senate's second-ranking Democrat:[295] "You can count on two hands the number of people in Congress who really know."[296] When all senators were invited to a classified briefing by senior national security officials to explain the NSA's surveillance programs, fewer than half attended.[297] Little wonder that in its review of congressional oversight for intelligence and counterterrorism—which it, again, described as "dysfunctional"[298]—the 9/11 Commission concluded that "[t]inkering with the existing structure is not sufficient."[299] "[T]he NSA," *The Economist* concluded, "lives under a simulacrum of judicial and legislative oversight."[300] And, it might have added, a simulacrum of honesty.

Before the leaks, James Clapper, Director of National Intelligence, testifying on behalf of the Obama administration before Feinstein's committee on March 12, 2013, was asked directly about the NSA surveillance by Senator Ron Wyden. "[D]oes the NSA collect any type of data at all on millions or hundreds of millions of Americans?" he asked. Clapper responded, "No, sir." Wyden followed up: "It does not?" Clapper replied, "Not wittingly. There are cases where they could inadvertently perhaps collect, but not wittingly."[301]

Following the Snowden disclosures, Clapper admitted that his testimony was false. On June 9, 2013, he described his response to NBC's Andrea Mitchell as "the least untruthful" statement he could give,[302] suggesting that he understood the question and deliberated on how it should be answered. Two weeks later, however, in a June 21 letter to Senator Dianne Feinstein, he suggested that he had been confused and, in his answer, had been thinking of the NSA's collection of Internet rather than telephony data.[303] The issue of intent is relevant, since the statement may have constituted a felony;[304] confused or not, Clapper had the often-exercised option of suggesting that the matter be discussed in executive session. Feinstein, who was presiding on June 11 when the initial statement was made and who had earlier been briefed on the programs, knew that statement was false and said nothing.[305] President Obama and other senior members of his administration also knew that it was false[306]—or, if the Madisonian model were functioning as intended, should have known it was false[307]—and also said nothing, allowing the falsehood to stand for months until leaks publicly revealed the testimony to be false.[308] Obama, finally caught by surprise, insisted that he "welcomed"[309] the debate that ensued, and his administration commenced active efforts to arrest the NSA employee whose disclosures had triggered it.[310] He downplayed the significance of collecting mere metadata[311] (although a former general counsel to the NSA said it "tells you everything"[312]). The President then proceeded to insist that the NSA was not "actually abusing its powers."[313] In fact, a May 2012 NSA audit revealed 2,776 incidents in the preceding twelve months where the agency engaged in "unauthorized collection, storage, access to or distribution of legally protected communications."[314]

The NSA also made misrepresentations to the FISC.[315] In a declassified 2011 opinion by the FISC's chief judge, U.S. District Court Judge John Bates, the court said that it was "troubled that the government's revelations...mark the third instance in less than three years in which the government has disclosed a substantial misrepresentation regarding the scope of a major collection program." His court's earlier approval of NSA's telephone records collection, Bates wrote, was based upon "a flawed depiction" of how the NSA uses metadata, a "misperception...buttressed by repeated inaccurate statements made in the government's submissions, and despite a government-devised and Court-mandated oversight regime." "Contrary to the government's repeated assurances," Bates continued, the "NSA had been routinely running queries of the metadata using querying terms that did not meet the required standard for querying. The court concluded that this requirement had been 'so frequently and systemically violated that it can fairly be said that this critical element of the overall…regime has never functioned effectively.' "[316]

As the surveillance controversy unfolded, "the NSA quietly removed from its website a fact sheet about its collection activities because it contained inaccuracies discovered by lawmakers."[317] Senator Ron Wyden, a member of the Senate Intelligence Committee, said that national security officials in the Obama administration were "actively" misleading the American public about domestic surveillance.[318] It was not clear whether he was referring to additional actions. After having claimed that the collection of bulk phone records was the primary tool in thwarting dozens of plots, a senior NSA official conceded that it had thwarted only one plot.[319]

On July 24, 2013, following an intense lobbying effort by Clapper and the NSA,[320] the House of Representatives by a vote of 205 to 217 defeated a measure, sponsored by Representatives Justin Amash and John Conyers Jr., that would have prevented the NSA from continuing its bulk phone records collection program within the United States.[321] The Obama administration "made common cause with the House Republican leadership to try to block it."[322] During the debate the chairman of the House Intelligence Committee, Representative Mike Rogers, revealed, perhaps unwittingly, the relationship between the oversight committees and the intelligence agencies. "What they're talking about doing," he said, "is turning off a program that after 9/11 we realized we missed—we the intelligence community—missed a huge clue," Rogers said.[323]

We the intelligence community: the overseers and the overseen had, at length, become one.

CHAPTER 5

⌒∿⌒

Plausible Alternative Explanations for Policy Continuity

Bagehot's notion of double government provides a lens that sharpens focus on the reasons why policies such as National Security Agency (NSA) surveillance have remained continuous from the Bush administration through the Obama administration. Double government is not, however, the only possible explanation. The most plausible competing alternatives, as noted earlier,[1] fall into two categories (which I borrow from the classic typology applied by Graham Allison and Philip Zelikow to explain events during the Cuban missile crisis[2]). The first suggests that continuity is simply the rational response to continuing security threats. The second suggests that continuity is merely another result of the *Sturm und Drang* of government politics.

For reasons that will become clear, neither is convincing. More powerful are the insights of organizational behaviorists— which reinforce Bagehot's theory and dovetail with the notion of a network within the United States' double government. A review of these three models follows.

THE RATIONAL ACTOR MODEL

The first plausible alternative explanation is straightforward: the reason that U.S. national security does not change is simply that the threats have not changed. Whatever else they may be, according to this argument, national security policymakers are rational actors, and U.S. national security policy is merely a rational response to the same continuing threats. This explanation recalls Palmerston's famous maxim that England has no eternal allies, only eternal interests.[3] The continuity of American national security, under this view, merely reflects the permanence of U.S. interests in addressing enduring security threats. This, the so-called "rational actor" model, supposes that the government comprises a unitary actor that engages in several analytic steps in coming to decisions to advance those interests. First, it identifies a policy objective. Then it puts together a range of options for achieving that objective. Next it weighs the costs and benefits of each option against the costs and benefits of the others. Finally, it rationally and freely chooses the option that is objectively optimal.[4]

The rational actor model is elegant and simple. It has a potent attraction: the policymaker's identity is irrelevant. Politics and personality count for naught. Given the same information, opportunity for deliberation, and decisional context, every rational policymaker can be expected to select the same option; any other option would be irrational. Indeed, prominent versions of the rational actor model (e.g., so-called "comprehensive rationality") go so far as to suggest that only one rational option exists and that a given policy can be explained entirely by decision makers' desires to maximize the single utility or preference underpinning that policy.[5] Some scholars lean toward this approach in analyzing terrorism.[6] Other, "thicker" variants (e.g., the "bounded rationality" approach) acknowledge multicausality and cognitive distortion—though at the cost of vastly expanding and complicating the required analysis and empirical spadework, and perhaps conjoining it with the governmental politics mode, discussed below.[7] Each of these two strands has been invoked to explain the Obama administration's continuation of Bush national security policies. Both strands, at bottom, predict that if the government's interest in maximizing security remains constant and if internal and external security threats also remain constant, one administration will respond to those threats by choosing the same national security options as another administration. Who happens to be President is of no consequence: the government acts rationally, and discontinuity under such conditions would be irrational.

Elegance and simplicity, however, don't always add up to truth. Thinking that policy continuity has been the result of rationality, it turns out, is like thinking that the cause of an automobile accident was two cars colliding with each other. The issue is, what *creates* the ostensible rationality? What *causes* policymakers to engage in behavior that is experienced as "rational"? The model has multiple, well-known flaws. There are, on analysis, five reasons to look beyond the rational actor model in attempting to explain policymakers' choices.

First, it provides no useful guidance as to what preference, value, or utility ought to be maximized. Consider the decision not to prosecute Bush administration officials who supervised and conducted waterboarding. The policy arguably rested on the judgment that domestic political stability, reconciliation, or simple forgiveness was more important than some conflicting value such as strict juridical consistency, sympathy for the victims, or international reputational interests. But why does one of those values have some foundational, hierarchical superiority over another? Why is one in some objective sense more "rational" than another?

Second, no one can know with certainty what particular objective is being pursued; in applying the rational actor model, ends are inferred from action that is inevitably ambiguous and capable of supporting multiple, conflicting inferences. To continue with the same example, one plausible goal of the policy of nonprosecution may have been to avoid making heroes out of the defendants. Another may have been to avoid the embarrassment of a possible not-guilty verdict. Another may have been to avoid putting friends or friends of friends or colleagues of friends on the docket. How can we know which factor determined the decision? For that matter, why is it not possible that the policy goal changes—that the mission creeps—as the process of executing that policy unfolds?

Third, the model's anthropomorphizing notwithstanding, the government is not a unitary actor with feelings and thoughts and purposes. It consists of individuals. People make decisions. The nonprosecution option emerged from groups of people. Who within the group made the decision? How can we identify who wrote the determinative email that triggered the determinative comment at the determinative teleconference that led to the determinative judgment? What was the triggering event? As Allison and Zelikow note, during the Cuban missile crisis, "thousands of people were performing actions that had, or could have had, significant impact on the event."[8] The same information, opportunity for deliberation and decisional context are *never present* from one administration to the next. The variables always differ. We can never identify them all, let alone which one really matters. The old verse well encapsulates the insurmountable problem of tracing causation and the way tiny, seemingly inconsequential events ultimately determine enormous outcomes:[9]

> For want of a nail, the shoe was lost;
> For want of a shoe, the horse was lost;
> For want of a horse, the rider was lost;
> For want of a rider, the battle was lost;
> For want of a battle, the kingdom was lost![10]

As Fernand Braudel put it, it is "an obvious and dangerous oversimplification" to think that we can "distinguish without difficulty the 'important events,' which means 'those which bore consequences.'"[11] The predictive value of the model is thus severely limited.

Fourth, the cost-benefit analysis that the model entails cannot dictate which factors are to be placed on the scales or how much weight each should be accorded. This point is different from the first in that it refers to means rather than ends, but the implication is similar: judgments as to the relative attractiveness of one means are inevitably subjective and vary from one decision maker to the next. Even if it were in some sense rational to prefer, say, domestic political stability over all other ends, why is nonprosecution the only rational option among competing alternatives capable of achieving that goal? Why exclude the possibility that prosecution might redound to domestic political stability in the long term by, for example, inducing the belief that governmental edicts are to be respected because the government holds itself and its officials to the same standards as private citizens? Why is not the alternative of a "truth commission" (which the Obama administration rejected[12]) one that produces fewer costs and greater benefits in pursuit of domestic political stability? Obviously a measure of guesswork is involved; how much risk is tolerable? Is every rational actor equally risk-averse? Doesn't personal political philosophy or organizational bias play some role? Might another option be available that hasn't been considered? These and many similar questions are of course debatable—which is precisely the point: reasonable people can differ. Human beings do not process information like computers and spit out an objectively optimal answer. One particular policy option is not the only sensible means to an agreed-upon end. Thomas Powers has pointed out that, to CIA Director William Casey, the Reagan administration's Nicaragua policy was entirely rational—even though "[h]is war killed people to no purpose; it squandered the nation's political energy in a fruitless repetition of old arguments; and it put the CIA through a ringer that it had barely survived for the first time around in the mid-1970s."[13] Much the same could be said of other ill-conceived national security initiatives from the Bay of Pigs to Vietnam to Bush's invasion of Iraq: the decisions all seemed rational at the time to those who made them.

Finally, rationality is indeed "bounded" by cognitive distortions. Daniel Kahneman and Amos Tversky pointed out the many ways that otherwise "rational" (if there really is such a thing) people behave irrationally. Our minds "are susceptible to systematic errors";[14] "[w]e are prone to overestimate how much we understand about the world and to underestimate the role of chance in events."[15] They documented twenty systematic errors in the thinking of normal people—biases traceable to deficiencies in cognition, not "the corruption of thought by emotion"[16] (such as fear, affection or hatred—which present another set of difficulties). We tend, for example, to believe things because others do (the "bandwagon bias"), we remember choices as being better than they actually were ("choice supportive bias"), we tend to be skeptical of contradictory evidence ("disconfirmation bias"), we tend to assume that others share our attitudes and beliefs ("projection bias") and fall victim to multiple, additional cognitive errors that skew our judgment.[17] Cognitive errors such as these pervade the decision-making process throughout the realm of national security and make prediction extraordinarily difficult, and it can never be fully anticipated when one or another such errors will pop up. What appears to its participants to be consensus-based rationality may in fact be an unnoticed, symbiosis-driven mind-meld created and reinforced by cognitive error. Not only can we be "blind to the obvious," as Kahneman has put it, "we are also blind to our blindness."[18]

We are blind, specifically, to our tendency to overestimate threats—a tendency that pervades the thinking of both the Trumanite network and the general public. Cass Sunstein has explained the phenomenon in the context of terrorism. "[E]xaggerated risk perceptions [are] a likely result" of a terrorist attack because people tend to measure probability, inaccurately, by recalling the most readily available example—the earlier terrorist attack.[19] The outcome can be "significantly exaggerated judgments of probable harm."[20] Further, new risks—risks that seem unfamiliar or uncontrollable—generate disproportionate fear, leading to large behavioral changes even though the magnitude of the risks does not justify those changes. (The United States could quickly and easily save 4,500 lives annually by banning the "familiar" risk posed by motorcycles.[21]) Finally, when their emotions are intensely engaged, people focus their attention on the bad outcome itself, "and they are inattentive to the fact that it is unlikely to occur."[22] Other studies confirm a natural human "predilection toward alarmist responses and excessive weighting of the worst case scenario."[23] We are, in short, *not* rational in some situations in which we most need to be; we tend to harbor, as one analyst put it, a "false sense of insecurity."[24]

These deficiencies in the rational actor model undermine its capacity to explain and predict policy continuity. What is true of the nonprosecution policy with respect to torture is true of other elements of national security policy as well: whatever the merits of any given element of the Bush/Obama national security policy, the contention that those policies are the only rational response to the same continuing threats is unconvincing.[25] Sound reasons might exist for one or more elements of that policy. But that judgment can be made only by examining the merits of each policy case by case, evaluating trade-offs, and by assessing side effects and opportunity costs, acceptable risk levels, short-term and long-term payoffs, value conflicts, urgency and the many other factors that weigh for or against a given policy.[26] My purpose is not, again, to address the merits of any of those issues. The point is that it is erroneous to think that the Bush/Obama national security policies necessarily represent the single rational or the most rational response to the same continuing threats. Something more is going on.

THE GOVERNMENT POLITICS MODEL

The government politics model attempts to remedy the flaws in the slim rational actor model by cramming in everything that might constitute that "something more."[27] The model is easily summarized: virtually everything that the rational actor model excludes, this model includes. It posits that government policy is a result not of purposive action directed at solution-finding but rather that policy emerges from a collage of separate decisions flowing from the "compromise, conflict, and confusion" of chaotic bargaining by "officials with diverse interests and unequal influence."[28] Myriad factors shape the turmoil that is policymaking: the identity of the "players"; their preferences, perceptions, and political philosophies—and all the variables that shape those factors; the "action channels" within which officials proceed; applicable legal and cultural rules; where the official sits organizationally, including hierarchical rank; and any evidence that is available or unavailable concerning why pertinent decision makers acted as they did. In attempting to explain the continuity of U.S. national security policy, the model therefore picks up the various personality-related and politically-contextual factors dominant in popular discourse. A president's supposed conflict-averseness, for example, and archetypal political vulnerabilities all would be seen as potentially causative.

The model's great strength thus lies in its realism. It recognizes the unavoidable difficulty of picking out what's causally relevant in driving human and therefore governmental behavior. Unlike the rational actor model, this model is not excessively parsimonious. But this strength is also a weakness. It fails to identify any one factor *but for* which the policy result would not have occurred. The government politics model "incorporates so many variables that it is an analytic kitchen sink," as Jonathan Bendor and Thomas Hammond put it. "Nothing of any possible relevance appears to be excluded...."[29] Again, Allison and Zelikow themselves acknowledge that, during the Cuban missile crisis, "thousands of people were performing actions that had, or could have had, significant impact on the event."[30] To a greater or lesser extent the same is true of every national security policy—innumerable actions by innumerable people shape the final outcome. Unless at least some greater simplification occurs, however, explanation is impossible. Whereas the rational actor model errs through underinclusiveness, the government politics model errs through overinclusiveness. A model is needed that more accurately isolates causes. The organizational behavior model—the prime tenets of which parallel those of Bagehot's approach—comes closer to filling that bill.

THE ORGANIZATIONAL BEHAVIOR MODEL

Unlike the government politics model, the organizational behavior model doesn't throw in the kitchen sink; unlike dominant strands of the rational actor model, it doesn't purport to present a neat, unicausal theory. Instead it lays out a series of characteristics common to the behavior of organizations of the sort that partake in the making of U.S. national security policy.[31]

Pertinent elements of modern organizational behavior theory, distilled from the writings of prominent scholars,[32] provide added insight into six key issues: how membership and the culture of its members' home organizations shape the Trumanite network's purposes; how standard operating procedures limit its capacity for change; how the network assesses risk; how power within the Trumanite network is allocated and enhanced; and how information flows and affects network outputs.[33]

Membership, Culture, and Purposes

Government consists of organizations and organizations consist of people; to understand how organizations behave requires understanding how their members behave. Access to organizations is selective. Appointments are made according to specialized qualifications tailored to the organization's purposes and the capabilities it needs to carry out those purposes. Attitudinal conformance is thus critical.

The organization's purposes are a function of the practices of its members. The original purposes given the organization by its creators are modified over time by its members, who confront unanticipated challenges that must be addressed. Newly emerging purposes are implicitly ratified by the creators, who later defer to the organization's expertise in evaluating those challenges and the capabilities needed to meet them.[34] Organizations resist new missions, however, that are seen as undercutting their culture or efficiency.

Members' practices are shaped by the organization's culture, which defines role expectations and duties, who is hired and how they are trained, what behavior is rewarded and what is penalized, organizational truth and virtue, and how what has happened to the organization should be interpreted.[35] Culture confers a sense of worth on members, generates loyalty, and motivates desired behaviors. Members' practices are also shaped by efficiency in addressing problems of cooperation and collective action, leading them, for example, to engage in free-riding when possible and aberrant behavior that risks tolerable penalties.

Standard Operating Procedures and Change

To control the organization's members and channel them in carrying out its purposes, standard operating procedures (SOPs) are adopted. These fixed SOPs are analogous to a football team's playbook; they are set routines that lay out a predetermined response to a given set of contingencies. Contingencies not in the playbook are analogized to those that are; the organization therefore responds to a contingency that is not within the playbook by adhering to an existing, familiar SOP. Most organizational behavior is governed by previously established procedures. Established routines for avoiding established routines are disfavored.[36] Capabilities are generated to carry out an organization's purposes, as implemented in its SOPs. For this reason capabilities induce analytic bias; organizational choice is a function of capability. Contingencies that might better be addressed with different capabilities are therefore addressed with existing, available capabilities. Missions change only incrementally. This produces stable expectations and reliability but also inflexibility and stasis.[37] SOPs change, but, barring a disaster, only gradually.[38] Adherence to existing SOPs is the usual standard of success; the menu of choice is therefore severely limited and is defined by short-term payoffs for the organization and its members, not long-term payoffs for the organization's creators or uninfluential third-parties.

Risk Assessment

The SOPs are fashioned, and action under SOPs occurs, based upon the likely consequences for the organization. Actions and SOPs with high organizational benefits are chosen over those with high costs. Costs and benefits are calculated by "retrieving experience preserved in the organization's files or individual memories."[39] Dramatic performance failures threaten an organization with dramatic change. Organizations therefore eschew risky ventures and avoid uncertainty. Outputs that incur predictable but acceptable costs are preferable to outputs that risk high costs for potentially greater benefits. Hence the tendency of organizations to "satisfice"[40]—to settle for an option that is satisfactory though not potentially the best.

Priority is given to immediate problems of probable importance over future problems of speculative importance.

Organizations are therefore reactive rather than proactive. Programs already undertaken are not dropped merely because costs outweigh benefits. Organizational inertia carries a program beyond the loss point.[41]

Power Allocation and Enhancement

Benefits take the form of enlarged budgets, personnel, missions;[42] costs take the form of retrenchments in each. Net enlargements minus retrenchments equal the organization's ability to get what it wants—its external power, or its ability, in Max Weber's words, to realize its "own will in communal action, even against the resistance of others."[43] Greater power leads to greater capabilities, and greater capabilities to greater power. Organizations seek to identify new problems that need to be addressed within their missions to justify greater capabilities. Clarity of mission trumps expansion, however; change is resisted because it threatens traditional expectations and SOPs along with organizational culture and efficiency.

Individuals within organizations seek, similarly, greater power. Each is "a little cog in the machine and, aware of this, his one preoccupation is whether he can become a bigger cog."[44] The organization acts externally through its upper layers, but lower layers shape upper layers' responses, for field-based learning and information acquisition come from the bottom.[45] Decision-making and data-gathering therefore occur at remote levels.

Information Flows and Network Outputs

Data is capability-enhancing in that it reduces uncertainty; it therefore is not shared with real or potential competitors, leading to secrecy, equivocation, and exclusivity. The process of filtering and reinterpreting data in the intermediate layers from collection to decision subjects the data to abbreviation, modification, and cognitive distortion (such as groupthink). The filters compromise the organization's aim of preserving its culture and efficiency. Organizational outputs thus constrain leaders to choose from a limited range of options in addressing problems. The problems are identified in lower organizational layers, and steps are taken to respond to those problems before leaders direct the organization to do so. Their choices often are anticlimactic.[46] These organizational tendencies produce consistent preferences that remain stable over time and are little influenced by the identity of the organization's members or even its leaders.

These are some of the principal tenets of organizational theory pertinent to the Trumanite network; there are of course more. Many overlap. Some are in tension with others. None is invariable; exceptions exist. Nonetheless, their relevance to the Trumanites, who were described more fully earlier,[47] need hardly be spelled out. Together, they reinforce Bagehot's theory and explain further why the Trumanite network keeps U.S. national security policy constant.

THE NETWORK MODEL

One key modification is needed, however. The organizational behavior model supposes the existence of a discrete "organization." A more apt description of the Trumanites' structure is that it comprises a network that straddles multiple organizations.[48] "Special networks are nothing new," one national security alumnus noted. They are not "found on the organizational charts of any agency." But it is often through a network that the "most important business of government gets done, and if a President does not establish networks of his own, they will likely be established to undermine him."[49] Similarly, Bagehot's concept of an "institution" implies a level of process and formality that its substance belies. The notion of a network seems better to capture the structure and complexity of multiple actors, policy determinants, and their interactions.[50]

The Trumanite structure[51] is more like a network than an organization or institution in six key respects. First, its boundaries are amorphous. Who on the margins is in or out at any given time is unclear. Its membership fluctuates as a function of how the problem is framed, the organizational position of the individual, the individual's interactions with other individuals in the network, and factors related to individual personality, professional history, reputation, and political preferences.

Second, the Trumanite structure has no formal powers as such. Its members exercise what authority they have as a result of factors exogenous to the network, including their organizational position, expertise, personal relationships, history, and professional credentials.

Third, the network has no formal routines. Rules are few. Unlike organizations, it has no standard operating procedures or established decision-making processes.

Fourth, the network has no explicit division of labor. Specialization exists but is often overlooked. Lawyers kibitz on policy, weapons experts on law, budgeteers on covert operations. Members are seen as experts but also as smart generalists.[52] They know each other, call on each other, and use each other; they are, in Hugh Heclo's phrase, "experts in using experts."[53]

Fifth, when one node becomes inoperable, a work-around develops. Inoperability can occur as a result of unavailability or intentional exclusion owing to disagreement; decisional power flows over and around those blockages.

And sixth, a network has no fixed, identifiable leaders. Different officials take on more or less responsibility as a function of an ever-shifting mélange of issues, personalities, relationships, and political imponderables.[54]

While the Trumanite network is unlike an organization in these respects, it is like an organization in one all-important sense: its members all are members of organizations, and the behavior of network members is conditioned by the patterns of behavior common to their organizations. This is particularly true of the Pentagon and intelligence community. "[T]he CIA, for all its legend and mystique, is at bottom a large federal bureaucracy."[55] While formal rules of the network are few, informal expectations are still powerful. Members are thus counted on, for example, to exhibit loyalty to existing decisions, avoid publicly embarrassing other members of the network, and demonstrate fidelity to commonly shared values and assumptions.

These and related characteristics explain the Trumanite network's susceptibility to what social psychologists refer to as "groupthink." The concept takes its name from Irving Janus's classic work by that title.[56] It refers to the stifled thinking that occurs within highly cohesive groups. Dissent is suppressed in a continuing drive for consensus that values loyalty to group mores against all else. Personal responsibility for the group's actions are downplayed, along with risk of failure; the merits of alternative policies are given short shrift; the least objectionable alternative—the status quo—often is rationalized as the safest. Glenn Carle, a former CIA analyst, described the tendency to "reject incongruous or contradictory facts as erroneous, because they do not conform to accepted reality...." The result was classic groupthink: one could always speak up—in principle—but the career consequences need hardly be spelled out: "Say what you want at meetings. It's your decision. But you are doing yourself no favors."[57] Groupthink creates an illusion that consensus is created by mere rationality—groupthink reinforces commitment to the rational actor model—but the consensus derives not from seeming rationality; it derives from the tacit premises that the group unconsciously shares.

The Trumanite network has thrived because "it takes a network to fight a network."[58] The terrorist threats that the Trumanites have confronted are nimble, shadowy, and quick-footed adversaries too agile to be fought by a bureaucracy strangling in its own red tape. Had the Trumanite network ever reified into a formal agency or department of the

U.S. government, it would have generated too much visibility to ensure its efficiency and survival. For external as well as internal reasons, then, the network structure has well-suited the Trumanites.

THE MYTH OF ALTERNATIVE
COMPETING HYPOTHESES

As these considerations suggest, the supposedly "alternative explanations" outlined above are not truly alternatives at all; they are not mutually exclusive in that they do not "compete." Analysis of competing hypotheses, or "ACH," is a method favored by CIA analysts to aid in weighing alternative explanations or conclusions. Its aim is to improve the analysis of issues that require a careful weighing of alternative explanations and to avoid a well-supported intuitive conclusion without first examining other possibilities. This is done by identifying other reasonable hypotheses, preparing a matrix that lists the evidence for and against each, weighing the diagnostic value of that evidence, attempting to disprove each hypothesis, and weighing those hypotheses' relative likelihood.[59] One of its advertised advantages is that it provides an "audit trail" to show step by step how analysts arrived at their judgment. The strength of the approach lies in the discreteness of the supposed alternatives: when one is confirmed, the others, if truly oppositional, are disconfirmed.

The problem with the ACH approach is that logical discreteness rarely exists. Explanations overlap. Aspects of one find their way into another. Evidence that supports one also supports another. The possibility that President Obama was insincere in claiming opposition to congressionally unauthorized war, for example, is not inconsistent with the possibility that U.S. participation in the military action against Libya represented either sound policy or, conversely, a chance for the President to shore up his image as a strong leader. The possibility that the administration chose to expend limited political capital fighting for a domestic agenda, similarly, is not inconsistent with the possibility that the Trumanite network's influence is too great to make it politically feasible to take it on. It may be less costly politically to alienate core supporters than to pay a big price for victories on issues that large segments of the public are not thought to care about. These possibilities are not inconsistent with the thesis of double government. Claims of unicausality, in short, are as suspect in popular political discourse as they are in scholarly modeling.[60]

Even acknowledging multicausality, it is almost never possible to know which variable really makes a difference. Predictive powers are seldom as advertised. Werner Heisenberg put it well: "What is wrong with the rigid formulation of the law of causality—'If we know the present exactly, we can calculate the future'—is not the final clause, but rather the premise. As a matter of principle, we cannot know all determinant elements of the present."[61] Daniel Kahneman makes the same point in suggesting why one could never hope to understand "what made Google succeed." "The ultimate test of an explanation is whether it would have made the event predictable in advance," he writes. "No story of Google's unlikely success will meet that test, because no story can include the myriad of events that would have caused a different outcome."[62] No story of the military action against Libya will meet that test either. Nor will any story of targeted killings, invocation of the state secrets privilege in litigation, or the subpoenas served on the Associated Press.

For similar reasons, it is rarely possible to know how any given counterfactual might come out. None of the three models outlined above can predict how the Soviets would have responded during the Cuban missile crisis had the U.S. Navy fired on a Soviet submarine challenging the blockade. Nor can the concept of double government predict whether, say, the Second Gulf War would have occurred had Al Gore been elected President rather than George Bush. A good theory of institutional behavior can predict, at best, only tendency over time. The notion of double government predicts only that national security policy will change little from one administration to the next. It does not predict with the same level of probability whether any given element of national security policy will remain constant. A good theory, whether in international relations, institutional evolution, foreign policy decision-making—or bird flight patterns—predicts reversion to a mean, not stand-alone, individual action.[63]

CHAPTER 6

ᴄᴠᴐ

Is Reform Possible? Checks, Smoke, and Mirrors

My aim thus far has been to explain the continuity in U.S. national security policy. An all-too-plausible answer, I have suggested, lies in Bagehot's concept of double government. Bagehot believed that double government could survive only so long as the general public remains sufficiently credulous to accept the superficial appearance of accountability, and only so long as the concealed and public elements of the government are able to mask their duality and thereby sustain public deference.[1] Bagehot analogized double government to a spinning top, or "cone," which survives in an "unstable equilibrium"; the political equilibrium will collapse if (in his words) the "ignorant class" is permitted to rule or if "the masses" see through the charade and become less respectful. As evidence of duality becomes plainer and public skepticism grows, the cone of governance will be "balanced on its point."[2] If "you push it ever so little," he wrote, "it will depart farther and farther from its position and fall to earth."[3]

If Bagehot's theory is correct, the United States now confronts a precarious situation. Maintaining the appearance that Madisonian institutions control the course of national security policy requires that those institutions play a large enough role in the decision-making process to maintain the illusion. But the Madisonians' role is too visibly shrinking, and the Trumanites' too visibly expanding, to maintain the plausible impression of Madisonian governance.[4] For this reason and others, public confidence in the Madisonians has sunk to new lows.[5] The Trumanites have resisted transparency far more successfully than have the Madisonians, with unsurprising results. The success of the whole dual institutional model depends upon the maintenance of public enchantment with the dignified/Madisonian institutions. This requires allowing no daylight to spoil their magic,[6] as Bagehot put it. An element of mystery must be preserved to excite public imagination. But transparency—driven hugely by modern Internet technology, multiple informational sources, and social media—leaves little to the imagination. "The cure for admiring the House of Lords," Bagehot observed, "was to go and look at it."[7] The public has gone and looked at Congress, the Supreme Court, and the President, and their standing in public opinion surveys is the result. Justices, senators, and presidents are not masters of the universe after all, the public has discovered. *They are just like us.* Enquiring minds may not have read enough of *Foreign Affairs*[8] to assess the Trumanites' national security policies, but they have read enough of *People Magazine*[9] to know that the Madisonians are not who they pretend to be. While the public's unfamiliarity with national security matters has no doubt hastened the Trumanites' rise, too many people will soon be too savvy to be misled by the Madisonian veneer,[10] and those people often exercise an influence on public opinion that is disproportionate to their numbers. There is no point in telling ghost stories, Holmes said, if people do not believe in ghosts.[11]

It might be supposed that existing, non-Madisonian, external restraints pose counterweights that compensate for the weakness of internal, Madisonian checks. The press, and the public sentiment it partially shapes, do constrain the abuse of power—but only up to a point. To the extent that the "marketplace of ideas" analogy ever was apt, that marketplace, like other marketplaces, is given to distortion. Public outrage is notoriously fickle, manipulable, and selective, particularly when driven by anger, fear, and indolence. Sizeable segments of the public—often egged on by public officials—lash out unpredictably at imaginary transgressors, failing even in the ability to identify sympathetic allies.[12] "[P]ublic opinion," Sorensen wryly observed, "is not always identical with the public interest."[13]

The influence of the media, whether to rouse or dampen, is thus limited. The handful of investigative journalists active in the United States today are the truest contemporary example of Churchill's tribute to the Royal Air Force.[14] In the end, though, access remains everything to the press. Explicit or implicit threats by the targets of its inquiries to curtail access often yield editorial surrender. Members of the public obviously are in no position to complain when a story *does not* appear. Further, even the best of investigative journalists confront a high wall of secrecy. Finding and communicating with (on deep background, of course) a knowledgeable, candid source within an opaque Trumanite network resistant to efforts to pinpoint decision makers[15] can take years. Few publishers can afford the necessary financial investment; newspapers are, after all, businesses, and the bottom line of their financial statements ultimately governs investigatory expenditures. Often, a second corroborating source is required. Even after scaling the Trumanite wall of secrecy, reporters and their editors often become victims of the deal-making tactics they must adopt to live comfortably with the Trumanites.[16] Finally, members of the mass media are subject to the same organizational pressures that shape the behavior of other groups. They eat together, travel together, and think together. A case in point was the Iraq War. The *Washington Post* ran twenty-seven editorials in favor of the war along with dozens of op-ed pieces, with only a few from skeptics.[17] The *New York Times, Time, Newsweek,* the *Los Angeles Times,* and the *Wall Street Journal* all marched along in lock-step.[18] As Senator Eugene McCarthy aptly put it, reporters are like blackbirds; when one flies off the telephone wire, they all fly off.[19]

More important, the premise—that a vigilant electorate fueled by a skeptical press together will successfully fill the void created by the hollowed-out Madisonian institutions—is wrong.[20] This premise supposes that those outside constraints operate *independently*, that their efficacy is not a function of the efficacy of internal, Madisonian checks.[21] But the internal and external checks are woven together and depend upon one another.[22] Nondisclosure agreements (judicially enforced gag orders, in truth) are prevalent among those best positioned to criticize.[23] Heightened efforts have been undertaken to crush vigorous investigative journalism and to prosecute and humiliate whistleblowers and to equate them with spies under the espionage laws. National security documents have been breathtakingly overclassified. The evasion of Madisonian constraints by these sorts of policies has the net effect of narrowing the marketplace of ideas, curtailing public debate, and gutting both the media and public opinion as effective restraints.[24] The vitality of external checks depends upon the vitality of internal Madisonian checks, and the internal Madisonian checks only minimally constrain the Trumanites.

Some suggest that the answer is to admit the failure of the Madisonian institutions, recognize that for all their faults the external checks are all that really exist, acknowledge that the Trumanite network cannot be unseated, and try to work within the current framework.[25] But the idea that external checks alone do or can provide the needed safeguards is false. If politics were the effective restraint that some have argued it is,[26] politics—intertwined as it is with law—would have produced more effective legalist constraints. It has not. The failure of law is and has been a failure of politics. If the press and public opinion were sufficient to safeguard what the Madisonian institutions were designed to protect, the story of democracy would consist of little more than a series of elected kings, with the rule of law having frozen with the signing of Magna Carta in 1215. Even with effective rules to protect free, informed, and robust expression—which is an enormous assumption—public opinion alone cannot be counted upon to protect what law is needed to protect. The hope that it can do so recalls earlier reactions to Bagehot's insights—the faith that "the people" can simply "throw off" their "deferential attitude and reshape the political system," insisting that the Madisonian, or dignified, institutions must "once again provide the popular check" that they were intended to provide.[27]

That, however, is exactly what many thought they were doing in electing Barack Obama as President. The results need not be rehearsed; little reason exists to expect that some future public effort to resuscitate withered Madisonian institutions would be any more successful. Indeed, the added power that the Trumanite network has taken on under the Bush/Obama policies would make that all the more difficult. It is simply naïve to believe that a large enough group of informed and intelligent voters can organize effectively to bring the Trumanite network within the system of Madisonian constraints. Those who believe that do not understand why that network was formed, how it operates, or why it survives. They want it, in short, to become more Madisonian. The Trumanite network, of course, would not mind *appearing* more Madisonian, but its enduring ambition is to become, in reality, less Madisonian.

It is not clear what precisely might occur should Bagehot's cone of governance "fall to earth." United States history provides no precedent. One possibility is a prolongation of what are now long-standing trends, with the arc of power continuing to shift gradually from the Madisonian institutions to the Trumanite network. Under this scenario, those institutions continue to subcontract national security decision-making to the Trumanites; a majority of the public remains satisfied with trade-offs between liberty and security; and members of a dissatisfied minority are at a loss to know what to do and are, in any event, chilled by widely feared Trumanite surveillance capabilities. The Madisonian institutions, in this future, fade gradually into museum pieces, like the British House of Lords and monarchy; Madisonians kiss babies, cut ribbons, and read Trumanite talking points, while the Trumanite network, careful to retain historic forms and familiar symbols, takes on the substance of a silent directorate.

Another possibility, however, is that the fall to earth could entail consequences that are profoundly disruptive, both for the government and the people. This scenario would be more likely in the aftermath of a catastrophic terrorist attack that takes place in an environment lacking the safety-valve checks that the Madisonian institutions once provided.[28] In this future, an initial "rally round the flag" fervor and associated crackdown are followed, later, by an increasing spiral of recriminatory reactions and counter-reactions. The government is seen increasingly by elements of the public as hiding what they ought to know, criminalizing what they ought to be able to do, and spying upon what ought to be private. The people are seen increasingly by the government as unable to comprehend the gravity of security threats, unappreciative of its security-protection efforts, and unworthy of its own trust. Recent public opinion surveys are portentous. A September 2013 Gallup Poll revealed that Americans' trust and confidence in the federal government's ability to handle international problems had reached an all-time low;[29] a June 2013 *Time* magazine poll disclosed that 70 percent of those age eighteen to thirty-four believed that Edward Snowden "did a good thing" in leaking the news of the National Security Agency (NSA)'s surveillance program.[30] This yawning attitudinal gap between the people and the government could reflect itself in multiple ways. Most obviously, the Trumanite network must draw upon the U.S. population to fill the five million positions needed to staff its projects that require security clearances.[31] That would be increasingly difficult, however, if the pool of available recruits comprises a growing and indeterminate number of Edward Snowdens—individuals with nothing in their records that indicates disqualifying unreliability but who, once hired, are willing nonetheless to act against perceived authoritarian tendencies by leaving open the vault of secrecy.

A smaller, less reliable pool of potential recruits would hardly be the worst of it, however. Lacking perceived legitimacy, the government could expect a lesser level of cooperation, if not outright obstruction, from the general public. Many national security programs presuppose public support for their efficient operation. This ranges from compliance with national security letters and library records disclosure under the PATRIOT Act to the design, manufacture, and sale of drones, and cooperation with counterintelligence activities and criminal investigations involving national security prosecutions. Moreover, distrust of government tends to become generalized; people who doubt governmental officials' assertions on national security threats are inclined to extend their skepticism. Governmental assurances concerning everything from vaccine and food safety to the fairness of stock-market regulation and IRS investigations (not without evidence[32]) become widely suspect. Inevitably, therefore, daily life would become more difficult. Government, after all, exists for a reason. It carries out many helpful and indeed essential functions in a highly specialized society. When those functions cannot be fulfilled, work-arounds emerge and social dislocation results. Most seriously, the protection of legitimate national security interests would itself suffer if the public were unable to distinguish between measures vital to its protection and those assumed to be undertaken merely through bureaucratic inertia or lack of imagination.

The government itself, meanwhile, could not be counted upon to remain passive in the face of growing public obduracy in response to its efforts to do what it thinks essential to safeguard national security. Here we do have historical precedents, and none is comfortably revisited. The Alien and Sedition Acts in the 1790s;[33] the Palmer Raids of 1919 and 1920;[34] the round-up of Japanese-American citizens in the 1940s;[35] governmental spying on and disruption of civil rights, draft protesters, and anti-war activists in the 1960s and 1970s;[36] and the incommunicado incarceration without charges, counsel, or trial of "unlawful combatants" only a few short years ago[37]— all are examples of what can happen when government sees limited options in confronting nerve-center security threats.[38] "[W]ar," Mackubin Owens reminds us, "is the great destroyer of free government." "The forces that contributed to the collapse of free government in Germany, Russia, China, and Japan in the twentieth century are the same ones that destroyed the possibility of free government among the ancient Greeks, as catalogued by Thucydides in his history of the Peloponnesian war."[39] No one can be certain, but the ultimate danger posed if the system were to fall to earth in the aftermath of a devastating terrorist attack could be intensely divisive and potentially destabilizing—not unlike what was envisioned by conservative Republicans in Congress who opposed Truman's national security programs when the managerial network was established.[40] Former Supreme Court Justice David Souter has expressed concern about a similar scenario, precipitated by America's "pervasive civic ignorance."[41]

It is therefore appropriate to move beyond explanation and to turn to possibilities for reform—to consider steps that might be taken to prevent the entire structure from falling to earth. Madison, as noted at the outset,[42] believed that a constitution must not only set up a government that can control and protect the people, but, equally important, must protect the people from the government.[43] Madison thus anticipated the enduring trade-off: the lesser the threat from government, the lesser its capacity to protect against threats; the greater the government's capacity to protect against threats, the greater the threat from the government.

Recognition of the dystopic implications of double government focuses the mind, naturally, on possible legalist cures to the threats that double government presents. Potential remedies fall generally into two categories. First, strengthen systemic checks, either by reviving Madisonian institutions—by tweaking them about the edges to enhance their vitality—or by establishing restraints directly within the Trumanite network. Second, cultivate civic virtue within the electorate.

STRENGTHENING SYSTEMATIC CHECKS

The first set of potential remedies aspires to tone up Madisonian muscles one by one with ad hoc legislative and judicial reforms, by, say, narrowing the scope of the state secrets privilege; permitting the recipients of national security letters at least to make their receipt public; broadening standing requirements; improving congressional oversight of covert operations, including drone killings and cyberoperations; or strengthening statutory constraints like the Foreign Intelligence Surveillance Act (FISA)[44] and the War Powers Resolution.[45] Law reviews brim with such proposals. But their stopgap approach has been tried repeatedly since the Trumanite network's emergence. Its futility is now glaring. Why such efforts would be any more fruitful in the future is hard to understand. The Trumanites are committed to the rule of law and their sincerity is not in doubt, but the rule of law to which they are committed, as suggested in chapter 4, is largely devoid of meaningful constraints.

This applies not only to domestic law but, it might quickly be noted, to international law as well. Indeed, international law affords even greater deflective possibilities; the United Nations Charter[46] and multilateral arrangements such as the NATO Treaty[47] provide ever-useful cover, which explains their continuing attraction to the Trumanites. The malleable, indeterminate, and oft-ignored "rules" of the Charter concerning use of force can plausibly be marshaled to support virtually any U.S. military action deemed in the national interest.[48] Limited or ambiguous U.N. Security Council approval, where available, is easily stretched. The mere observation that "the Security Council approved" normally is enough to carry the day; neither the public nor the press typically is eager to dig out and then examine the fine print to determine exactly *what* the Council approved.

It has been claimed, for example, that the Council approved NATO's overthrow of the government of Libya. The facts suggest otherwise. The Council approved use of force against Libya on March 17, 2011.[49] China, Russia, Brazil, India, and Germany abstained. The resolution authorized use of force for two and only two purposes: "to protect civilians...under threat of attack" and to enforce a no-fly zone. On March 28, 2011, President Obama underscored the narrow limits on force permitted by the resolution.[50] The U.N. mandate, he said, was only "to protect the Libyan people from immediate danger, and to establish a no-fly zone...."[51] "If we tried to overthrow Qaddafi by force," he said, "our coalition would splinter."[52] It would therefore be a mistake, he said, to try to "bring down Qaddafi and usher in a new government."[53] Nonetheless, NATO military action came to be directed at precisely the objective that the President said the Security Council did not approve— regime change. Messrs. Obama, Cameron, and Sarkozy publicly acknowledged as much. According to an op-ed piece coauthored by the three leaders on April 14, 2011, NATO's real objective was to ensure that "the Libyan people can choose their own future." [54] "Qaddafi must go and go for good," they wrote.[55]

NATO is a particular Trumanite favorite in the conduct of overt military operations. The Organization provides credibility, flexibility, and anonymity in equal doses. Its Council has no substantive written rules of procedure. It issues no legal guidance or guidelines that might restrict member states. It exercises no stand-alone authority, since member states have delegated none, but serves, rather, as an instrument for member states in the conduct of their military operations; no internal rules exist that would render "NATO," as such, responsible for a violation of international law. Yet the Organization's long-standing policy, according to a high-ranking NATO official, is not to reveal which member state participated in a given military operation. These elements combine to give NATO its greatest asset—its capacity to serve as a veil. NATO shields member states from legal and political accountability. Thus press reports in wars such as the one NATO fought in Libya invariably describe bombings, missile strikes, and other attacks carried out only by "NATO," with responsibility deflected from the unidentified, actual author(s) of the operation.[56] No congressional or parliamentary inquiries, no demonstrations outside embassies, and no justiciable legal actions threaten member states that have donned NATO's convenient mask. Accordingly, reform of the feckless international rules governing use of force is not pushed by the world's militarily powerful governments, which regard themselves as benefiting from the rules' elasticity.

Strengthening the domestic rule of law that constrains national security policy, therefore, is the central enterprise of knowledgeable reformers. Lawsuits, amendments, and lobbying efforts directed at securing assistance from the courts, Congress, and the President make up the implicit universe of action. Occasionally the reformers win, as Bagehot's theory would predict; they win just often enough to keep playing, like the gambler who realizes the dealer is stacking the deck but is led on by an occasional winning hand. Yet continued focus on domestic legalist Band-Aids merely buttresses the illusion that the Madisonian institutions are alive and well—and with that illusion has come an entire narrative premised on the assumption that it is merely a matter of identifying a traditional legalist, rule-of-law solution and looking to the Madisonian institutions to effect it. What poses a threat to the Trumanite network is not the rule of law, however; the rule of law in the national security realm is an element of the Madisonian myth system. What poses a mortal danger is the collapse of the myth system that sustains Madisonian credibility and, with it, Trumanite authority. "The power in any society," as Philip Roth observed, "is with those who get to impose the fantasy."[57]

The fantasy that the Madisonian institutions are in control deflects attention from the underlying malady. What is needed, if Bagehot's theory is correct, is a fundamental change in the very discourse within which U.S. national security policy is made. For the question is no longer: What should the *government* do? The questions now are: What should be done *about* the government? What *can* be done about the government? What are the responsibilities not of the government but of *the people*?[58]

A second approach would inject legalist limits directly into the Trumanites' operational core by, for example, setting up de facto judges within the network, or at least lawyers able to issue binding legal opinions, before certain initiatives could be undertaken.[59] Another proposed reform would attempt to foster intranetwork competition among the Trumanites by creating Madisonian-like checks and balances that operate directly within the Trumanite network.[60] The difficulty with these and similar ideas is that the checks they propose would merely replicate and relocate failed Madisonian institutions without controlling the forces that led to the hollowing-out of the *real* Madisonian institutions. There is scant reason to believe that pseudo-Madisonian checks would fare any better. Why would the Trumanite network, driven as it is to maintain and strengthen its autonomy, subject itself behind the scenes to *internal* Madisonian constraints any more readily than it publicly has subjected itself to *external* Madisonian constraints? Why, in Bagehot's terms, would the newly established intra-Trumanite institutions not become, in effect, a new, *third* institutional layer that further disguises where the real power lies?

Indeed, intra-Trumanite checks have already been tried. When questions arose whether Justice Department lawyers inappropriately authorized and oversaw warrantless electronic surveillance in 2006, its Office of Professional Responsibility commenced an investigation—until its investigators were denied the necessary security clearances, blocking the inquiry.[61] The FBI traditionally undertakes an internal investigation when an FBI agent is engaged in a serious shooting; "from 1993 to early 2011, FBI agents fatally shot about seventy 'subjects' and wounded about eighty others—and every one of those [shootings] was justified," its inspectors found.[62]

Inspectors general were set up within federal departments and agencies in 1978 as safeguards against waste, fraud, abuse, and illegality,[63] but the positions have remained vacant for years in some of the government's largest cabinet agencies, including the departments of Defense, State, Interior, and Homeland Security.[64] The best that can be said of these inspectors general is that, despite the best of intentions, they had no authority to overrule, let alone penalize, anyone. The worst is that they were trusted Trumanites who snored through everything from NSA's bulk domestic phone records collection programs[65] to arms sales to the Nicaraguan contras to Abu Ghraib[66] to the waterboarding of suspected terrorists.[67] To look to Trumanite inspectors general as a reliable check on unaccountable power would represent the ultimate triumph of hope over experience.

"Blue-ribbon" executive commissions also have been established, but they have done little to check the power of the Trumanite network. Following disclosures of illegal CIA domestic surveillance by the *New York Times*,[68] President Ford created a commission within the executive branch to, as he put it, "[a]scertain and evaluate any facts relating to activities conducted within the United States by the Central Intelligence Agency which give rise to questions of compliance with the" law.[69] Vice President Nelson Rockefeller headed the commission.[70] Rockefeller's driving resolve to "ascertain and evaluate" was disclosed in a confidential comment to William Colby, then Director of Central Intelligence, that Colby recalled in his memoirs. "Bill," Rockefeller asked him privately, "do you really have to present all this material to us?" [71] He continued: "We realize that there are secrets that you fellows need to keep and so nobody here is going to take it amiss if you feel that there are some questions that you can't answer quite as fully as you feel you have to."[72] The commission's report said nothing about the CIA's efforts to assassinate Fidel Castro, though it did reaffirm the findings of the Warren Commission.[73]

Following the NSA surveillance disclosures, President Obama (after having insisted immediately afterward that "we've struck the right balance"[74]) announced the creation of his own "independent"[75] panel to ensure that civil liberties were being respected and to restore public confidence.[76] The panel, it turned out, consisted of trusted friends and advisers[77] who operated as an arm of the Office of the Director of National Intelligence, James Clapper—the same James Clapper who oversees the NSA.[78] Clapper quietly exempted the panel from U.S. rules that require federal committees to conduct their business and their meetings in ways the public can observe.[79] The panel's report declined to address coherently the legality of NSA's activities[80] (despite the presence of two prominent law professors in the group) and made "recommendations" without identifying current practices, which in many instances made it impossible to know what changes, if any, were actually being proposed.[81] Its tacit objective seemed to be to enhance public confidence and trust rather than to enhance actual security or privacy, or to outline a better balance.[82] The panel acknowledged the assistance of "personnel from throughout the government," without indicating who assisted, how much they assisted, or what assistance was given.[83] The report did, however, nudge the national debate away from the question of *whether* the NSA should collect certain metadata to the question of *where* such data, once collected, should be housed.[84]

A third internal "check," the Foreign Intelligence Surveillance Court, subsists formally outside the executive branch but for all practical purposes might as well be within it; as noted earlier, it approved 99.9 percent of all warrant requests between 1979 and 2011.[85] In 2013, it approved the NSA collection of the telephone records of tens of millions of Americans, none of whom had been accused of any crime.[86] An authentic *check* is one thing; smoke and mirrors are something else.

The first difficulty with such proposed checks on the Trumanite network is circularity; all rely upon Madisonian institutions to restore power to Madisonian institutions by exercising the very power that Madisonian institutions lack. All assume that the Madisonian institutions, in which all reform proposals must necessarily originate, can somehow magically impose those reforms upon the Trumanite network or that the network will somehow merrily acquiesce. All suppose that the forces that gave rise to the Trumanite network can simply be ignored. All assume, at bottom, that Madison's scheme can be made to work—that an equilibrium of power can be achieved—without regard to the electorate's fitness.

Yet Madison's theory, again,[87] presupposed the existence of a body politic possessed of civic virtue. It is the personal ambition only of officeholders *who are chosen by a virtuous electorate* that can be expected to translate into institutional ambition. It is legislators *so chosen*, Madison believed, who could be counted upon to resist encroachments on, say, Congress's power to approve war or treaties because a diminution of Congress's power implied a diminution of their own individual power. Absent a virtuous electorate, personal ambition and institutional ambition no longer are coextensive. Members' principal ambition[88] then becomes political survival, which means accepting, not resisting, Trumanite encroachments on congressional power. The Trumanites' principal ambition, meanwhile, remains the same: to broaden their ever-insufficient "flexibility" to deal with unforeseen threats—that is, to enhance their own power. The net effect is imbalance, not balance.

This imbalance has suffused the development of U.S. counterterrorism policy. Trumanites express concerns about convergence, about potentially dangerous link-ups among narco-terrorists, cybercriminals, human traffickers, weapons traders, and hostile governments.[89] Yet their concerns focus largely, if not entirely, on only one side of Madison's ledger—the government's need to protect the people from threats—and little, if at all, on the other side: the need to protect the people from the government.[90] As a result, the discourse, dominated as it is by the Trumanites, exaggerates potential threats and downplays trade-offs that must be accepted to meet those threats. The

Madisonians themselves are not troubled about new linkages forged among the newly created components of military, intelligence, homeland security, and law enforcement agencies—linkages that together threaten civil liberties and personal freedom in ways never before seen in the United States. The earlier "stovepiping" of those agencies was seen as contributing to the unpreparedness that led to the September 11 attacks,[91] and after the wearying creation of the Department of Homeland Security and related reorganizations, the Madisonians have little stomach for re-drawing box charts yet again. And so the cogs of the national security apparatus continue to tighten while the scaffolding of the Madisonian institutions continues to erode.

It is no answer to insist that, whatever the system's faults, the Madisonian accountability mechanisms have at least generated a political consensus.[92] First, even if consensus exists among the Madisonians themselves, the existence of an authentic public consensus on national security policy is at best doubtful.[93] Second, if the application of Bagehot's theory to U.S. national security policy is correct, whatever consensus does exist at the political level is contrived and synthetic in that it derives not from contestation among the three branches of the federal government but from efforts of the Madisonian institutions to remain in sync with the Trumanite network. That network is the moving force behind any consensus. It has forged the policies that the consensus supports; it has orchestrated Madisonian support. Third, even if real, the existence of a Madisonian/Trumanite consensus says nothing about the *content* of the consensus—nothing about whether Madison's second great goal of protecting the people from the government has been vindicated or defeated. Autocracy can be consensus-based. The notion of a benign modern-day consensus on national security policy is, indeed, reminiscent of the observation of Richard Betts and Leslie Gelb who, reviewing agreements that emerged from national security deliberations during the Johnson administration, concluded that "the system worked."[94] Well, perhaps; the result was Vietnam.

The second difficulty with legal and public-opinion–based checks on the Trumanite network is the assumption in Madison's theory that the three competing branches act independently. "[I]t is evident that each department should have a will of its own," says *The Federalist*.[95] This is achieved by ensuring that each is "so constituted that the members of each should have as little agency as possible in the appointment of the members of the others."[96] Different policy preferences will obtain because the three Madisonian branches will act upon different motives.

But when it counts, the branches do not. Each branch has the same ultimate incentive: to bring its public posture into sync with the private posture of the Trumanites.[97] The net effect is "balance," after a fashion, in the sense that the end result is outward harmony of a sort easily mistaken for Madisonian-induced equipoise. But the balance is not an equilibrium that results from competition for power among three branches struggling "for the privilege of conducting American foreign policy," as Edward S. Corwin memorably put it.[98] The "system" that produces this ersatz consensus is a symbiotic tripartite co-dependence in which the three Madisonian branches fall over themselves to keep up with the Trumanites. The ostensible balance is artificial; it reflects a juridical legerdemain created and nurtured by the Trumanite network, which shares, defends, and begins with the same static assumptions. Bagehot relates the confidential advice of Lord Melbourne to the English Cabinet: "It is not much matter which we say, but mind, we must all say *the same*."[99] The Madisonian institutions and the Trumanite network honor the same counsel.

There is a third, more fundamental, more worrisome reason why the Madisonian institutions have been eclipsed, as noted earlier.[100] It is the same reason that repairs of the sort enumerated above are not likely to endure. And it is not a reason that can be entirely laid at the feet of the Trumanites. It is a reason that goes to the heartbeat of democratic institutions. The reason is that Madisonian institutions rest upon a foundation that has proven unreliable: a general public possessed of civic virtue. The United States today is beset by, to repeat Justice Souter's words, a "pervasive civic ignorance."[101]

Civic virtue, in Madison's view, required acting for the public interest rather than one's private interest.[102] Madison, realist that he was, recognized that deal-making and self-interest would permeate government; this could be kept in check *in part* by clever institutional design, with "ambition...to counteract ambition"[103] among governmental actors to maintain a power equilibrium. But no such institutional backup is available if the general public itself lacks civic virtue—meaning the capacity to participate intelligently in self-government and to elect officials who are themselves virtuous.[104] Indeed, civic virtue is thus even more important,[105] Madison believed, for the public at large than for public officials; institutional checks are necessary but not sufficient. Ultimately, the most important check on public officials is, as Madison put it, "virtue and intelligence in the community...."[106] Institutional safeguards, Madison believed, cannot be relied upon to protect liberty absent a body politic possessed of civic virtue.[107]

Madison was not alone in this belief, though other leading political theorists have since put it differently. Minimal levels of economic well-being, education, and political intelligence,[108] Bagehot believed, are essential conditions for the universal franchise and "ultra-democracy," as he called it, that has come to exist in the United States.[109] Lord Bryce observed that "[t]he student of institutions as well as the lawyer is apt to overrate the effect of mechanical contrivances in politics."[110] The various repairs that have been proposed—and, ultimately, the very Madisonian institutions themselves—are in the end mechanical contrivances. Whatever their elegance, these "parchment barriers," as Madison described laws that stand alone,[111] cannot compensate for a want of civic virtue. Bagehot concurred: "No polity can get out of a nation more than there is in the nation...." "[W]e must first improve the English nation," he believed, if we expect to improve Parliament's handiwork.[112]

This insight was widely shared among nineteenth-century English constitutionalists. John Stuart Mill (whose work on the English Constitution was published shortly before Bagehot's) shared Bagehot's and Bryce's doubts about the ultimate impotence of free-standing legal rules. "In politics as in mechanics," Mill wrote, "the power which is to keep the engine going must be sought for outside the machinery; and if it is not forthcoming, or is insufficient to surmount the obstacles which may reasonably be expected, the confidence will fail."[113] The force of these insights was not lost on prominent American jurists. Learned Hand wrote that "[l]iberty lies in the hearts of men and women; when it dies there, no constitution, no law, no court can save it."[114] A virtuous electorate, on the other hand, would in Bagehot's view be governed well whatever the structure of its constitution.[115] But the tendency in modern societies, Bagehot believed, was "to raise the average and to lower—comparatively, and perhaps absolutely to lower—the summit"[116]—a forecast ominously elaborated sixty years later by Jose Ortega y Gasset in *The Revolt of the Masses*.[117]

GOVERNMENT CULTIVATION OF CIVIC VIRTUE

In light of these realities, should the United States, as a matter of governmental policy, actively cultivate civic virtue of the sort that permits a robust, single institutional structure of government?

It is barely possible to touch upon the main themes in this recurring debate, but the question does bear directly upon the amenability of double government to reform. The case for inculcating at least some elements of civic virtue—for attempting to foster, in Robert Dahl's term, the "adequate citizen"[118]—is an argument from principles of civic republicanism, from the notion that individual fulfillment depends upon liberty, liberty upon self-government, and self-government upon collective deliberation concerning the common good.[119] On this view, effective deliberation—participation in the public sphere—requires civic virtue. Civic virtue gives citizens the *capacity* to participate. One of government's responsibilities is to help them acquire that capacity. Individuals cannot fully develop absent a supportive public sphere. Participation in self-government, and the exercise of judgment, discernment, and the responsibility that active participation entails, is not only a means to the good life but also an end in itself, an indispensable part of human social interaction and self-expression that promotes feelings of community and empathy. The net result is a public sphere in which the individual thrives.

However much republican[120] principles may actually have influenced the Framers—a question on which scholarly opinion is divided[121]—there can be little doubt that in the years following the Constitution's adoption, a competing liberal tradition has dominated American political thought. Though not all strands of liberalism and republicanism are incompatible, core principles of each are hard to reconcile. Liberalism places few demands on citizens.[122] It suggests that government ought to take no position on what constitutes the good life. It sees individuals as free and independent, capable of deciding for themselves what ends to seek. No reason exists, liberals argue, to think that government knows better than the individual what character, disposition, or habits of mind are preferable. Government's role is to respect people's right to choose their own ends, not to interfere with their choices; unfettered individual development and fulfillment requires not governmental meddling but governmental neutrality. People acting in their own self-interest will create an aggregate order that maximizes individual satisfaction and creates a political equilibrium that is self-correcting.[123] Governmental interference—governmental preference-shaping—would open the door to tyranny. No minimal knowledge of government or public affairs is required to vote; indeed, voting itself and all other forms of political participation are optional.

Liberalism's conflicting commands, however, create a paradox for those interested in diffusing concentrated Trumanite power. On the one hand, the liberal tradition counsels alarm at the rise of unaccountable power—yet on the other hand, liberal principles also counsel alarm at the image of government propagandizing citizens to adopt *the government's* ideas about what constitutes good government. The same liberalism that recoils at the specter of undifferentiated mass surveillance also breeds fear and loathing of local school boards and state textbook review committees spelling out a politically correct answer to what constitutes virtuous participation in accountable governance. Can the threat of concentrated governmental power be repulsed by further concentrating governmental power to address that threat? It is one thing to recognize the essentiality of civic virtue but quite another to believe that government is responsible for sustaining it.

Moreover, as a practical matter, it would be difficult to overcome voter ignorance that is in important respects entirely rational. Consider more closely three of the prerequisites for intelligent participation in governance: minimal intellectual acumen, sound judgment concerning policy alternatives, and an adequate informational base. The first two elements are in many respects already widely present. The fact is that "Joe Six-Pack" is neither unintelligent nor irrational. No one familiar with the rules of American football—surely among the most complicated sports in the world—can doubt the raw intelligence of anyone able to weigh the pros and cons of the nickel defense. Its moral dimensions notwithstanding, the decision whether to run a play-action fake on third-and-two is not a *conceptually* more difficult question than the decision whether to strike a high-value target located in a car in Yemen with four unidentified companions. Different types of research obviously are required, but neither matter is beyond the intellectual grasp of a person of common intelligence. The moral implications are also, of course, different, but what reason is there to believe that the Trumanites have any greater moral expertise than the average voter? It is often said that the public lacks access to the requisite information. The reality, however, is that all the material needed to make an informed judgment on the wisdom of drone strikes as a general policy—as well as 95 percent of the other issues the Trumanites confront—is readily available to anyone who can access the Internet. One reason that the public does not do so is that, given competing demands on its time, there is no obvious reason to become more informed. National security policy remains the same from one president to the next, whomever one votes for, and even in the most politically accountable of worlds, the public still would necessarily be excluded from sensitive national security deliberations. Why waste time learning about things one cannot affect?[124] American voters may not have read Voltaire, but they know that there are gardens to be tended.[125] Theirs is, in key respects, rational ignorance.[126]

This is the nub of the negative feedback loop in which the United States is now locked. Resuscitating the Madisonian institutions requires an informed, engaged electorate, but voters have little reason to be informed or engaged if their efforts are for naught—and as they become more uninformed and unengaged, they have all the more reason to continue on that path. The Madisonian institutions thus continue to atrophy, the power of the Trumanite network continues to grow, and the public continues to disengage. If this trend continues, it takes no great prescience to see what lies ahead: the term *Orwellian* will have little meaning to a people who have never known anything different, who have scant knowledge of history, civics, or public affairs, and who in any event have never heard of George Orwell.[127]

CHAPTER 7

༺ঌ

Conclusion

U.S. national security policy has scarcely changed from the Bush to the Obama administration. The theory of Walter Bagehot explains why. Bagehot described the emergence in nineteenth-century Britain of a "disguised republic" consisting of officials who actually exercised governmental power but remained unnoticed by the public, which continued to believe that visible, formal institutions exercised legal authority.[1] Dual institutions of governance, one public and the other concealed, were referred to by Bagehot as "double government."[2] A similar process of bifurcated institutional evolution has occurred in the United States, but in reverse: a network has emerged within the federal government that exercises predominant power with respect to national security matters. It has evolved in response to structural incentives rather than invidious intent, and it consists of the several hundred executive officials who manage the military, intelligence, diplomatic, and law enforcement agencies responsible for protecting the nation's security. These officials are as little disposed to stake out new policies as they are to abandon old ones. They define security more in military and intelligence terms than in political or diplomatic ones.

Enough examples exist to persuade the public that the network is subject to judicial, legislative, and executive constraints. This appearance is important to its operation, for the network derives legitimacy from the ostensible authority of the public, constitutional branches of the government. The appearance of accountability is, however, largely an illusion fostered by those institutions' pedigree, ritual, intelligibility, mystery, and superficial harmony with the network's ambitions. The courts, Congress, and even the President in reality impose little constraint. Judicial review is negligible, congressional oversight dysfunctional, and presidential control nominal. Past efforts to revive these institutions have thus fallen flat. Future reform efforts are no more likely to succeed, relying as they must upon those same institutions to restore power to themselves by exercising the very power that they lack. External constraints—public opinion and the press—are insufficient to check it. Both are manipulable, and their vitality depends heavily upon the vigor of constitutionally established institutions, which would not have withered had those external constraints had real force. Nor is it likely that any such constraints can be restored through governmental efforts to inculcate greater civic virtue, which would ultimately concentrate power even further. Institutional restoration can come only from an energized body politic. The prevailing incentive structure, however, encourages the public to become less, not more, informed and engaged.

For many, inculcated in the hagiography of Madisonian checks and balances and oblivious of the reach of Trumanite power, the response to these realizations will be denial. The image of a double national security government will be shocking. It cannot be right. It sounds of conspiracy, "a state within," and other variations on that theme. "The old notion that our Government is an extrinsic agency," Bagehot wrote, "still rules our imaginations."[3] That the Trumanite network could have emerged in full public view and without invidious intent makes its presence all the more implausible. Its existence challenges all we have been taught.

There is, however, little room for shock. The pillars of America's double government have long stood in plain view. We *have* learned about significant aspects of what Bagehot described—from some eminent thinkers. Max Weber's work on bureaucracies showed that, left unchecked, the inexorability of bureaucratization can lead to a "polar night of icy darkness" in which humanitarian values are sacrificed for abstract organizational ends.[4] Friedrich Hayek's work on political organization led him to conclude that "the greatest danger to liberty today comes from the men who are most needed and most powerful in government, namely, the efficient expert administrators exclusively concerned with what they regard as the public good."[5] Eric Fromm's work on social psychology showed how people unconsciously adopt societal norms as their own to avoid anxiety-producing choices, so as to "escape from freedom."[6] Irving Janis's work on group dynamics showed that the greater a group's *esprit de corps*, "the greater the danger that independent critical thinking will be replaced by groupthink, which is likely to result in irrational and dehumanizing actions directed against out-groups."[7] Michael Reisman's work on jurisprudence has shown how de facto operational codes can quietly arise behind publicly embraced myth systems, allowing for governmental conduct that is not approved openly by the law.[8] C. Wright Mills' 1956 work on power elites showed that the centralization of authority among officials who hold a common worldview and operate in secrecy can produce a "military metaphysic" directed at maintaining a "permanent war economy."[9] One person familiar with Mills' work was political scientist Malcolm Moos, the presidential speechwriter who five years later wrote President Eisenhower's prophetic warning.[10] "In the councils of government," Eisenhower said, "we must guard against the acquisition of unwarranted influence, whether sought or unsought, by the military-industrial complex. The potential for the disastrous rise of misplaced power exists and will persist."[11]

Bagehot anticipated these risks. Bureaucracy, he wrote, is "the most unimproving and shallow form of government,"[12] and the executive that commands it "the most dangerous."[13] "If it is left to itself," he observed, "without a mixture of special and non-special minds," decisional authority "will become technical, self-absorbed, self-multiplying."[14] The net result is responsibility that is neither fixed nor ascertainable but diffused and hidden,[15] with implications that are beyond historical dispute. "The most disastrous decisions in the twentieth century," in Robert Dahl's words, "turned out to be those made by authoritarian leaders freed from democratic restraints."[16]

The benefits derived by the United States from double government—enhanced technical expertise, institutional memory and experience, quick-footedness, opaqueness in confronting adversaries, policy stability, and insulation from popular political oscillation and decisional idiosyncrasy—need hardly be recounted. Those benefits, however, have not been cost-free. The price lies in well-known risks flowing from centralized power, unaccountability, and the short-circuiting of power equilibria. Indeed, in this regard the Framers thought less in terms of risk than certainty. John Adams spoke for many: "The nation which will not adopt an equilibrium of power must adopt a despotism. There is no other alternative."[17]

The trivial risk of sudden despotism, of an abrupt turn to a police state or dictatorship installed with coup-like surprise, has created a false sense of security in the United States.[18] That a strongman of the sort easily visible in history could suddenly burst forth is not a real risk. The risk, rather, is the risk of slowly tightening centralized power, growing and evolving organically beyond public view, increasingly unresponsive to Madisonian checks and balances.[19] Madison wrote, "There are more instances of the abridgment of the freedom of the people by gradual and silent encroachments of those in power than by violent and sudden usurpations."[20] Recent history bears out his insight. Dahl has pointed out that in the twentieth century—the century of democracy's great triumph—some seventy democracies collapsed and quietly gave way to authoritarian regimes.[21] A want of civic virtue, in the form of political

ignorance, amplifies that risk. "If a nation expects to be ignorant and free, in a state of civilization," Thomas Jefferson
wrote, "it expects what never was and never will be."[22] What
form of government ultimately will emerge from the United
States' experiment with double government is uncertain. The
risk is considerable, however, that it will not be a democracy.
A former security official suggested to me that this trajectory is
broadly accepted *faute de mieux*—for want of something better.
Perhaps. But if American democracy has contracted a potentially fatal illness, and if it has gone through all the antibiotics
in the institutional medicine cabinet, and if its condition has
continued to worsen, is that really any comfort?

The objection will no doubt be heard that the need for specialization and the appeal of "technocracy"—rule by experts—
is nothing new. Indeed, "the roots of technocracy go back to the
Enlightenment, with its emphasis on reason, science, technical
rationality, and technology."[23] Other realms of law, policy, and
business also have come to be dominated by specialists, made
necessary and empowered by ever-increasing divisions of labor;
other expert and nonexpert communities also have polarized.[24]
Organizational control within them also has become more
centralized.[25] Is not national security duality merely a contemporary manifestation of the challenge long posed to democracy
by the administrative state[26]-*cum*-technocracy?[27]

There is validity to this intuition and no dearth of examples of
the frustration confronted by Madisonians who are left to shrug
their shoulders when presented with complex policy options,
the desirability of which cannot be assessed without high levels
of technical expertise. International trade issues, for example,
turn frequently upon esoteric econometric analysis beyond the
grasp of all but a few Madisonians. Climate change and global
warming present questions that depend ultimately upon the
validity of one intricate computer model versus another. The
financial crisis of 2008 posed similar complexity when experts
insisted to hastily gathered executive officials and legislators that—absent massive and immediate intervention—the

nation's and perhaps the world's entire financial infrastructure would face imminent collapse.[28] In these and a growing number of similar situations, the "choice" made by the Madisonians is increasingly hollow; the real choices are made by technocrats who present options to Madisonians that the Madisonians are in no position to assess. Why is national security any different?

It is different for a reason that I described in 1981: the organizations in question "do not regulate truck widths or set train schedules. They have the capability of radically and permanently altering the political and legal contours of our society."[29] An unrestrained security apparatus has throughout history been one of the principal reasons that free governments have failed. The Trumanite network holds within its power something far greater than the ability to recommend higher import duties or more windmills or even gargantuan corporate bailouts: it has the power to kill and arrest and jail, the power to see and hear and read peoples' every word and action,[30] the power to instill fear and suspicion, the power to quash investigations and quell speech, the power to shape public debate or to curtail it, and the power to hide its deeds and evade its weak-kneed overseers. The Trumanite network holds, in short, the power of *irreversibility*. No democracy worthy of its name can permit that power to escape the control of the people.

NOTES

CHAPTER 1

1. *See* ROBERT J. SPITZER, COMPARING THE CONSTITUTIONAL
   PRESIDENCIES OF GEORGE W. BUSH AND BARACK OBAMA:
   WAR POWERS, SIGNING STATEMENTS, VETOES 2 (2012);
   Richard M. Pious, *Obama's Use of Prerogative Powers in the
   War on Terrorism, in* OBAMA IN OFFICE 255, 256 (James
   A. Thurber ed., 2011); Richard M. Pious, *Prerogative Power in
   the Obama Administration: Continuity and Change in the War on
   Terrorism*, 41 PRESIDENTIAL STUD. Q. 263, 264 (June 2011).
   While this book considers only national security policy, note
   that elements of national security policy bear directly upon
   U.S. foreign policy generally and, indeed, upon domestic
   policy. The Bush/Obama view that "homeland security [is]
   the be-all and end-all of grand strategy," for example, has
   required maintaining "the security apparatus that supported drone attacks on Al Qaeda targets" in countries such
   as Yemen, which in turn has shaped U.S. engagement in the
   Middle East and the muted U.S. response to the Arab Spring.
   "Drones, not democracy, drive American policy." VALI NASR,
   THE DISPENSABLE NATION: AMERICAN FOREIGN POLICY IN
   RETREAT 180–81 (2013).

2. David Johnston, *U.S. Says Rendition to Continue, but with
   More Oversight*, N.Y. TIMES, Aug. 24, 2009, http://www.
   nytimes.com/2009/08/25/us/politics/25rendition.html,
   [http://www.perma.cc/09SBNcUFE4B/].

3. Peter Baker, *Obama to Use Current Law to Support Detentions*, N.Y. TIMES, Sept. 23, 2009, http://www.nytimes. com/2009/09/24/us/politics/24detain.html?_r=0, [http:// www.perma.cc/0j8wrqrjEVL] ("The Obama administration has decided not to seek new legislation from Congress authorizing the indefinite detention of about 50 terrorism suspects being held without charges at Guantanamo Bay, Cuba, officials said Wednesday. Instead, the administration will continue to hold the detainees without bringing them to trial based on the power it says it has under the Congressional resolution passed after the attacks of Sept. 11, 2001, authorizing the President to use force against forces of Al Qaeda and the Taliban."); *see also* Matthew C. Waxman, *Administrative Detention: Integrating Strategy and Institutional Design, in* LEGISLATING THE WAR ON TERROR: AN AGENDA FOR REFORM 43, 45 (Benjamin Wittes ed., 2009) (describing how the Obama administration has "continued to defend a broad authority to detain suspected al Qaeda and affiliated terrorists based on the law of war.").

4. *See* Anne E. Kornblut & Carrie Johnson, *Obama Will Help Select Location of Khalid Sheik Mohammed Terrorism Trial*, WASH. POST, Feb. 12, 2010, http://www.washingtonpost.com/ wp-dyn/content/article/2010/02/11/AR2010021105011_ pf.html, [http://www.perma.cc/0PSRibPn6Wi] ("President Obama is planning to insert himself into the debate about where to try the accused mastermind of the Sept. 11, 2001, attacks, three administration officials said . . . .").

5. *Guantanamo Bay Still Unresolved*, NPR.ORG (Jan. 14, 2013, 12:00 PM), http://www.npr.org/2013/01/14/169334679/ guantanamo-bay-still-unresolved, [http://www.perma. cc/0iLHqVYKmJf/].

6. *See* Gov't Brief at 3, Bostan v. Obama, 674 F. Supp. 2d 9 (D.D.C. Apr. 9, 2009) (No. 1:05-cv-00883).

7. Charlie Savage, *Judge Rejects New Rules on Access to Prisoners*, N.Y. TIMES, Sept. 6, 2012, http://www.nytimes. com/2012/09/07/us/judge-rejects-limits-on-lawyers-

access-to-guantanamo-prisoners.html?_r=0, [http://www. perma.cc/0ua3YPrxbSS/] ("Accusing the Obama administration of 'an illegitimate exercise of executive power,' a federal judge on Thursday rejected the government's effort to impose new restrictions on lawyers' access to prisoners at Guantanamo Bay, Cuba, if they were no longer actively challenging the prisoners' detention in federal court.").

8. Charlie Savage, *Obama Upholds Detainee Policy in Afghanistan*, N.Y. TIMES, Feb. 21, 2009, http://www. nytimes.com/2009/02/22/washington/22bagram.html?_ r=0, [http://www.perma.cc/0QcYjY9QLE3/] ("The Obama administration has told a federal judge that military detainees in Afghanistan have no legal right to challenge their imprisonment there, embracing a key argument of former President Bush's legal team."). None of the sixty-seven non-Afghan prisoners held at Bagram Air Force base has been formally tried. Kevin Sieff, *In Afghanistan, a Second Guantanamo*, WASH. POST, Aug. 5, 2013, http:// www.washingtonpost.com/world/in-afghanistan-a-second-guantanamo/2013/08/04/e33e8658-f53e-11e2-81fa-8e83b3864c36_print.html, [http://www.perma.cc/ 0gmuzShiTwz]. Many have been cleared for release by informal military review boards, but most of those were never freed. *Id.*

9. Gov't Brief, *supra* note 6 ("Congress has recently and unambiguously precluded reliance on or invocation of the Geneva Conventions in habeas cases or in any other civil action; the Military Commissions Act of 2006 ('MCA') reflects the well-established principle that the Geneva Conventions are not judicially enforceable by private individuals.").

10. Alissa J. Rubin, *Afghans Detail Detention in "Black Jail" at U.S. Base*, N.Y. TIMES, Nov. 28, 2009, http://www.nytimes.com/ 2009/11/29/world/asia/29bagram.html?pagewanted=all, [http://www.perma.cc/0ptmkdcFGpG/] ("An American military detention camp in Afghanistan is still holding inmates, sometimes for weeks at a time, without access to

the International Committee of the Red Cross, according to human rights researchers and former detainees held at the site on the Bagram Air Base.").

11. *See* Charlie Savage & Mark Landler, *White House Defends Continuing U.S. Role in Libya Operation*, N.Y. TIMES, June 15, 2011, http://www.nytimes.com/2011/06/16/us/politics/16powers.html?pagewanted=all, [http://www.perma.cc/0p5uDsF7tMf/] ("The White House, pushing hard against criticism in Congress over the deepening air war in Libya, asserted Wednesday that President Obama had the authority to continue the military campaign without Congressional approval because American involvement fell short of full-blown hostilities.").

12. *See* ANDREW FUTTER, BALLISTIC MISSILE DEFENSE AND U.S. NATIONAL SECURITY POLICY: NORMALIZATION AND ACCEPTANCE AFTER THE COLD WAR 134–58 (2013).

13. Sarah Moughty, *Top CIA Official: Obama Changed Virtually None of Bush's Controversial Programs*, FRONTLINE (Sept. 1, 2011, 11:02 AM), http://www.pbs.org/wgbh/pages/frontline/iraq-war-on-terror/topsecretamerica/top-cia-official-obama-changed-virtually-none-of-bushs-controversial-programs/, [http://www.perma.cc/0sdUgvQfkEr/] (quoting former CIA Acting General Counsel John Rizzo: "With a notable exception of the enhanced interrogation program, the incoming Obama administration changed virtually nothing with respect to existing CIA programs and operations.").

14. Peter Bergen & Megan Braun, *Drone Is Obama's Weapon of Choice*, CNN.COM (Sept. 19, 2012, 10:37 AM), http://www.cnn.com/2012/09/05/opinion/bergen-obama-drone, [http://www.perma.cc/0RFNWZGDoM8/] ("[President Obama] has already authorized 283 strikes in Pakistan, six times more than the number during President George W. Bush's eight years in office. As a result, the number of estimated deaths from the Obama administration's drone strikes is more than four times what it was during the

Bush administration—somewhere between 1,494 and 2,618.").

15. *See* Scott Shane, *No Charges Filed on Harsh Tactics Used by the C.I.A.*, N.Y. TIMES, Aug. 30, 2012, http://www.nytimes.com/2012/08/31/us/holder-rules-out-prosecutions-in-cia-interrogations.html?_r=2&pagewanted=1&pagewanted=all&, [http://perma.cc/0kL2rS3VBWE] ("Attorney General Eric H. Holder Jr. announced Thursday that no one would be prosecuted for the deaths of a prisoner in Afghanistan in 2002 and another in Iraq in 2003, eliminating the last possibility that any criminal charges will be brought as a result of the brutal interrogations carried out by the C.I.A..... [T]he decision will disappoint liberals who supported President Obama when he ran in 2008 and denounced what he called torture and abuse of prisoners under his predecessor."). "I never had any indication that [José Rodriquez] suffered any repercussions from his unilateral decision to destroy the tapes [of waterboarding of detainees]." JOHN RIZZO, COMPANY MAN: THIRTY YEARS OF CONTROVERSY AND CRISIS IN THE CIA 22 (2014).

16. Mark Mazzetti, Charlie Savage, & Scott Shane, *How a U.S. Citizen Came to Be in America's Cross Hairs*, N.Y. TIMES, Mar. 9, 2013, http://www.nytimes.com/2013/03/10/world/middleeast/anwar-al-awlaki-a-us-citizen-in-americas-cross-hairs.html?pagewanted=all, [http://www.perma.cc/0thgVJziYSx/] ("For what was apparently the first time since the Civil War, the United States government had carried out the deliberate killing of an American citizen as a wartime enemy and without a trial.").

17. *See* Charlie Savage, *Secret U.S. Memo Made Legal Case to Kill a Citizen*, N.Y. TIMES, Oct. 8, 2011, http://www.nytimes.com/2011/10/09/world/middleeast/secret-us-memo-made-legal-case-to-kill-a-citizen.html?pagewanted=all, [http://www.perma.cc/0tDjQbpbLFc/].

18. Scott Shane & Mark Mazzetti, *White House Tactic for C.I.A. Bid Holds Back Drone Memos*, N.Y. TIMES, Feb. 20,

2013, http://www.nytimes.com/2013/02/21/us/politics/ strategy-seeks-to-ensure-bid-of-brennan-for-cia.html? pagewanted=all, [http://www.perma.cc/03bnHH29pzk/] ("The White House is refusing to share fully with Congress the legal opinions that justify targeted killings.... The refusal so far to share more of the opinions with Congress, or to make redacted versions of the memos public, comes despite a pledge of greater transparency by President Obama in his State of the Union address on Feb. 12.").

19. Walter Pincus, *White House Threatens Veto on Intelligence Activities Bill*, WASH. POST, Mar. 16, 2010, http://www.wash-ingtonpost.com/wp-dyn/content/article/2010/03/15/ AR2010031503720.html?hpid=sec-politics, [http://www. perma.cc/0vqJVN4sCKV/] ("The White House has renewed its threat to veto the fiscal 2010 intelligence authorization bill over a provision that would force the administration to widen the circle of lawmakers who are informed about covert operations and other sensitive activities.").

20. Karen DeYoung & Greg Jaffe, *U.S. "Secret War" Expands Globally as Special Operations Forces Take Larger Role*, WASH. POST, June 4, 2010, http://www.washingtonpost.com/ wp-dyn/content/article/2010/06/03/AR2010060304965_ pf.html, [http://perma.cc/0EPuhJEqXCL] ("Beneath its commitment to soft-spoken diplomacy and beyond the combat zones of Afghanistan and Iraq, the Obama adminis-tration has significantly expanded a largely secret U.S. war against al-Qaeda and other radical groups, according to senior military and administration officials.").

21. MARK MAZZETTI, THE WAY OF THE KNIFE: THE CIA, A SECRET ARMY, AND A WAR AT THE ENDS OF THE EARTH 225 (2013).

22. *See* DAVID E. SANGER, CONFRONT AND CONCEAL: OBAMA'S SECRET WARS AND SURPRISING USE OF AMERICAN POWER 188–203 (2013).

23. Adam Liptak, *Justices Turn Back Challenge to Broader U.S. Eavesdropping*, N.Y. TIMES, Feb. 26, 2013, http://

www.nytimes.com/2013/02/27/us/politics/supreme-court-rejects-challenge-to-fisa-surveillance-law.html, [http://www.perma.cc/0f6RQErGey7/] (describing how the Supreme Court ruled "that the journalists, lawyers and human rights advocates who challenged the constitutionality of the [Foreign Intelligence Surveillance Act (FISA) amendments] could not show they had been harmed by it and so lacked standing to sue" and how "[t]he Obama administration defended the law in court, and a Justice Department spokesman said the government was 'obviously pleased with the ruling.'").

24. Charlie Savage, *Obama's War on Terror May Resemble Bush's in Some Areas*, N.Y. TIMES, Feb. 17, 2009, http://www.nytimes.com/2009/02/18/us/politics/18policy.html?pagewanted=all, [http://www.perma.cc/0EuB1yXzZFY/]; *see* Ryan Devereaux, *Is Obama's Use of State Secrets Privilege the New Normal?*, NATION, Sept. 29, 2010, http://www.thenation.com/article/155080/obamas-use-state-secrets-privilege-new-normal#, [http://www.perma.cc/0ViNXrCjZDi/]. *See also* Louis Fisher, *Government Errors Are Shrouded in Secrecy*, NATIONAL LAW JOURNAL, Mar. 10, 2014 ("Following the pattern of the Bush administration, Obama and the Justice Department have been willing at every step to invoke the state-secrets privilege to prevent any type of judicial relief for individuals wronged by the executive branch.").

25. Scott Wilson & Anne Gearan, *Obama Didn't Know about Surveillance of U.S.-Allied World Leaders until Summer, Officials Say*, WASH. POST, Oct. 30, 2013, http://www.washingtonpost.com/politics/obama-didnt-know-about-surveillance-of-us-allied-world-leaders-until-summer-officials-say/2013/10/28/0cbacefa-4009-11e3-a751-f032898f2dbc_story.html, [http://perma.law.harvard.edu/0Udk99ndnJm/]; Alison Smale, Melissa Eddy, & David E. Sanger, *Data Suggests Push to Spy on Merkel Dates to '02*, N.Y. TIMES, Oct. 28, 2013, http://www.nytimes.com/2013/10/28/world/europe/

data-suggests-push-to-spy-on-merkel-dates-to-02.html?_
r=0, [http://perma.law.harvard.edu/0WjiCMF31p1/].

26. Adam Liptak, *Court Case Asks If "Big Brother" Is Spelled GPS*, N.Y. TIMES, Sept. 10, 2011, http://www.nytimes.com/2011/09/11/us/11gps.html, [http://www.perma.cc/0jEBCJDuAi5/] (describing how the Obama administration argued that "requiring a warrant to attach a GPS device to a suspect's car 'would seriously impede the government's ability to investigate leads and tips on drug trafficking, terrorism and other crimes.'").

27. *See* United States v. Jones, 132 S. Ct. 945, 949 (2012) ("We hold that the Government's installation of a GPS device on a target's vehicle, and its use of that device to monitor the vehicle's movements, constitutes a 'search.'"); *see also* Adam Liptak, *Justices Say GPS Tracker Violated Privacy Rights*, N.Y. TIMES, Jan. 23, 2012, http://www.nytimes.com/2012/01/24/us/police-use-of-gps-is-ruled-unconstitutional.html?pagewanted=all&_r=0, [http://www.perma.cc/0ENtVZv7e6r/]. ("The Supreme Court on Monday ruled unanimously that the police violated the Constitution when they placed a Global Positioning System tracking device on a suspect's car and monitored its movements for 28 days.").

28. Charlie Savage, *F.B.I. Focusing on Security over Ordinary Crime*, N.Y. TIMES, Aug. 23, 2013, http://www.nytimes.com/2011/08/24/us/24fbi.html?_r=0, [http://www.perma.cc/U8JM-4BKC]. From 2009 to 2011, the FBI logged 82,325 such assessments. *Id.*

29. *See* Michael S. Schmidt, *Ex-C.I.A. Officer Sentenced to 30 Months in Leak*, N.Y. TIMES, Jan. 25, 2013, http://www.nytimes.com/2013/01/26/us/ex-officer-for-cia-is-sentenced-in-leak-case.html?ref=waterboarding, [http://www.perma.cc/0JZzFgyAtME/] ("A former Central Intelligence Agency officer was sentenced on Friday to 30 months in prison for disclosing the identity of a covert agency officer to a freelance writer, representing the first

time that a C.I.A. officer will serve prison time for disclosing classified information to the news media. The sentencing in federal court here of John C. Kiriakou, 48, who served as an agency analyst and counterterrorism officer from 1990 to 2004, was the latest development in the Obama administration's unprecedented crackdown on government leaks.").

30. Elizabeth Shell & Vanessa Dennis, *11 "Leakers" Charged with Espionage*, PBS NEWSHOUR, Aug. 21, 2013, http://www.pbs. org/newshour/multimedia/espionage/, [http://perma.cc/ E27L-KRMY].

31. Ellen Nakashima, *White House Proposal Would Ease FBI Access to Records of Internet Activity*, WASH. POST, July 29, 2010, http://www.washingtonpost.com/wp-dyn/content/ article/2010/07/28/AR2010072806141.html, [http:// perma.law.harvard.edu/0o9xk1AifSe] ("To critics, the move is another example of an administration retreating from campaign pledges to enhance civil liberties in relation to national security.").

32. Charlie Savage & James Risen, *Federal Judge Finds N.S.A. Wiretaps Were Illegal*, N.Y. TIMES, Mar. 31, 2010, http:// www.nytimes.com/2010/04/01/us/01nsa.html, [http:// perma.law.harvard.edu/0bWyABEng2m] ("A federal judge ruled Wednesday that the National Security Agency's program of surveillance without warrants was illegal, rejecting the Obama administration's effort to keep shrouded in secrecy one of the most disputed counterterrorism policies of former President George W. Bush. In a 45-page opinion, Judge Vaughn R. Walker ruled that the government had violated a 1978 federal statute requiring court approval for domestic surveillance when it intercepted phone calls of Al Haramain, a now-defunct Islamic charity in Oregon, and of two lawyers representing it in 2004.").

33. Charlie Savage, *Phone Records of Journalists Seized by U.S.*, N.Y. TIMES, May 13, 2013, http://www.nytimes.com/ 2013/05/14/us/phone-records-of-journalists-of-the-

associated-press-seized-by-us.html?pagewanted=all&_
r=0, [http://perma.cc/0DS9VmcDerU].

34. Glenn Greenwald, *NSA Collecting Phone Records of
    Millions of Verizon Customers Daily*, THE GUARDIAN,
    June 5, 2013, http://www.guardian.co.uk/world/2013/
    jun/06/nsa-phone-records-verizon-court-order, [http://
    perma.law.harvard.edu/02efbNFu6kz]; *see* Charlie Sa
    vage & Edward Wyatt, *U.S. Is Secretly Collecting Records
    of Verizon Calls*, N.Y. TIMES, June 5, 2013, http://www.
    nytimes.com/2013/06/06/us/us-secretly-collecting-
    logs-of-business-calls.html, [http://perma.law.harvard.
    edu/0XwUvKmBN1N]; Ellen Nakashima, *Verizon Providing
    All Call Records to U.S. under Court Order*, WASH. POST, June
    6, 1013, http://articles.washingtonpost.com/2013-06-05/
    world/39766583_1_court-order-secret-court-verizon,
    [http://perma.law.harvard.edu/0h9ns6o3WPz]. For fur-
    ther discussion, see pages 105–109.

35. Barton Gellman & Laura Poitras, *Documents: U.S., British
    Intelligence Mining Data from Nine U.S. Internet Companies
    in Broad Secret Program*, WASH. POST, June 6, 2013,
    http://www.washingtonpost.com/investigations/us-
    intelligence-mining-data-from-nine-us-internet-
    companies-in-broad-secret-program/2013/06/06/
    3a0c0da8-cebf-11e2-8845-d970ccb04497_print.html,
    [http://perma.cc/03Ln5QPBWr]; James Ball & Spencer
    Ackerman, *NSA Loophole Allows Warrantless Search for US
    Citizens' Emails and Phone Calls*, THE GUARDIAN, Aug. 9,
    2013, http://www.theguardian.com/world/2013/aug/09/
    nsa-loophole-warrantless-searches-email-calls, [http://
    perma.law.harvard.edu/0ETnqUSornG/].

36. James Risen & Laura Poitras, *N.S.A. Gathers Data on Social
    Connections of U.S. Citizens*, N.Y. TIMES, Sept. 28, 2013,
    http://www.nytimes.com/2013/09/29/us/nsa-examines-
    social-networks-of-us-citizens.html?pagewanted=all,
    [http://perma.law.harvard.edu/0oMAghojGHo/].

37. These included Dennis Blair, President Obama's Director of National Intelligence from 2009 to 2010, who served as Commander-in-Chief of the U.S. Pacific Command in the Bush administration; John Brennan, CIA Director and former Assistant to the President for Homeland Security in the Obama administration, who served in the Bush administration as Chief of Staff to CIA Director George Tenet, Deputy Director of the CIA, and Director of the National Counterterrorism Center; James B. Comey, FBI Director in the Obama administration, who served as Deputy Attorney General in the Bush administration; James Clapper, Obama's Director of National Intelligence since 2010, who served as President Bush's Under Secretary of Defense for Intelligence; Robert Gates, Secretary of Defense in the Obama administration from 2009 to 2011 and also in the Bush administration; Stephen Kappes, Deputy Director of the CIA in the Obama administration from 2009 to 2010, who served in that same position in the Bush administration; Michael Leiter, Director of the National Counterterrorism Center under Obama from 2009 to 2011 and earlier under President Bush; Douglas Lute, Obama's coordinator for Afghanistan and Pakistan on the National Security Staff from 2009 to 2013, who served in the Bush administration as Assistant to the President and Deputy National Security Advisor for Iraq and Afghanistan; Stanley A. McChrystal, Commander, International Security Assistance Force (ISAF) in Afghanistan in the Obama administration, who served in the Bush administration as Director of the Joint Staff from August 2008 to June 2009 and as Commander of the Joint Special Operations Command from 2003 to 2008; William McCraven, who served as Obama's Commander of the Joint Special Operations Command (JSOC) from 2009 to 2011 and also in the Bush administration; Michael Mullen, who served as Obama's Chairman of the Joint Chiefs of Staff

from 2009 to 2011 and also in the Bush administration; Michael Morrell, Obama's Deputy Director of the CIA from 2010 to 2013, who served as Associate Deputy Director in the Bush administration; Robert Mueller, Obama's FBI Director from 2009 to 2013 and also in the Bush administration; Victoria Nuland, Obama's State Department spokesperson, who served as Deputy National Security Advisor to Vice President Dick Cheney; David Petraeus, Obama's Director of the Central Intelligence Agency from 2011 to 2012, who served in the Bush administration as Commander of United States Central Command, U.S. Forces in Afghanistan, and the Multinational Force in Iraq; and John Rizzo, the CIA's general counsel in the Obama administration in 2009 and also in the Bush administration. *See* JACK GOLDSMITH, POWER AND CONSTRAINT: THE ACCOUNTABLE PRESIDENCY AFTER 9/11, at 27–28 (2012); MAZZETTI, *supra* note 21, at ix–xi; Jeremy W. Peters, *Senate Backs F.B.I. Chief and Considers Other Picks*, N.Y. TIMES, July 29, 2013, http://www.nytimes.com/2013/07/30/us/politics/senate-approves-comey-to-lead-the-fbi.html, [http://perma.law.harvard.edu/0CFLXbX9yAE/]. Gates reports that he "knew from experience that, when all was said and done, there would be far more continuity than the new team realized in its first, heady days." ROBERT M. GATES, DUTY: MEMOIRS OF A SECRETARY AT WAR 282 (2014).

38. While I focus on the continuation of Bush administration policies by the Obama administration, earlier administrations also have adhered to preexisting national security programs. Among the more prominent examples are the prosecution of the war in Vietnam and the pursuit of a system of anti-ballistic missile defense. *See generally* FUTTER, *supra* note 12; R. W. KOMER, BUREAUCRACY DOES ITS THING: INSTITUTIONAL CONSTRAINTS ON U.S.-GVN PERFORMANCE IN VIETNAM (1972); *see also* COLUMBA PEOPLES, JUSTIFYING BALLISTIC MISSILE DEFENCE: TECHNOLOGY, SECURITY AND CULTURE (2010).

39. Even national security insiders have professed bewilderment. Robert Gates, for example, expressed puzzlement over the Bush administration's failure to review the need to continue policies concerning Guantánamo and interrogation techniques:

    > The key question for me was why, several years after 9/11 and after so many of those information gaps had been filled and the country's defenses had dramatically improved, there was not a top-to-bottom review of policies and authorities with an eye to culling out those that were most at odds with our traditions, culture, and history, such as renditions and "enhanced interrogations." I once asked Condi that question, and she acknowledged that they probably should have done such a review, perhaps after the 2004 election, but it just never happened.

    Robert M. Gates, Duty: Memoirs of a Secretary at War 93–94 (2014).

40. President Obama and his White House team, Goldsmith has written, were "sobered by the terrorist threat they fully appreciated only when they assumed power...." Jack Goldsmith, Power and Restraint: The Accountable Presidency after 9/11 xiii (2012). They were, similarly, persuaded by the soundness of the Bush policy responses, Goldsmith suggests, once they were educated with respect to the reasons behind those policies. Claiming the state secrets privilege, for example, made sense to the Obama team once the justification was "convincingly explained" in CIA documentation. *Id.* at 26. "President Obama has done nothing to change the policies of the Bush administration in the war on terrorism. And I mean practically nothing," said New Jersey Governor Chris Christie. "And you know why? 'Cause they work." Jonathan Martin, *Christie Assails Libertarian Shift on National Security by Some in the G.O.P.*, N.Y. Times, July 27, 2013.

41. *See* chapter 5.
42. *See* chapter 5.
43. *See* Walter Bagehot, The English Constitution (Cornell University Press 1966) (1867).
44. *See* M. A. Goldberg, *Trollope's* The Warden: *A Commentary on the "Age of Equipoise*," 17 Nineteenth-Century Fiction 381, 381 (1963).
45. Bagehot's theory is still analyzed today. *See, e.g.*, Gerard N. Magliocca, *The Constitution Can Do No Wrong*, 2012 U. Ill. L. Rev. 723, 726 (2012) ("Walter Bagehot's *The English Constitution* is a classic study of the parliamentary system during the 1860s, but his work is timeless due to its emphasis on function over form. While *The Federalist* was the first modern study on how constitutions should be organized, *The English Constitution* was the first to ask why people obey their constitutions."); Thomas O. Sargentlich, *The Limits of the Parliamentary Critique of the Separation of Powers*, 34 Wm. & Mary L. Rev. 679, 688 (1993) ("[Woodrow] Wilson's critique in the 1880s was directly influenced by Bagehot's study of the English Constitution, which was published in 1867 and in the United States in 1877. Indeed, Wilson specifically noted his intellectual debt to Bagehot."); Adam Tomkins, *The Republican Monarchy Revisited*, 19 Const. Comment. 737, 738 (2002) ("Bagehot matters, even now. His work is of great importance to contemporary constitutional scholarship, both in Britain and to some extent also in the United States.").
46. *See, e.g.*, Terry M. Moe & Michael Caldwell, *The Institutional Foundations of Democratic Government: A Comparison of Presidential and Parliamentary Systems*, 150 J. Institutional & Theoretical Econ. 171, 171–72 (1994) ("It is telling that the most widely cited analyses [include] Walter Bagehot's *The English Constitution* [1873].... [t]he modern literature has echoed these same themes....").
47. Bagehot, *supra* note 43, at 176.
48. *Id.* at 67–68, 82–86, 89.

49. *Id.* at 61.
50. *Id.* at 250.
51. *Id.* at 61.
52. *Id.* at 66–68.
53. *Id.* at 65.
54. *Id.* at 266.
55. *Id.* at 97, 248–51, 255.
56. *Id.* at 176.
57. *Id.*
58. *See id.* at 176–77.
59. *Id.* at 263.
60. R. H. S. Crossman, *Introduction* to WALTER BAGEHOT, THE ENGLISH CONSTITUTION 27 (Cornell University Press 1963) (1867).
61. This was the inference of the eminent Bagehot scholar R. H. S. Crossman, writing in 1963. Crossman, *Introduction, supra* note 60, at 25–26 (referring to "conscious concealment," "organized deception," and "mass deception").
62. BAGEHOT, *supra* note 43, at 97.
63. *Id.* at 249.
64. *Id.* at 63.
65. *Id.*
66. *Id.* at 250.
67. *Id.* at 248.
68. *Id.* at 251.
69. *Id.* at 248.
70. *Id.* at 249.
71. These realities seem hard to square with the suggestion that politics and public opinion provide constraints that can substitute for the rule of law, resting as they do on the acknowledged premise that "a wealthy and educated population is a strong safeguard of democracy." ERIC A. POSNER & ADRIAN VERMEULE, THE EXECUTIVE UNBOUND: AFTER THE MADISONIAN REPUBLIC 14 (2010).
72. *Census: U.S. Poverty Rate Spikes, Nearly 50 Million Americans Affected*, CBS DC (Nov. 15, 2012, 10:01 AM), http://

washington.cbslocal.com/2012/11/15/census-u-s-poverty-rate-spikes-nearly-50-million-americans-affected/, [http://perma.law.harvard.edu/0b3qiirRh4W/]. In 2012, the poverty level for a family of four was $23,050 in total yearly income. *Computations for the 2012 Annual Update of the HHS Poverty Guidelines for the 48 Contiguous States and the District of Columbia*, U.S. DEP'T OF HEALTH & HUM. SERVICES, http://aspe.hhs.gov/poverty/12computations. shtml, [http://perma.law.harvard.edu/0RNu9XipUH1/] (last updated Feb. 9, 2012).

73. Lindsey Layton, *Study: Poor Children Are Now the Majority in American Public Schools in South, West*, WASH. POST, Oct. 16, 2013, http://www.washingtonpost.com/local/education/study-poor-children-are-now-the-majority-in-american-public-schools-in-south-west/2013/10/16/34eb4984-35bb-11e3-8a0e-4e2cf80831fc_story.html.

74. Greg Toppo, *Literacy Study: 1 in 7 U.S. Adults Are Unable to Read This Story*, USA TODAY, Jan. 8, 2009, http://usatoday30.usatoday.com/news/education/2009-01-08-adult-literacy_N.htm, [http://perma.law.harvard.edu/0ubbK5zDPb7/].

75. *Renewing America—Remedial Education: Federal Education Policy*, COUNCIL ON FOREIGN REL. (June 2013), http://www.cfr.org/united-states/remedial-education-federal-education-policy/p30141, [http://perma.law.harvard.edu/07e5QqRd5mV/].

76. *7/1: Independence Day—Seventeen Seventy When?*, MARIST POLL (July 1, 2011), http://maristpoll.marist.edu/71-independence-day-dummy-seventeen-seventy-when/, [http://perma.law.harvard.edu/0QYaZAeM15H/] ("[A]bout one in four Americans doesn't know from which *country* the United States declared its independence.").

77. *Take the Quiz: What We Don't Know*, NEWSWEEK, Apr. 4, 2011, at 58.

78. *New National Poll Finds: More Americans Know Snow White's Dwarfs Than Supreme Court Judges, Homer Simpson Than*

Homer's Odyssey, and Harry Potter Than Tony Blair, Bus. Wire (Aug. 14, 2006, 9:00 AM), http://www.businesswire. com/news/home/20060814005496/en/National-Poll- Finds-Americans-Snow-Whites-Dwarfs, [http://perma. cc/6VU5-V48G].

79. *CNN Poll: Americans Believe Iran Has Nuclear Weapons*, CNN. com (Feb. 19, 2010, 12:00 PM), http://politicalticker.blogs. cnn.com/2010/02/19/cnn-poll-american-believe-iran- has-nuclear-weapons/, [http://perma.law.harvard.edu/ 0hxzacRqVRf].

80. Kathy Frankovic, *Polls, Truth Sometimes at Odds*, CBSNews. com (Feb. 11, 2009, 4:15 PM), http://www.cbsnews. com/2100-501863_162-3253552.html, [http://perma.law. harvard.edu/0MjaPmmoEYD].

81. National Geographic-Roper Public Affairs, *2006 Geographic Literacy Study* 22–24 (May 2006), *available at* http://www.nationalgeographic.com/roper2006/pdf/ FINALReport2006GeogLitsurvey.pdf, [http://perma.law. harvard.edu/0T7nCc74Q9p].

82. *Id.* at 24–25.

83. *Id.* at 22.

84. Bradley Graham, Hit to Kill: The New Battle over Shielding America from Missile Attack xxvi, 390 (2002).

85. *See Newspaper: Butterfly Ballot Cost Gore White House*, CNN.com (Mar. 11, 2001, 8:43 AM), http://edition.cnn. com/2001/ALLPOLITICS/03/11/palmbeach.recount/, [http://perma.law.harvard.edu/0Aiwr7KNj6Z] ("Voters confused by Palm Beach County's butterfly ballot cost Al Gore the presidency, The Palm Beach Post concluded Sunday.").

CHAPTER 2

1. Walter Bagehot, The English Constitution 196 (Cornell University Press 1963) (1867). For a recent, comprehensive treatment of the problem of political ignorance, *see generally*

ILYA SOMIN, DEMOCRACY AND POLITICAL IGNORANCE: WHY SMALLER GOVERNMENT IS SMARTER (2013).

2. BAGEHOT, *supra* note 1, at 196.

3. MICHAEL H. HUNT, THE AMERICAN ASCENDANCY: HOW THE UNITED STATES GAINED AND WIELDED GLOBAL DOMINANCE 149 (2007) (quoting WALTER LAFEBER, AMERICAN POLICY-MAKERS, PUBLIC OPINION, AND THE OUTBREAK OF THE COLD WAR, 1945–50, at 60 (1977)).

4. The diplomatic historian Thomas A. Bailey wrote in 1948 that "[d]eception of the people may become increasingly necessary, unless we are willing to give our leaders in Washington a freer hand.... Just as the yielding of some of our national sovereignty is the price that we must pay for effective international organization, so the yielding of some of our democratic control of foreign affairs is the price that we may have to pay for greater physical security." THOMAS A. BAILEY, THE MAN IN THE STREET 13 (1948). Walter Lipmann, then the nation's preeminent columnist, wrote in 1955 that the "people have imposed a veto upon the judgments of informed and responsible officials.... Mass opinion... has shown itself to be a dangerous master of decisions when the stakes are life and death." WALTER LIPPMANN, THE PUBLIC PHILOSOPHY 20 (Transaction Publishers 1989) (1955). George Kennan wrote that he felt a "distaste amounting almost to horror for the chaotic disorder of the American political process." GEORGE F. KENNAN, MEMOIRS: 1950–1963, at 322 (1972). Irving Kristol, godfather of modern neoconservatism, said that "the notion that there should be one set of truths available to everyone is a modern democratic fallacy. It doesn't work." There are, he contended, "different truths for different kinds of people." *Quoted in* Ronald Bailey, *Origin of the Specious: Why Do Neoconservatives Doubt Darwin?*, 29 REASON 22, 24 (1997).

5. The "foreign service," said Dean Rusk, "does not share their view that the world was created at the last presidential

election or that a world of more than 160 nations will somehow be different because we elected one man rather than
another as president." BARRY RUBIN, SECRETS OF STATE 99
(1985).

6. Acheson's "philosophical tendencies aligned him with the
Establishment, which, at home and abroad, represented the
status quo," Justice Douglas wrote. WILLIAM O. DOUGLAS,
THE COURT YEARS 1939–1975: THE AUTOBIOGRAPHY OF
WILLIAM O. DOUGLAS 289 (1980). "Under Acheson," said
Douglas, "the nation set its foot on the dreary path it was
to follow for the next decades." *Id.*

7. *See generally* EDWARD M. BURNS, JAMES MADISON,
PHILOSOPHER OF THE CONSTITUTION (1938); RALPH
KETCHAM, JAMES MADISON: A BIOGRAPHY (1971);
ADRIENNE KOCH, MADISON'S ADVICE TO MY COUNTRY
(1966); JACK N. RAKOVE, JAMES MADISON AND THE
CREATION OF THE AMERICAN REPUBLIC (3d ed. 2007);
ROBERT A. RUTLAND, JAMES MADISON, THE FOUNDING
FATHER (1987).

8. U.S. CONST. art. I, § 8, cl. 12.

9. *Id.* art. I, § 8, cl. 13.

10. *Id.* art. I, § 8, cl. 14.

11. *Id.* art. I, § 8, cl. 15.

12. *Id.* art. I, § 8, cl. 16.

13. *Id.* art. II, § 2, cl. 1.

14. *Id.* art. II, § 2, cl. 2.

15. *Id.* art. III, § 2, cl. 1.

16. *See* THE FEDERALIST No. 10 (James Madison).

17. *Id.*

18. *See* pages 105–109.

19. *Id.*

20. For an account of the origins and growth of the
U.S. national security apparatus, *see* MICHAEL J. HOGAN,
A CROSS OF IRON: HARRY S. TRUMAN AND THE ORIGINS OF
THE NATIONAL SECURITY STATE, 1945–1954 (1998).

21. National Security Act of 1947, 50 U.S.C.A. §§ 3002–3003, 3021 (West 2013).
22. *See* S. Rep. No. 94–755, at 736 (1976). For a discussion of the NSA's role in the surveillance of domestic communications, *see* pages 65–72.
23. Justice William O. Douglas, for example, expressed concern about the growing influence of the military on U.S. foreign policy. Douglas, *supra* note 6, at 292.
24. Hogan, *supra* note 20, at 330.
25. 97 Cong. Rec. 2854, 3098 (1951).
26. *Id.*
27. *Id.*
28. 97 Cong. Rec. 247 (1951).
29. *See* 97 Cong. Rec. 244–47 (1951).
30. 93 Cong. Rec. 5246, 5247 (1947).
31. 93 Cong. Rec. 8320 (1947).
32. Hogan, *supra* note 20, at 154.
33. *Id.* at 319–20.
34. *Id.* at 155.
35. 97 Cong. Rec. 3374 (1951).
36. Hogan, *supra* note 20, at 321.
37. 97 Cong. Rec. 6982 (1951), *quoted in* Hogan, *supra* note 20, at 338.
38. *Quoted in* Hogan, *supra* note 20, at 255.
39. *Quoted in id.*
40. National Security Act of 1947, 50 U.S.C.A. § 3036(d)(1) (West 2013). *See generally* Douglas T. Stuart, Creating the National Security State: A History of the Law That Transformed America (2012).
41. Hogan, *supra* note 20, at 37.
42. *Id.*
43. *See generally id.* at 36–37.
44. *Quoted in id.* at 109.
45. *Quoted in id.*
46. NSC 68, the report of the State Department's policy planning staff sent to Truman on April 14, 1950, has been

regarded as a foundational blueprint for U.S. grand strategy during the Cold War. "In order to 'sell' the idea of a major military buildup—in this case, to Truman himself—the document exaggerated the threats the United States confronted." Acheson himself acknowledged the exaggeration; the purpose of the report was "to bludgeon the mind of 'top government'" by making its points "clearer than truth...." JOHN LEWIS GADDIS, GEORGE F. KENNAN: AN AMERICAN LIFE 390–91 (2011).

47. THE COMMISSION ON ORGANIZATION OF THE EXECUTIVE BRANCH OF THE GOVERNMENT, THE NATIONAL SECURITY ORGANIZATION: A REPORT TO THE CONGRESS 11 (1949), *available at* http://www.foia.cia.gov/sites/default/files/document_conversions/45/national_sec_org.pdf.

48. *Id.* at 9.

49. *See* Aaron L. Friedberg, *Why Didn't the United States Become a Garrison State?*, 16 INT'L SEC. 109, 123–31 (1992). For a discussion of the broader historical evolution of the "garrison state," *see generally* MILTON J. ESMAN, THE EMERGING AMERICAN GARRISON STATE (2013); Harold D. Lasswell, *The Garrison State, in* HAROLD D. LASSWELL ON POLITICAL SOCIOLOGY (Dwayne Marvick ed., 1977).

50. HUNT, *supra* note 3, at 149.

51. *See Top Secret America: Government Organizations*, WASH. POST, http://projects.washingtonpost.com/top-secret-america/gov-orgs/, [http://perma.law.harvard.edu/0tjWr3B3gJd/] (last visited Apr. 13, 2013); *see generally* DANA PRIEST & WILLIAM M. ARKIN, TOP SECRET AMERICA: THE RISE OF THE NEW AMERICAN SECURITY STATE (2011).

52. Dana Priest & William M. Arkin, *A Hidden World, Growing beyond Control*, WASH. POST, July 19, 2010, http://projects.washingtonpost.com/top-secret-america/articles/a-hidden-world-growing-beyond-control/print, [http://perma.law.harvard.edu/0aNktQ4JCum/] ("Some 1,271 government organizations and 1,931 private companies

work on programs related to counterterrorism, homeland
security and intelligence in about 10,000 locations across
the United States.").

53. *See, e.g.*, GORDON ADAMS & CINDY WILLIAMS, BUYING
NATIONAL SECURITY: HOW AMERICA PLANS AND PAYS
FOR ITS GLOBAL ROLE AND SAFETY AT HOME 1 (2010)
("Including the cost of operations in Iraq and Afghanistan,
combined spending for national security, including
national defense, international affairs, and homeland security, was more than three-quarters of a trillion dollars in
fiscal year (FY) 2009, about 80 percent more in real terms
than in FY 2001."); Chris Hellman & Mattea Kramer, *Our
Insanely Big $1 Trillion National Security Budget*, MOTHER
JONES (May 23, 2012, 3:00 AM), http://www.motherjones.
com/politics/2012/05/national-security-budget-1-trillion-
congress, [http://perma.law.harvard.edu/0UFkLYtVjSU/]
(totaling the budgets of all national security–related agencies in the federal government—including those that support veterans—and concluding that "the national security
budget in fiscal 2013 will be nearly $1 trillion").

54. Saul Pett, *Henry A. Kissinger: Loyal Retainer or Nixon's
Svengali?*, WASH. POST, Aug. 2, 1970, at B3.

55. *See, e.g.*, Lyndsey Layton & Lois Romano, *"Plum Book" Is
Obama's Big Help-Wanted Ad*, WASH. POST, Nov. 13, 2008,
http://articles.washingtonpost.com/2008-11-13/politics/
36810686_1_plum-book-executive-secretary-job-seekers,
[http://perma.law.harvard.edu/084DcU22qjN/] (describing how "[a]bout one-third" of the more than 8,000 jobs
in the "Plum Book" "are strictly presidential appointments—that is, patronage positions that will go largely
to Democrats who know how to network"); Camille
Tuutti, *How to Become a Presidential Appointee*, FCW
(Nov. 9, 2012), http://fcw.com/articles/2012/11/09/hire-
presidential-appointees.aspx, [http://perma.law.harvard.
edu/0JDFgRBqEyv/] ("Not all of the jobs listed in the Plum
Book can be filled at the discretion of the administration,

however. There are roughly 4,200 jobs that can be filled at the discretion, Palguta said, and 500 to 600 of them have some special statutory exceptions or are time limited.").

56. David E. Lewis, The Politics of Presidential Appointments: Political Control and Bureaucratic Performance 82 (2008).

57. *See* Alan G. Whittaker et al., Nat'l Def. Univ., The National Security Policy Process: The National Security Council and Interagency System 14 (2011), *available at* http://www.virginia.edu/cnsl/pdf/national-security-policy-process-2011.pdf.

58. Christopher C. Shoemaker, The NSC Staff: Counseling the Council 1 (1991).

59. Robert M. Gates, Duty: Memoirs of a Secretary at War 587 (2014).

60. Jack Goldsmith, Power and Constraint: The Accountable Presidency after 9/11, at 29 (2012).

61. Stuxnet was a computer worm believed to have been released by the United States and Israel as part of a cyber-operation to damage Iran's nuclear facilities. *See generally In Classified Cyberwar against Iran, Trail of Stuxnet Leak Leads to White House*, Wash. Times, Aug. 18, 2013, http://www.washingtontimes.com/news/2013/aug/18/trail-of-stuxnet-cyberwar-leak-to-author-leads-to-/?page=all, [http://perma.cc/WD4V-MYEP].

62. *See* C. Wright Mills, The Power Elite 354 (1956).

63. Anthony Trollope, The Warden 190 (Bernhard Tauchnitz 1859) (1855). However, "their prestige is a sort of ex-officio prestige," in the words of a more contemporary observer, "awarded for performance and function and revocable for lack of it." William H. Whyte Jr., The Organization Man 343 (1957).

64. Max Weber, *Bureaucracy, in* From Max Weber: Essays in Sociology 196, 214 (Hans Gerth & Charles Mills eds. & trans., Routledge 2009) (1948).

65. Bagehot, *supra* note 1, at 159.

66. *Id.* at 160.
67. *Id.* at 151.
68. *Id.* at 159.
69. It is their "mushiness on the most sensitive issues [that] makes them acceptable." Hugh Heclo, *Issue Networks and the Executive Establishment, in* THE NEW AMERICAN POLITICAL SYSTEM 106 (Anthony King ed., 1978).
70. MILLS, *supra* note 62, at 222. James Carroll has suggested that by 1965, "[f]or the first time in [American] history, military assumptions undergirded America's idea of itself." JAMES CARROLL, HOUSE OF WAR: THE PENTAGON AND THE DISASTROUS RISE OF AMERICAN POWER 29 (2006).
71. DAVID HALBERSTAM, THE BEST AND THE BRIGHTEST 60 (1972).
72. Les Gelb & Jeanne-Paloma Zelmati, *Mission Unaccomplished*, 13 DEMOCRACY 10, 24 (2009).
73. VALI NASR, THE DISPENSABLE NATION: AMERICAN FOREIGN POLICY IN RETREAT 36 (2013).
74. BOB WOODWARD, OBAMA'S WARS 319 (2010).
75. *Id.* at 247. The President's staff were furious after a meeting with the President and military leaders. "The generals and admirals are systematically playing him," they said, "boxing him in." *Id.* at 173.
76. President Eisenhower was aware of those costs:

> Every gun that is made, every warship launched, every rocket fired signifies, in the final sense, a theft from those who hunger and are not fed, those who are cold and not clothed. This world in arms is not spending money alone. It is spending the sweat of its laborers, the genius of its scientists, the hopes of its children.... This is not a way of life at all in any true sense. Under the cloud of threatening war, it is humanity hanging from a cross of iron.

> Dwight D. Eisenhower, "The Chance for Peace" Delivered Before the American Society of Newspaper Editors (Apr.

16, 1953), *available at* http://www.eisenhower.archives.gov/ all_about_ike/speeches/chance_for_peace.pdf, [http:// perma.law.harvard.edu/0dDgSZnNkrE].

77. President Eisenhower wrote:

> Some day there is going to be a man sitting in my present chair who has not been raised in the military services and who will have little understanding of where slashes in their estimates can be made with little or no damage. If that should happen while we still have the state of tension that now exists in the world, I shudder to think of what could happen in this country....

Letter from Dwight D. Eisenhower to Everett E. Hazlett (Aug. 20, 1956), *quoted in* WILLIAM BRAGG EWALD JR., EISENHOWER THE PRESIDENT 248 (1981) (date of letter provided by Eisenhower Library, Abilene, Kansas).

78. JEFFREY ROSEN, THE NAKED CROWD 222 (2004).

79. *Id.* at 79.

80. SEYMOUR M. HERSH, CHAIN OF COMMAND: THE ROAD FROM 9/11 TO ABU GHRAIB 97 (2004).

81. *See generally* Robert Jervis, *Cooperation Under the Security Dilemma*, 30 WORLD POL. 167 (1978). NATO expansion was a case in point. Russia's resentment toward the United States and the crisis that erupted in March 2014 with Russia's occupation of Crimea were not unrelated to the Clinton administration's insistence in the 1990s that NATO be expanded to Russia's borders. Strobe Talbott, Deputy Secretary of State at the time, reports that Russian President Boris Yeltsin "openly expressed bitterness toward the U.S. and toward Clinton personally. 'Why,' he kept asking, 'had 'our friend Bill' unleashed 'this monster'?'" STROBE TALBOTT, THE RUSSIA HAND: A MEMOIR OF PRESIDENTIAL DIPLOMACY 224 (2003). French President Jacques Chirac warned at the time that "the U.S. was not 'taking full account of Russian sensitivities,' especially 'a traditional fear of encirclement as well as a fear of

humiliation.'" *Id.* at 225. Chirac was not the only voice urging caution. "It seemed like virtually everyone I knew from the world of academe, journalism, and foreign policy think-tanks was against enlargement," Talbott recounts. *Id.* at 119–20. Following a speech on the subject at the Harriman Institute at Columbia University, "[o]ne eminent guest after another rose to register his distaste for the policy. Several expressed disappointment in me for defending it." *Id.* at 220. One of the most prominent was George Kennan, who later termed enlargement a "strategic blunder of potentially epic proportions." *Id.* In an op-ed, Kennan elaborated. "[E]xpanding NATO would be the most fateful error of American policy in the entire post-cold-war era," he wrote. "Such a decision may be expected to inflame the nationalistic, anti-Western and militaristic tendencies in Russian opinion; to have an adverse effect on the development of Russian democracy; to restore the atmosphere of the cold war to East-West relations, and to impel Russian foreign policy in directions decidedly not to our liking." George F. Kennan, *A Fateful Error*, N.Y. TIMES, Feb. 5, 1997. Curiously, not even the most astute analysts have been able to pinpoint when the U.S. government made the decision to expand NATO, who made it, or even why it was made. *See, e.g.*, James M. Goldgeier, *NATO Expansion: The Anatomy of a Decision, in* THE DOMESTIC SOURCES OF AMERICAN FOREIGN POLICY: INSIGHTS AND EVIDENCE 396 (James M. McCormick ed., 2012) ("Readers may find it unsatisfying that I have not uncovered either *the* moment of decision or the president's ulterior motive.") (emphasis in original). *See also* JAMES M. GOLDGEIER, NOT WHETHER BUT WHEN: THE U.S. DECISION TO ENLARGE NATO (1999). What does seem clear is that the decisive voice was not the President's. "Clinton complained that the national security system wasn't working well enough and that he hadn't been adequately involved in the decisions." ELIZABETH DREW, ON THE EDGE: THE CLINTON PRESIDENCY 336 (1994).

82. DAVID E. SANGER, CONFRONT AND CONCEAL: OBAMA'S SECRET WARS AND SURPRISING USE OF AMERICAN POWER 417 (2013).
83. *Id.*
84. *Id.*
85. *Id.* at 418.
86. *Id.*
87. *Id.*
88. Since, as we have seen, doing so would lead to prosecution. David Carr, *Blurred Line Between Espionage and Truth*, N.Y. TIMES, Feb. 26, 2012, http://www.nytimes. com/2012/02/27/business/media/white-house-uses-espionage-act-to-pursue-leak-cases-media-equation.html, [http://perma.law.harvard.edu/0JyHP2USEcP] ("The Espionage Act, enacted in 1917 to punish those who gave aid to our enemies, was used three times in all the prior administrations to bring cases against government officials accused of providing classified information to the media. It has been used six times since the current president took office."). One of the rare exceptions to threat inflation has been Glenn Carle, the former CIA officer and Deputy National Intelligence Officer for Transnational Threats on the National Intelligence Council. The CIA, he concluded, has been "spinning in self-referential circles" in which "our premises were flawed, our facts used to fit our premises, our premises determined, and our fears justified our operational actions, in a self-contained process that arrived at a conclusion dramatically at odds with the facts." GLENN L. CARLE, THE INTERROGATOR: AN EDUCATION 275 (2011). Yet the participants in this process have deluded themselves into believing in their rationality. Their analyses "were all sincerely, ardently held to have constituted a rigorous, rational process to identify terrorist threats...." *Id.* Scholars of the process of intelligence analysis confirm that the conformist instinct is pervasive. "Like other bureaucrats," Steve Chan observed, "intelligence analysts

have to conform with the regime's basic views about the nature and morality of international relations if they wish to be treated as 'responsible' and 'serious.'" Steve Chan, *Intelligence Stupidity: Understanding Failures in Strategic Warning*, 73 AMERICAN POLITICAL SCIENCE REVIEW 178 (Mar. 1979).

89. The elastic concept of "terrorism" fits readily into claimed emergencies, which are easily attributed to terrorists of one stripe or another. *See* Michael J. Glennon, *Terrorism and International Law*, Center for Studies and Research in International Law and International Relations, The Hague Academy of International Law 105 (2006).

90. *See* John J. Mearsheimer, *America Unhinged*, THE NATIONAL INTEREST 9, 26 (Jan./Feb. 2014), http://nationalinterest. org/article/america-unhinged-9639 ("The taproot of the problem is that a democracy constantly preparing for and fighting wars, as well as extolling the virtues of using force, will eventually transform itself into a national-security state.").

91. J. William Fulbright, *Foreword* to MICHAEL J. GLENNON, CONSTITUTIONAL DIPLOMACY (1990), at xiv.

92. BAGEHOT, *supra* note 1, at 65, 68, 90, 100, 248, 249.

93. *Quoted in* TED GUP, NATION OF SECRETS: THE THREAT TO DEMOCRACY AND THE AMERICAN WAY OF LIFE 14 (2008).

94. A "SCIF" is a "sensitive compartmented information facility." Dana Priest & William M. Arkin, *A Hidden World, Growing Beyond Control*, WASH. POST, July 19, 2010, http://projects.washingtonpost.com/top-secret-america/ articles/a-hidden-world-growing-beyond-control/print, [http://perma.law.harvard.edu/0JayDShhKua] (describing SCIFs as "special rooms encased in metal or permanent dry wall, impenetrable to eavesdropping tools and protected by alarms and a security force capable of responding within 15 minutes.").

95. Jack M. Balkin, *The Constitution in the National Surveillance State*, 93 Minn. L. Rev. 1, 17–18 (2008).

96. Approximately 5,000 documents were stolen by Yeoman Charles Radford, who worked in the Chiefs' liaison office at the National Security Council in the White House. One of the documents Radford stole was a "President's Eyes Only" summary of Kissinger's meetings with Chou En-lai, which was passed to Admiral Thomas H. Moorer, the Chiefs' chairman. *See* Seymour M. Hersh, The Price of Power: Kissinger in the White House 380, 465 (1983). On at least one trip Radford ransacked Kissinger's personal luggage looking for material. *Id.* at 469. There was no doubt that the senior military officers around Admiral Moorer also knew what was happening, Radford said. *Id.* at 467. He did it, he said, because "I was loyal to the 'cause'—the Navy," and because he believed it would lead to a promotion. *Id.* When investigators from the Defense Investigative Service discovered what was going on, one recalled that "[w]e walked out thinking this was *Seven Days in May*." *Id.* at 472. The Senate Armed Services Committee held hearings on the matter in February and March of 1974 but the hearings were halted because their continuation, Committee Chairman John Stennis said, could "destroy the Pentagon." *Id.* at 466, n. *. Attorney General John Mitchell was assigned the role of covering up the mess, and Nixon decided not to prosecute Radford or the admirals who oversaw him. *Id.* at 473.

97. Thomas Powers, Intelligence Wars: American Secret History from Hitler to Al Qaeda 358 (2004).

98. "[M]ultiple independent organizations" normally are involved in national security decisions, and multiple officials within each organization, with the result that "there isn't a simple answer as to who should bear responsibility. . . ." Robert M. Gates, Duty: Memoirs of a Secretary at War 146 (2014).

99. The CIA's executive director/comptroller described with some amazement the ability of Richard Helms to leave no paper trail. "Do you realize," he said, "that there isn't one piece of paper in this whole Agency about the Bay of Pigs with Helms's signature on it?" THOMAS POWERS, THE MAN WHO KEPT SECRETS: RICHARD HELMS AND THE CIA 329, n. 4 (1979).

100. *See generally* PAUL C. LIGHT, THICKENING GOVERNMENT: FEDERAL HIERARCHY AND THE DIFFUSION OF ACCOUNTABILITY (1994).

101. Consolidated Appropriations Act, 2012, P.L. 112–74, § 708, 125 Stat. 786, 930.

102. *Diplomacy in Action*, U.S. Department of State, Daily Press Briefing, Washington, D.C., July 26, 2013 *available at* http://www.state.gov/r/pa/prs/dpb/2013/07/212484. htm#EGYPT, [http://perma.law.harvard.edu/02gX3aezqC8].

103. Three scholars have captured the network's fluidity in describing the President's national security team as consisting of "barons" and "courtiers." I. M DESTLER, LESLIE GELB, & ANTHONY LAKE, OUR OWN WORST ENEMY: THE UNMAKING OF U.S. FOREIGN POLICY 156 (1984). Members of the NSC staff described the national security bureaucracy as populated by "tribes" representing different organizational interests, policy views, and personal loyalties. *See* WOODWARD, *supra* note 74, at 173. One of those tribes is the NSC staff itself, "which has emerged as . . . largely independent of the president's use of the NSC itself as a decisional body." CHRISTOPHER C. SHOEMAKER, THE NSC STAFF: COUNSELING THE COUNCIL 3 (1991). National security policy thus materializes from a shifting series of feedback loops among the tribes and their members. Lower-level Trumanites influence higher-level Trumanites, and vice versa, as one tribe, or subnetwork, influences another until a decision ultimately emerges. The locus of decision-making lies below Madisonian

officials, to whom "consensus" is often presented after being hashed out by lower-level officials. FINAL REPORT OF THE NATIONAL COMMISSION ON TERRORIST ATTACKS UPON THE UNITED STATES, THE 9/11 COMMISSION REPORT 199 (2004) ("In the NSC during the first Bush administration, many tough issues were addressed at the level of the Deputies Committee. Issues did not go to the principals unless the deputies had been unable to resolve them."); *see id.* at 210 (describing how the Bush administration's initial policy towards covert action against al Qaeda in Afghanistan came "from [Richard] Clarke and the NSC senior director for intelligence, Mary McCarthy," both Clinton administration holdovers, and was then reviewed by CIA Director George Tenet, himself a Clinton appointee); ALAN G. WHITTAKER ET AL., NAT'L DEFENSE UNIV., THE NATIONAL SECURITY POLICY PROCESS: THE NATIONAL SECURITY COUNCIL AND INTERAGENCY SYSTEM 27 (2011), *available at* http://www.virginia.edu/cnsl/pdf/national-security-policy-process-2011.pdf ("[National Security Advisors] Rice and Hadley sought to hammer out a general agreement among Principals and departments before bringing a decision paper with a recommended policy to President Bush for a final decision."). Networks arise within the network; not all presidential advisers necessarily sit within any of them. *See generally* FATEFUL DECISIONS: INSIDE THE NATIONAL SECURITY COUNCIL (Karl F. Inderfurth & Loch K. Johnson eds., 2004).

104. Emails released by the White House following the Benghazi attack revealed fierce internal jostling over draft talking points between the State Department and CIA and also within the CIA. Mark Landler, Eric Schmitt, & Michael D. Shear, *Early E-Mails on Benghazi Show Internal Divisions*, N.Y. TIMES, May 16, 2013, http://www.nytimes.com/2013/05/16/us/politics/e-mails-show-jostling-over-benghazi-talking-points.html, [http://perma.law.harvard.edu/0rST5477BjP/].

105. *See generally* RICHARD K. BETTS, SOLDIERS, STATESMEN, AND COLD CRISES (1991).
106. MILLS, *supra* note 62, at 190. The military mind, Mills continued, "points to the product of a specialized bureaucratic training…a system of formal selection and common experiences and friendships and activities…instant and stereotyped obedience…a common outlook, the basis of which is the metaphysical definition of reality as essentially military reality." *Id.* at 195.
107. WOODWARD, *supra* note 74, at 186.
108. Josh Gerstein, *Obama Lawyers Set to Defend Yoo*, ASSOCIATED PRESS, Jan. 28, 2009. Hugh Heclo has described the presidency's "deep structure" as comprising those elements that remain the same when the administration changes. Hugh Heclo, *The Changing Presidential Office, in* THE MANAGERIAL PRESIDENCY (James P. Pfiffner ed., 1999).
109. "Most are interested in the philosophical only to the extent of finding out what the accepted view is in order that they may accept it and get on to the practical matters." WHYTE, *supra* note 63, at 72.
110. Former Pennsylvania Governor Ed Rendell considered Janet Napolitano ideally suited to head the Department of Homeland Security. "Janet's perfect for that job," he said. "Because for that job, you have to have no life. Janet has no family. Perfect. She can devote, literally, 19, 20 hours a day to it." Jimmy Orr, *Ed Rendell on Janet Napolitano: Perfect Because She Has No Life!*, CHRISTIAN SCIENCE MONITOR, Dec. 3, 2008, *available at* http://www.csmonitor.com/USA/Politics/The-Vote/2008/1203/ed-rendell-on-janet-napolitano-perfect-because-she-has-no-life, [http://perma.law.harvard.edu/0e5bpgwEZ7h]. The typical Trumanite, a classic organization man, cannot distinguish between his work and the rest of his life. WHYTE, *supra* note 63, at 164.

111. "[I]t is characteristic of an age of turmoil that it produces so many immediate issues that little time is left to penetrate their deeper meaning." Henry A. Kissinger, American Foreign Policy: Three Essays by Henry A. Kissinger 50 (1969). For a similar point, *see* Mark Mazzetti, The Way of the Knife: The CIA, a Secret Army, and a War at the Ends of the Earth 14 (2013) (CIA has become more tactical as analysts seek career advancement by working on terrorism issues that will appear in the President's morning intelligence briefing).

112. Robert S. McNamara, In Retrospect xvii (1995).

113. President Reagan's defense secretary, Caspar W. Weinberger, was reported to be "swamped," "overwhelmed," and "left with not enough time to look forward." Theodore H. White, *Weinberger on the Ramparts*, N.Y. Times Magazine, Feb. 6, 1983.

114. James C. Thomson Jr., *How Could Vietnam Happen?*, Atlantic Monthly, Apr. 1968, at 52.

115. The economist Robert Higgs has described the role of crisis in promoting the "ratchet effect," the difficulty in dismantling or reversing governmental programs initially established to meet transient conditions such as economic crisis or war. *See* Robert Higgs, Crisis and Leviathan (1986). Ratcheting can occur, however, even in the absence of crisis and emergency; consider President Clinton's changed plans concerning ABM deployment. "[V]ery little had changed in the international system between 1993 and 1997: no immediate new threat had emerged, Russia was subdued and China was only beginning its drive to modernity." Yet Clinton, who had tried to kill the ABM program in 1993, "almost entirely reversed" course in 1996, announcing that the United States would embark upon a huge new ABM development and deployment program. *See* Andrew Futter, Ballistic Missile Defense and U.S. National Security Policy:

NORMALIZATION AND ACCEPTANCE AFTER THE COLD
WAR 46–47 (2013).

116. WHYTE, *supra* note 63, at 172.
117. ROBERT E. HUNTER, PRESIDENTIAL CONTROL OF FOREIGN
POLICY: MANAGEMENT OR MISHAP 72 (1982).
118. *Id.*
119. KISSINGER, *supra* note 111, at 18. "What passes for planning is frequently the projection of the familiar into the
future." *Id.* at 19.
120. Senator Dianne Feinstein described the efforts of the
CIA's acting general counsel to intimidate the staff of the
Senate Intelligence Committee by filing a crimes report in
connection with the Committee's acquisition and reten-
tion of certain documents. The acting general counsel, it
turned out, was one of the individuals whose conduct was
placed at issue in the documents:

> I should note that for most, if not all, of the CIA's
> Detention and Interrogation Program, the now
> acting general counsel was a lawyer in the CIA's
> Counterterrorism Center—the unit within which
> the CIA managed and carried out this program.
> From mid-2004 until the official termination of the
> detention and interrogation program in January
> 2009, he was the unit's chief lawyer. He is mentioned
> by name more than 1,600 times in our study.

Senator Dianne Feinstein, *Statement on Intel Committee's
CIA Detention, Interrogation Report*, Mar. 11, 2014, http://
www.feinstein.senate.gov/public/index.cfm/press-
releases?ID=db84e844-01bb-4eb6-b318-31486374a895.
121. HALBERSTAM, *supra* note 71, at 212.
122. BRUCE PALMER, THE 25-YEAR WAR: AMERICA'S MILITARY
ROLE IN VIETNAM 213 n.26 (1978).
123. BAGEHOT, *supra* note 1, at 195.
124. *Id.*

125. "Self-co-optation" is the term Mills applies. Mills, *supra* note 62, at 348. Even some defenders of NSA surveillance acknowledge that the oversight committees cannot be trusted. "Clearly, they've been co-opted," said Senator John McCain. "There's no doubt about that." Darren Samuelsohn, *Hill Draws Criticism over NSA Oversight*, POLITICO, Mar. 2, 2014, http://www.politico.com/story/2014/03/hill-draws-criticism-over-nsa-oversight-104151.html?hp=r2.

126. KISSINGER, *supra* note 111, at 17.

127. *Id.*

128. GOLDSMITH, *supra* note 60, at 27.

129. *See generally* Taylor C. Boas, *Conceptualizing Continuity and Change: The Composite-Standard Model of Path Dependence*, 19(1) JOURNAL OF THEORETICAL POLITICS 33 (2007); Scott E. Page, *Path Dependence*, 1 QUARTERLY JOURNAL OF POLITICAL SCIENCE 87 (2006).

130. VICTOR A. THOMPSON, MODERN ORGANIZATION 91 n.1 (1961).

131. James Carroll refers to the bureaucracy's "grooved thinking" as its "metapersonal dynamics," conditions under which "ideology and organizational loyalties and history trump[] the most acute present analysis." CARROLL, *supra* note 70, at 302.

132. *See generally* MORTON H. HALPERIN, BUREAUCRATIC POLITICS AND FOREIGN POLICY 99 (1974). One example of the need to change many smaller policies when changing a bigger policy is the debate over closing the Guantánamo military prison.

133. "The alternative to the status quo is the prospect of repeating the whole anguishing process of arriving at decisions. This explains to some extent the curious phenomenon that decisions taken with enormous doubt and perhaps with a close division become practically sacrosanct once adopted." KISSINGER, *supra* note 111, at 20.

134. *Quoted in* MAZZETTI, *supra* note 111, at 43.
135. 2 HARRY S. TRUMAN, YEARS OF TRIAL AND HOPE 165 (1956).
136. *Id.*
137. RICHARD E. NEUSTADT, PRESIDENTIAL POWER: THE POLITICS OF LEADERSHIP 9 (1960) (emphasis added).
138. Sheehan was the *New York Times* reporter who obtained the Pentagon Papers and won a Pulitzer Prize for his reporting on Vietnam.
139. HALBERSTAM, *supra* note 71, at 409.
140. "What starts out as an aid to decision-makers often turns into a practically autonomous organization whose internal problems structure and sometimes compound the issues which it was originally designed to solve." KISSINGER, *supra* note 111, at 20. The phenomenon is not unique to the United States. Former U.K. appeal court judge Sir Stephen Sedley expressed his apprehension about a statutory surveillance regime shrouded in secrecy, part of a growing constitutional model which has led some of us to wonder whether the tripartite separation of powers—legislature, judiciary, executive—conventionally derived from Locke, Montesquieu, and Madison, still holds good.

The security apparatus is today able in many democracies to exert a measure of power over the other limbs of the state that approaches autonomy: procuring legislation which prioritizes its own interests over individual rights, dominating executive decision-making, locking its antagonists out of judicial processes and operating almost free of public scrutiny.

Stephen Sedley, *Beware of Kite-Flyers*, LONDON REVIEW OF BOOKS, Sept. 12, 2013, http://www.lrb.co.uk/v35/n17/stephen-sedley/beware-kite-flyers. *See also* Alan Rusbridger, *The Snowden Leaks and the Public*, N.Y. REVIEW OF BOOKS, Nov. 21, 2013, at 31.

CHAPTER 3

1. "We have a chance to establish our own foreign policy," CIA
   Director William Casey told Bob Woodward in the fall of
   1985. "We're on the cutting edge. We are the action agency
   of the government." THOMAS POWERS, INTELLIGENCE
   WARS: AMERICAN SECRET HISTORY FROM HITLER TO AL
   QAEDA 279 (2004) (quoting Bob Woodward's account of an
   interview with Casey). Casey's remark came a decade after
   Senator Frank Church had famously described the CIA as a
   "rogue elephant on a rampage without command." Editorial,
   Let Congress Chain This Rogue Elephant, DAYTONA BEACH
   MORNING JOURNAL, Sept. 12, 1975, *available at* http://news.
   google.com/newspapers?nid=1873&dat=19750912&id=t9
   AhAAAAIBAJ&sjid=-54FAAAAIBAJ&pg=1863,3766177,
   [http://perma.law.harvard.edu/0dBxnMkani]. "[I]n the
   '50s and '60s...it apparently was [true], to a large extent"
   that the CIA "did whatever it wanted, whenever it wanted,
   regardless of the law." JOHN RIZZO, COMPANY MAN:
   THIRTY YEARS OF CONTROVERSY AND CRISIS IN THE CIA 47
   (2014).
2. Walter Bagehot, THE ENGLISH CONSTITUTION 90 (Cornell
   University Press 1963) (1867).
3. *Id.* at 249.
4. *Id.*
5. *Id.*
6. *Id.* at 255.
7. For contemporary elaboration of this theme see Hugh
   Heclo, *Introduction: The Presidential Illusion, in* THE ILLUSION
   OF PRESIDENTIAL GOVERNMENT 2 (Hugh Heclo & Lester
   M. Salamon eds., 1981) ("If the president is widely believed
   to be in charge, then he may gain real power to perform in
   accord with the illusion.").
8. *Id.* at 82–98.
9. *Id.* at 91–93.

10. For example, in 1878 Gladstone commented that the document was "the most wonderful work ever struck off at a given time by the brain and purpose of man." W. E. Gladstone, *Kin Beyond Sea*, 127 N. AM. REV. 179, 185 (1878).

11. BAGEHOT, *supra* note 2, at 82.

12. C. WRIGHT MILLS, THE POWER ELITE 351 (1956).

13. BAGEHOT, *supra* note 2, at 248.

14. *Id.*

15. *Id.* at 90.

16. *Id.*

17. *Id.* at 207.

18. *See* Theodore Sorensen, *Political Perspective: Who Speaks for the National Interest?, in* THE TETHERED PRESIDENCY 3, 12–13 (Thomas M. Franck ed., 1981).

19. MILLS, *supra* note 12, at 201.

20. *See* THOMAS POWERS, THE MAN WHO KEPT SECRETS: RICHARD HELMS AND THE CIA 58–59, 63 (1979).

21. *See generally* LYNNE OLSON, THOSE ANGRY DAYS: ROOSEVELT, LINDBERGH, AND AMERICA'S FIGHT OVER WORLD WAR II, 1939–1941 (2013).

22. *See generally* MICHAEL FULLILOVE, RENDEZVOUS WITH DESTINY: HOW FRANKLIN D. ROOSEVELT AND FIVE EXTRAORDINARY MEN TOOK AMERICA INTO THE WAR AND INTO THE WORLD (2013); OLSON, *supra* note 21.

23. BAGEHOT, *supra* note 2, at 173.

24. The idea of mining Nicaragua's harbors reportedly was conceived by a CIA official, Dewey Clarridge, "while sitting alone [one] night . . . with a glass of gin on the rocks." RIZZO, *supra* note 1, at 83.

25. Robert Dallek, based upon recent revelations, has provided an unsettling account of the role of U.S. military and intelligence leaders in the Bay of Pigs debacle. *See* ROBERT DALLEK, CAMELOT'S COURT: INSIDE THE KENNEDY WHITE HOUSE (2013). CIA director Allen Dulles told President Kennedy after his inauguration that Castro planned to export communism to other Western Hemisphere countries. *Id.* at

132. His successor, John McCone, privately told Attorney General Robert Kennedy that "[i]f Cuba succeeds, we can expect most of Latin America to fall." *Id.* at 288. Castro, CIA and military leaders believed, was the advance wave of Soviet control of the hemisphere. *Id.* at 134. They believed that an invasion of Cuba by the U.S.-supported exiles would touch off a civil war and that Kennedy would be compelled to take direct military action if the invasion faltered. *Id.* In fact, CIA planners did not believe the invasion would succeed without direct U.S. military intervention—though they did not report this to Kennedy. *Id.* at 135, 136, 144. Kennedy later reflected that he had made the mistake of thinking that "the military and intelligence people have some secret skill not available to ordinary mortals." *Id.* at 149. The lesson that he took away was, "never rely on the experts." *Id.* Kennedy followed that counsel two years later during the Cuban missile crisis. It was "striking" that he did not consult directly with the military chiefs before deciding upon a blockade—aware, as he was, that their preference was for a surprise air strike. *Id.* at 315. In fact, even after the Soviets backed down, the Chiefs recommended a full-scale air strike and invasion barring "irrefutable evidence" that the missiles were being removed. *Id.* at 330. LeMay called the resolution of the crisis "the greatest defeat in our history," *id.* at 331; the Chiefs described themselves as ready to use "nuclear weapons for limited war operations in the Cuban area," *id.* at 362, and the CIA actively opposed Kennedy's initiatives aimed at achieving a reconciliation or rapprochement with the Cubans.

Thomas Powers also expressed skepticism that Agency planners could have been unaware that the invasion plan would fail absent U.S. intervention, or of the pressure that impending embarrassment would place on Kennedy. It is "hard to see," he suggests, how they could not have relied on the assumption that "Kennedy's hand would be forced" once it became clear that not intervening would mean publicly abandoning the trapped and isolated exiles. THOMAS POWERS, THE MAN WHO KEPT SECRETS: RICHARD HELMS AND THE CIA 117 (1979).

26. Authorization for Use of Military Force of 2001, Pub. L. No. 107-40, 115 Stat. 224 (2001).

27. *See* Sarah Moughty, *Top CIA Official: Obama Changed Virtually None of Bush's Controversial Programs,* FRONTLINE (Sept. 1, 2011, 11:02 AM), http://www.pbs.org/wgbh/pages/frontline/iraq-war-on-terror/topsecretamerica/top-cia-official-obama-changed-virtually-none-of-bushs-controversial-programs/, [http://www.perma.cc/0sdUgvQfkEr/].

28. Mark Landler, Eric Schmitt, & Michael D. Shear, *Early E-Mails on Benghazi Show Internal Divisions,* N.Y. TIMES, May 16, 2013, http://www.nytimes.com/2013/05/16/us/politics/e-mails-show-jostling-over-benghazi-talking-points.html?pagewanted=print, [http://perma.law.harvard.edu/0GPLqqA8Q7Q].

29. Hugh Heclo, *Introduction: The Presidential Illusion, in* THE ILLUSION OF PRESIDENTIAL GOVERNMENT 8 (Hugh Heclo & Lester M. Salamon eds., 1981).

30. MILLS, *supra* note 12, at 242.

31. *See* ANDREW J. BACEVICH, WASHINGTON RULES: AMERICAS' PATH TO PERMANENT WAR 30 (2010).

32. *See* JOHN R. HIBBING & ELIZABETH THEISS-MORSE, CONGRESS AS PUBLIC ENEMY: PUBLIC ATTITUDES TOWARD AMERICAN POLITICAL INSTITUTIONS 44–45 (1995).

33. *Id.*

34. *Id.*

35. *See* PAUL C. LIGHT, A GOVERNMENT ILL-EXECUTED 87–88 (2008). It took, in fact, ten months until all of President Obama's nominees took office. *See* EDWARD LUCE, TIME TO START THINKING: AMERICA IN THE AGE OF DESCENT 153 (2012). A nominee who serves as acting head of an office and whose nomination is rejected by Congress may (like a nominee for CIA general counsel) continue "heading the

office again in everything but title." RIZZO, *supra* note 1, at 21.

36. BAGEHOT, *supra* note 2, at 85.

37. Elmar Brok of Germany, the chairman of the European Parliament's foreign affairs committee, described the U.S. security establishment "as a creepy 'state within a state.'" Alison Smale, *Amid New Storm in U.S.-Europe Relationship, a Call for Talks on Spying*, N.Y. TIMES, Oct. 25, 2013, http://www.nytimes.com/2013/10/26/world/europe/fallout-over-american-spying-revelations.html.

38. "Hardened cynics will find it hard to believe, but bureaucrats want to do the right thing." JAMES Q. WILSON, BUREAUCRACY: WHAT GOVERNMENT AGENCIES DO AND WHY THEY DO IT 275 (1989).

39. *Id.* at 176.

CHAPTER 4

1. "The problem that besets us now," he wrote, "is not: how can this evolution be changed?—for that is impossible, but: what will come of it?" *Quoted in* J. P. MAYER, MAX WEBER AND GERMAN POLITICS 127 (2nd ed. 1956).

2. WALTER BAGEHOT, THE ENGLISH CONSTITUTION 66, 97 (Cornell University Press 1963) (1867).

3. "The main virtue of the system lies in its ability to self-correct...." JACK GOLDSMITH, POWER AND CONSTRAINT: THE ACCOUNTABLE PRESIDENCY AFTER 9/11, xv (2012); "Self-correction is an apt description of the events of the last decade." *Id.* at 209.

4. THE FEDERALIST No. 78 (Alexander Hamilton).

5. Marcus Raskin, without apparent familiarity with Bagehot, wrote with unusual insight in 1976:

> We know when examining the decisions of the courts that the judiciary has handled precious few cases involving the CIA or the National Security Agency (NSA). The courts are frightened of the Dual State,

> hoping that the problem will go away if no attention
> is paid to it. Furthermore, where such cases have been
> presented to the courts, judges have been reluctant or
> unable for institutional reasons, to rule against the
> secret agencies or to inquire as to their activities.

Marcus G. Raskin, *Democracy versus the National Security State*, 40 LAW & CONTEMPORARY PROBLEMS 189, 205–6 (Summer 1976).

6. According to Senator Richard Blumenthal, a former U.S. Attorney and state prosecutor, judges who come from the executive branch are "more likely to share a 'get the bad guys' mind-set and defer to the Justice Department." Charlie Savage, *Roberts's Picks Reshaping Secret Surveillance Court*, N.Y. TIMES, July 25, 2013, http://www.nytimes. com/2013/07/26/us/politics/robertss-picks-reshaping-secret-surveillance-court.html?pagewanted=all, [http:// perma.law.harvard.edu/0zJeAXR3MvB]. An occasional memoir provides a glimpse of the behind-the-scenes connections. The CIA's general counsel during the Reagan administration "left the CIA to join the federal bench as a district court judge...thanks in large part to [CIA Director] Casey's strong backing." JOHN RIZZO, COMPANY MAN: THIRTY YEARS OF CONTROVERSY AND CRISIS IN THE CIA 116 (2014).

7. *See generally* JOHN W. DEAN, THE REHNQUIST CHOICE: THE UNTOLD STORY OF THE NIXON APPOINTMENT THAT REDEFINED THE SUPREME COURT (2001).

8. *Id.* at xiii.

9. Stuart Taylor, *Rehnquist Critics Press Charges that He was Unethical on Court*, N.Y. TIMES, Sept. 11, 1986, http://www. nytimes.com/1986/09/11/us/rehnquist-s-critics-press-charges-that-he-was-unethical-on-court.html, [http:// perma.law.harvard.edu/0t88LQgzyJx].

10. *See* Glen Elsasser, *Scholar's Question Rehnquist's Candor*, CHI. TRIB., Sept. 9, 1986, http://articles.chicagotribune.

com/1986-09-09/news/8603070116_1_mr-rehnquist-justice-william-rehnquist-office-of-legal-counsel, [http://perma.law.harvard.edu/0ducjF4NksZ].

11. Federal Data Banks, Computers and the Bill of Rights, Part 1: Hearing Before the Subcomm. on Constitutional Rights, S. Comm. on the Judiciary, 92nd Cong. 620 (1971).
12. Taylor, *supra* note 9.
13. Ken Hughes, *Presidential Recordings Program*, MILLER CENTER (Sept. 25, 2013), http://whitehousetapes.net/exhibit/nixon-and-supreme-court-appointment-william-h-rehnquist,[http://perma.law.harvard.edu/0KstGeHNhuf].
14. Laird v. Tatum, 408 U.S. 1 (1972).
15. *Id.* at 1.
16. *See id.*
17. *Id.* at 14–15.
18. *See* Note, *Justice Rehnquist's Decision to Participate in Laird v. Tatum*, 73 COLUM. L. REV. 106 (1973); Ralph Michael Stein, Laird v. Tatum: *The Supreme Court and a First Amendment Challenge to Military Surveillance of Lawful Civilian Political Activity*, 1 HOFSTRA L. REV. 244 (1973); 132 CONG. REC. 22594 (Sept. 10, 1986) (letter from Floyd Feeney and Barry Mahoney to Hon. Strom Thurmond, U.S. Senate, Sept. 5, 1986 and accompanying memorandum, An Analysis of the Public Records Concerning Justice Rehnquist's Participation in Laird v. Tatum).
19. *Antonin Scalia*, LEGAL INFORMATION INSTITUTE (Sept. 25, 2013), http://www.law.cornell.edu/supct/justices/scalia.bio.html, [http://perma.law.harvard.edu/0smQrc7a8eV].
20. *Quoted in* CHARLIE SAVAGE, TAKEOVER: THE RETURN OF THE IMPERIAL PRESIDENCY AND THE SUBVERSION OF AMERICAN DEMOCRACY 30 (2007).
21. *Id.*
22. JOAN BISKUPIC, AMERICAN ORIGINAL: THE LIFE AND CONSTITUTION OF SUPREME COURT JUSTICE ANTONIN SCALIA 52 (2009).
23. SAVAGE, *supra* note 20, at 269.

24. *See generally* Herring v. United States, 424 F.3d 384 (3d Cir. 2005).
25. *John Roberts*, Legal Information Institute (Sept. 25, 2013), http://www.law.cornell.edu/supct/justices/roberts.bio.html, [http://perma.law.harvard.edu/0TnQQvxYmEC].
26. *See* Tony Mauro, *The Year Roberts Had Rehnquist's Ear*, Legal Times, Aug. 1, 2005.
27. 453 U.S. 654 (1981).
28. *See id.* at 686.
29. Savage, *supra* note 20, at 257.
30. *Id.*
31. *Id.* at 260.
32. *Roberts, supra* note 25.
33. Hamdan v. Rumsfeld, 415 F.3d 33 (D.C. Cir. 2005).
34. 548 U.S. 557 (2006).
35. *See "Hamdan v. Rumsfeld": Legal Issues & Ramifications*, Nat'l Pub. Radio (June 29, 2006), http://www.npr.org/templates/story/story.php?storyId=5521073, [http://perma.law.harvard.edu/0rAgxrMgv2].
36. Acree v. Republic of Iraq, 370 F.3d 41 (D.C. Cir. 2004).
37. *See generally* James B. Staab, The Political Thought of Justice Antonin Scalia: A Hamiltonian on the Supreme Court 95–136 (2006); David A. Schultz & Christopher E. Smith, The Jurisprudential Vision of Justice Antonin Scalia 82–90 (1996).
38. These are international agreements made by the President alone, without the approval of Congress or the Senate. *See* U.S. Senate, Congressional Oversight of Executive Agreements—1975: Hearings before the Subcomm. on Separation of Powers of the Committee on the Judiciary, 94th Cong.167–203, 302–05 (1975); Congressional Review of International Agreements: Hearings before the Subcomm. on International Security and Scientific Affairs of the Committee on International Relations, 94th Cong. 182–200 (1976).

39. Ramirez de Arellano v. Weinberger, 745 F.2d 1500, 1562 (D.C. Cir. 1984) (Scalia, J., dissenting).
40. In *Ramirez*, the plaintiff, a U.S. citizen, claimed that the U.S. military had occupied his Honduran cattle ranch to train Salvadoran soldiers, depriving him of his property without due process of law. The court's majority found the action to be justiciable; Judge Scalia (joined by Judges Robert Bork and Kenneth Starr) charged that that decision "reflect[ed] a willingness to extend judicial power into areas where we do not know, and have no way of finding out, what serious harm we may be doing." *Id.* at 1551.
41. Sanchez-Espinoza v. Reagan, 770 F.2d 202, 205 (D.C. Cir. 1985).
42. War Powers Resolution, 87 Stat. 555, 50 U.S.C. §§ 1541–48 (amended 1982).
43. For a chart of the unclassified Boland Amendments, *see* 133 Cong. Rec. H4982–H4987 (daily ed. June 15, 1987).
44. *Id.*
45. *Sanchez-Espinoza*, 770 F.2d at 208.
46. United States v. Stuart, 489 U.S. 353, 376 (1989) (Scalia, J., dissenting).
47. 542 U.S. 446 (2004).
48. *Id.* at 506.
49. 548 U.S. 557 (2006).
50. *Id.* at 655 (Scalia, J., dissenting).
51. 553 U.S. 723 (2008).
52. Matthew Barakat, *Scalia Expects NSA Program to End Up in Court*, Associated Press, Sept. 25, 2013, http://news.yahoo.com/scalia-expects-nsa-wiretaps-end-court-145501284--politics.html, [http://perma.law.harvard.edu/0yuzeWJX9nE].
53. "In more than a dozen classified rulings," the *New York Times* reported, "the nation's surveillance court has created a secret body of law giving the National Security Agency the power to amass vast collections of data on Americans

while pursuing not only terrorism suspects, but also people possibly involved in nuclear proliferation, espionage and cyberattacks.... [I]t has quietly become almost a parallel Supreme Court...." Eric Lichtblau, *In Secret, Court Vastly Broadens Powers of N.S.A*, N.Y. TIMES, July 7, 2013, http://www.nytimes.com/2013/07/07/us/in-secret-court-vastly-broadens-powers-of-nsa.html?_r=0, [http://perma.law.harvard.edu/0rXuMcN8BSj].

54. Foreign Intelligence Surveillance Act of 1978, Pub. L. No. 95-511, 92 Stat. 1783 (codified as amended at 50 U.S.C. § 1801 *et seq.* (2006)).

55. *Id.* § 1803.

56. *Id.*

57. *Id.*

58. Peter Wallsten, Carol D. Leonnig, & Alice Crites, *For Secretive Surveillance Court, Rare Scrutiny in Wake of NSA Leaks*, WASH. POST, June 22, 2013, http://www.washingtonpost.com/politics/for-secretive-surveillance-court-rare-scrutiny-in-wake-of-nsa-leaks/2013/06/22/df9eaae6-d9fa-11e2-a016-92547bf094cc_print.html, [http://perma.law.harvard.edu/0JWxWwyQ9jH/].

59. Charlie Savage, *Roberts's Picks Reshaping Secret Surveillance Court*, N.Y. TIMES, July 25, 2013, http://www.nytimes.com/2013/07/26/us/politics/robertss-picks-reshaping-secret-surveillance-court.html?pagewanted=all, [http://perma.law.harvard.edu/03YWpWeDvGk/]. Five judges on the court had prosecutorial experience. *Id.*

60. *See* 50 U.S.C. § 1802(a)(3), 1803(c); *see also* FISC R. P. 3.

61. "For about 30 years," the *Washington Post* reported, "the court was located on the sixth floor of the Justice Department's headquarters, down the hall from the officials who would argue in front of it." Carol Leonnig, Ellen Nakashima, & Barton Gellman, *Secret-Court Judges Upset at Portrayal of "Collaboration" with Government*, WASH. POST, June 29, 2013, http://www.washingtonpost.com/politics/secret-court-judges-upset-at-portrayal-of-

collaboration-with-government/2013/06/29/ed73fb68-e01b-11e2-b94a-452948b95ca8_print.html, [http://perma. law.harvard.edu/02ig1iUrqEW].

62. *See* Charlie Savage & Laura Poitras, *How a Court Secretly Evolved, Extending U.S. Spies' Reach*, N.Y. TIMES, Mar. 11, 2014, http://www.nytimes.com/2014/03/12/us/how-a-courts-secret-evolution-extended-spies-reach.html (describing the evolution of the FISC from surveillance approval to law interpretation, and in the process weakening restrictions on the sharing of private information about Americans).

63. "It is transparent," Obama said of the review procedures. "That's why we set up the FISA court." Greg Miller, *Misinformation on Classified NSA Programs Includes Statements by Senior U.S. Officials*, WASH. POST, July 1, 2013, http://www.washingtonpost.com/world/national-security/misinformation-on-classified-nsa-programs-includes-statements-by-senior-us-officials/2013/06/ 30/7b5103a2-e028-11e2-b2d4-ea6d8f477a01_print.html, [http://perma.law.harvard. edu/08Rt7uj2KJ8].

64. *Id.*

65. Carol D. Leonnig, *Court: Ability to Police U.S. Spying Program Limited*, WASH. POST, Aug. 16, 2013, http://www.washingtonpost.com/politics/court-ability-to-police-us-spying-program-limited/2013/08/15/4a8c8c44-05cd-11e3-a07f-49ddc7417125_print.html, [http://perma.law.harvard.edu/0Zo8bfYbZtS/].

66. Barton Gellman, *NSA Broke Privacy Rules Thousands of Times Per Year, Audit Finds*, WASH. POST, Aug. 16, 2013, http://www.washingtonpost.com/world/national-security/nsa-broke-privacy-rules-thousands-of-times-per-year-audit-finds/2013/08/15/3310e554-05ca-11e3-a07f-49ddc7417125_print.html, [http://perma.law.harvard.edu/0TpFZJGW9jv/].

67. *See* note 95, page 228.

68. *See* United States v. Richardson, 418 U.S. 166 (1974).
69. U.S. CONST., art. I, § 9, cl. 7.
70. *See* Schlesinger v. Reservists Comm. to Stop the War, 418 U.S. 208 (1974).
71. U.S. CONST., art. I, § 6, cl. 2.
72. Clapper v. Amnesty Int'l, 133 S. Ct. 1138 (2013). The Court found the plaintiffs' concern that their communications would be intercepted to be "too speculative" in that they were unable to show that they had been subjected to surveillance, *id.* at 1143—which of course no one could show, because the surveillance was secret. It turned out that activities that the Court labeled "speculative" were in fact occurring as its opinion was announced. Letter from Mark Udall, Ron Wyden, Martin Heinrich, U.S. Senators, to Donald Verrelli, U.S. Solicitor Gen. 1–2 (Nov. 20, 2013), *available at* http://www.scribd.com/doc/186024665/Udall-Wyden-Heinrich-Urge-Solicitor-General-to-Set-Record-Straight-on-Misrepresentations-to-U-S-Supreme-Court-in-Clapper-v-Amnesty (explaining that the FISA Amendments Act has been secretly interpreted to authorize collection of communications merely about a targeted overseas foreigner and that this collection accordingly likely results in the collection "tens of thousands" of wholly domestic communications annually).
73. Clapper, *id.*, at 1153. When he argued the case before the Supreme Court, Donald Verrelli, the Solicitor General, assured the Justices that if the government wanted to use information gathered in the surveillance program in a criminal prosecution, the source of the information would have to be disclosed. In a number of subsequent prosecutions, however, federal prosecutors refused to make the promised disclosures. Adam Liptak, *A Secret Surveillance Program Proves Challengeable in Theory Only*, N.Y. TIMES, Jan. 15, 2013, http://www.nytimes.com/2013/07/16/us/double-secret-surveillance.html?pagewanted=all.
74. *See generally Laird*, 408 U.S. 1.

75. U.S. CONST., amend. I.
76. *See* Dellums v. Bush, 752 F. Supp. 1141 (D.D.C. 1990).
77. U.S. CONST. art. I, § 8, cl. 11.
78. *Dellums*, 752 F. Supp at 1150.
79. Pub. L. No. 93-148, 87 Stat. 55 (1973) (codified at 50 U.S.C. §§ 1541–48 (1982)).
80. *See* Lowry v. Reagan, 676 F. Supp. 333 (D.D.C. 1982), *aff'd*, No. 87-5426 (D.C. Cir. 1988) (per curiam); Crockett v. Regan, 720 F.2d 1355 (D.C. Cir. 1983), *aff'g*, 558 F. Supp. 893 (1982).
81. *See* United States v. Reynolds, 345 U.S. 1 (1953).
82. *See* Sterling v. Tenet, 416 F.3d 338 (4th Cir. 2005).
83. *See* El-Masri v. United States, 479 F.3d 296 (4th Cir. 2007).
84. *See id.* at 302.
85. In 1928, the Supreme Court found that if Congress wrote a law that contained an "intelligible principle" for subsequent interpretation, "such legislative action is not a forbidden delegation of legislative power." J.W. Hampton, Jr., & Co. v. United States, 276 U.S. 394, 409 (1928).
86. The only two instances in U.S. history where a congressional delegation of authority was overruled by the Supreme Court occurred in 1935. *See generally* Panama Refining Co. v. Ryan, 293 U.S. 388 (1935); A.L.A. Schechter Poultry Corp. v. United States, 293 U.S. 495 (1935).
87. *See* Dames & Moore v. Regan, 453 U.S. 654, 686 (1981) ("In light of all of the foregoing—the inferences to be drawn from the character of the legislation Congress has enacted in the area ... and from the history of acquiescence in executive claims settlement—we conclude that the President was authorized to suspend pending claims pursuant to Executive Order No. 12294."). Congress now routinely delegates power to executive departments and agencies to define and punish even minor criminal offenses. One federal appeals court recently expressed concern that "the Code of Federal Regulations today finds itself crowded with so many 'crimes' that scholars actually debate their

number." United States v. Baldwin, No. 13-1198, D.C. No. 1:11-CR-00018-PAB-1(10th Cir., Feb. 18, 2014), http://www.ca10.uscourts.gov/opinions/13/13-1198.pdf.

88. *See* pages 22 and 43.

89. Congress and the Administration's Secrecy Pledges: Hearing Before the Subcomm. on Legislation and Nat'l Sec. of the H. Comm. on Gov't Operations, 100th Cong. 93 (1988) (statement of Rep. Jack Brooks, Chairman, H. Subcomm. on Legislation and Nat. Sec.) ("According to the General Accounting Office statement to be presented today, approximately 3 million secrecy pledges have been signed as of the end of last year.").

90. United States v. Curtiss-Wright Export Corp., 299 U.S. 304, 320 (1936). The executive continues to rely upon this ill-considered case even where narrower and more defensible support is available. *See, e.g.,* Brief for the Respondent in Opposition at 13, 23, Zivotofsky v. Kerry, No. 13-628 (U.S. Supreme Court, Feb. 2014) (arguing in the alternative that the executive is "sole organ" of the nation in foreign affairs and that an unbroken, unchallenged practice of presidential recognition of foreign nations invalidates congressional interference). *See* Michael J. Glennon, *Two Views of Presidential Foreign Affairs Power: Little v. Barreme or Curtiss-Wright?,* 13 YALE J. INT'L L. 5 (1988).

91. *Id.* at 318 ("It results that the investment of the federal government with the powers of external sovereignty did not depend upon the affirmative grants of the Constitution. The powers to declare and wage war, to conclude peace, to make treaties, to maintain diplomatic relations with other sovereignties, if they had never been mentioned in the Constitution, would have vested in the federal government as necessary concomitants of nationality.").

92. Youngstown Sheet & Tube Co. v. Sawyer, 343 U.S. 579, 588–89 (1952).

93. Solicitor General Erwin Griswold argued in the *Pentagon Papers* case that publication would cause "great and

irreparable harm to the security of the United States." Twenty-eight years later he acknowledged that no such threat existed:

> I have never seen any trace of a threat to the national security from the publication. Indeed, I have never seen it even suggested that there was such an actual threat.... It quickly becomes apparent to any person who has considerable experience with classified material that there is massive overclassification and that the principal concern of the classifiers is not with national security, but rather with governmental embarrassment of one sort or another.

Erwin Griswold, *Secrets Not Worth Keeping: The Courts and Classified Information*, WASH. POST, Feb. 15, 1989, at A25.
94. New York Times Co. v. United States, 403 U.S. 713, 714 (1971) (per curiam). The Court had initially, for the first time in U.S. history, enjoined publication. *Id.* at 715 (Black, J., concurring).
95. Hamdan v. United States, 548 U.S. 557, 567 (2006) ("[W]e conclude that the military commission convened to try Hamdan lacks power to proceed because its structure and procedures violate both the UCMJ and the Geneva Conventions.").
96. Boumediene v. Bush, 553 U.S. 723, 732–33 (2008) (holding that the procedures enacted as part of the Detainee Treatment Act of 2005 "are not an adequate and effective substitute for habeas corpus" and that "[t]herefore §7 of the Military Commissions Act of 2006 ... operates as an unconstitutional suspension of the writ").
97. Klayman v. Obama, No. 1:13 Civ. 0851 (D.D.C. Dec. 16, 2013), http://legaltimes.typepad.com/files/obamansa.pdf. The opinion was written by Judge Richard Leon. Another federal district court, however, quickly reached the opposite conclusion. ACLU v. Clapper, No. 13 Civ. 3994 (S.D.N.Y. Dec. 27, 2013) (opinion of Judge William H. Pauley III),

http://apps.washingtonpost.com/g/documents/world/
us-district-judge-pauleys-ruling-in-aclu-vs-clapper/723/.

98. Holtzman v. Schlesinger, 414 U.S. 1304, 1316 (1973)
(Douglas, J.) (holding case justiciable and vacating stay of
injunction against use of armed force in Cambodia).

99. *Id.* at 1304.

100. WILLIAM O. DOUGLAS, THE COURT YEARS 1939–1975: THE
AUTOBIOGRAPHY OF WILLIAM O. DOUGLAS 235–37
(1980).

101. *See* Korematsu v. United States, 342 U.S. 885 (1945).

102. Kim Lane Scheppele, *The New Judicial Deference*, 92 B.U.
L. REV. 89, 91 (2012) ("In major decisions both designed
to attract public attention and filled with inspiring language about the reach of the Constitution even in times of
peril, the Supreme Court, along with some lower courts,
has stood up to the government and laid down limits on
anti-terror policy in a sequence of decisions about the
detention and trial of suspected terrorists. But, at the
same time, these decisions have provided few immediate
remedies for those who have sought the courts' protection. As a result, suspected terrorists have repeatedly prevailed in their legal arguments, and yet even with these
court victories, little changed in the situation that they
went to court to challenge.").

103. Aziz Huq, *What Good Is Habeas?*, 26 CONST. COMM. 385,
429 (2010).

104. Sean Murphy described the post-9/11 preventive strategy
as follows:

> Such arrests—which were on a scale not seen in the
> United States since the Second World War—were con-
> ducted under great secrecy. Gag orders and other rules
> (including rules relating to the grand jury and to the
> detainees' privacy) prevented officials from discussing
> the detainees, and defense lawyers were sometimes
> allowed to see documents only at the courthouse.

A Washington Post analysis of 235 detainees revealed that the largest groups came from Egypt, Pakistan, and Saudi Arabia; virtually all were men in their twenties and thirties; and the greatest concentration were in U.S. states with large Islamic populations that included what law enforcement officials identified as Al Qaeda sympathizers: California, Florida, Michigan, New Jersey, New York, and Texas. Many were arrested because they were in the same places or engaged in the same kinds of activities as the hijackers (for example, taking flying lessons); many others apparently were detained because they came from certain countries or had violated U.S. immigration law. Further, the Justice Department announced a new policy that it would monitor communications between lawyers and persons being held on suspicion of being terrorists.

SEAN D. MURPHY, UNITED STATES PRACTICE IN INTERNATIONAL LAW, VOL. 1: 1999–2001 437 (2002) (footnotes omitted).

105. *See, e.g.*, Adam Liptak, *Justices Block Suit over Use of Material Witness Law against Detainee*, N.Y. TIMES, May 31, 2011, http://www.nytimes.com/2011/06/01/us/01scotus.html?pagewanted=all&_r=0, [http://perma.cc/J922-UNHW] ("The Supreme Court unanimously ruled Tuesday that a man detained after the Sept. 11 attacks may not sue John D. Ashcroft, the former attorney general, for asserted misuse of the federal material witness law."); *see also* Donald Q. Cochran, *Material Witness Detention in a Post-9/11 World: Mission Creep or Fresh Start?*, 18 GEO. MASON L. REV. 1, 10 (2010) ("Material witness proceedings and records were sealed at the government's request, and the government did not initially reveal how many persons were detained on material witness warrants. The government has subsequently admitted to holding forty to fifty material witnesses. According to

research by Human Rights Watch and the American Civil Liberties Union, however, at least seventy individuals— all male and all but one Muslim—were detained as material witnesses after 9/11.").

106. 28 C.F.R. § 50.10.

107. *See* pages 45–46.

108. *Foreign Intelligence Surveillance Act Court Orders 1979–2011*, Electronic Privacy Info. Ctr., http://epic.org/privacy/wiretap/stats/fisa_stats.html, [http://perma.cc/GXH8-8CH3].

109. Marc Ambinder, *U.S. Responds to NSA Disclosures*, THE WEEK, June 6, 2013, at http://theweek.com/article/index/245243/us-responds-to-nsa-disclosures, [http://perma.cc/T9DE-ZFUU].

110. ZBIGNIEW BRZEZINSKI, POWER AND PRINCIPLE 477 (1983).

111. *See supra* pages 19–22.

112. *See, e.g.*, Spencer Ackerman, *Intelligence Committee Withheld Key File before Critical NSA Vote, Amash Claims*, THE GUARDIAN, Aug. 12, 2013, http://www.theguardian.com/world/2013/aug/12/intelligence-committee-nsa-vote-justin-amash, [http://perma.cc/04i8gcTQcpt]. Bulk surveillance "certainly was approved by Congress," said Representative Jan Schakowsky. "Was it approved by a fully knowing Congress? That is not the case." Wallsten, *supra* note 58.

113. Jack Goldsmith, *Congress Must Figure Out What Our Government Is Doing in the Name of the AUMF*, Lawfare blog, May 17, 2013, http://www.lawfareblog.com/2013/05/congress-must-figure-out-what-our-government-is-doing-in-the-name-of-the-aumf/, [http://perma.cc/0dfCRyuPCS9].

114. Authorization for Use of Military Force, Pub. L. No. 107-40, 115 Stat. 224 (2001).

115. This was done, for example, during the Carter presidency when the White House counsel, Lloyd Cutler, became so concerned at the number of presidential

"Findings"—which authorized covert operations—that he agreed with the CIA to call many of them by the "deceptively innocuous term" "Memorandum of Notification." The term is still used. RIZZO, *supra* note 6, at 75.

116. *See* Curtis A. Bradley & Trevor W. Morrison, *Historical Gloss and the Separation of Powers*, 126 HARV. L. REV. 411, 421 (2012) (interbranch rivalry is less likely under contemporary political conditions).

117. *See* page 12.

118. *Id.*

119. THE FEDERALIST NO. 51 (James Madison).

120. *See* DAVID R. MAHEW, CONGRESS: THE ELECTORAL CONNECTION (1974).

121. "[L]ike the wily manservant in *The Marriage of Figaro*, [the bureaucracy] is constantly working to manipulate its master so as to achieve mutually profitable arrangements." JAMES Q. WILSON, BUREAUCRACY: WHAT GOVERNMENT AGENCIES DO AND WHY THEY DO IT 251 (1989).

122. *See* INS v. Chadha, 462 U.S. 919, 957–59, 967–68, 1002 (1983) (White, J., dissenting) (lamenting the excessively broad sweep of the holding invalidating the "legislative veto").

123. *Id.* at 954–55 ("Disagreement with the Attorney General's decision on Chadha's deportation—that is, Congress' decision to deport Chadha—no less than Congress' original choice to delegate to the Attorney General the authority to make that decision, involves determinations of policy that Congress can implement in only one way: bicameral passage followed by presentment to the President.").

124. David L. Boren, *The Winds of Change at the CIA*, 101 YALE L.J. 853, 856–57 (1992) (describing President George H. W. Bush's veto of the 1991 Intelligence Authorization Bill, which would have "tighten[ed] the definitions of 'covert actions' and 'timely notice'"). Sometimes committees do continue to review policy initiatives under informal "gentlemen's agreements" with executive agencies, though the formal legality of the practice is doubtful.

125. 50 U.S.C. 413(a)(1).

126. Jack Goldsmith, for example, has written that "[n]othing of significance happens in American intelligence without the intelligence committees, or some subset, knowing about it." GOLDSMITH, *supra* note 3, at 90.

127. My own experience as the legal counsel to the Senate Foreign Relations Committee, dating to the earliest days of the congressional intelligence committees' operations, led me to a very different conclusion, though the details remain classified.

128. *Quoted in* LOCH K. JOHNSON, SECRET AGENCIES: U.S. INTELLIGENCE IN A HOSTILE WORLD 117 (1996).

129. *Quoted in* LOCH K. JOHNSON, A SEASON OF INQUIRY: THE SENATE INTELLIGENCE INVESTIGATION 263 (1985).

130. "The White House has been withholding for five years more than 9,000 top-secret documents sought by the Senate Select Committee on Intelligence for its investigation into the now-defunct CIA detention and interrogation program, even though President Barack Obama hasn't exercised a claim of executive privilege," a McClatchy investigation revealed. "In contrast to public assertions that it supports the committee's work, the White House has ignored or rejected offers in multiple meetings and in letters to find ways for the committee to review the records...." Jonathan S. Landay, Ali Watkins, & Marisa Taylor, *White House Withholds Thousands of Documents from Senate CIA Probe, Despite Vows of Help* | National Security & Defense | McClatchy DC, Mar. 13, 2014, http://www.mcclatchydc.com/2014/03/12/221033/despite-vows-of-help-white-house.html.

131. Senator Dianne Feinstein, *Statement on Intel Committee's CIA Detention, Interrogation Report*, Mar. 11, 2014, http://www.feinstein.senate.gov/public/index.cfm/press-releases?ID=db84e844-01bb-4eb6-b318-31486374a895. A year later, she said, "we read about the tapes destruction

in the newspapers" when it was revealed by the *New York Times*. *Id*.

132. *Transcript: Senate Intelligence Hearing on National Security Threats*, WASH. POST, Jan. 29, 2014, http://www.washingtonpost.com/world/national-security/transcript-senate-intelligence-hearing-on-national-security-threats/2014/01/29/b5913184-8912-11e3-833c-33098f9e5267_story.html.

133. *Id*. He continued:

> These statements did not protect sources and methods that were useful in fighting terror. Instead, they hid bad policy choices and violation of the liberties of the American people.
>
> For example, the director of the NSA said publicly that the NSA doesn't hold data on U.S. citizens. That was obviously untrue.
>
> Justice Department officials testified that Section 215 of the Patriot Act is analogous to grand jury subpoena authority, and that deceptive statement was made on multiple occasions.
>
> Officials also suggested that the NSA doesn't have the authority to read Americans' emails without a warrant. But the FISA Court opinions declassified last August showed that wasn't true either.

Id.

134. "The Intelligence Committee knew, and members [of Congress] could go into the Intelligence Committee room and read the documents," said a former Wyden staffer. "But they couldn't bring staff, they couldn't take notes, they couldn't consult outside legal scholars." Robert Barnes, Timothy B. Lee, & Ellen Nakashima, *Government Surveillance Programs Renew Debate about Oversight*, WASH. POST, June 9, 2013, http://articles.washingtonpost.com/2013-06-08/politics/39834570_1_oversight-

programs-government-surveillance, [http://perma.cc/0SLNFgSLk1G].

135. CIA Director Richard Helms, instructing a subordinate who was to testify before a congressional committee, told him to "tell them as succinctly as possible the answer to the question they asked. Not the question they should have asked." THOMAS POWERS, THE MAN WHO KEPT SECRETS: RICHARD HELMS AND THE CIA 221 (1979).

136. Jennifer Kibbe, *Congressional Oversight of Intelligence: Is the Solution Part of the Problem?*, 25 INTELLIGENCE AND NATIONAL SECURITY 24, 34, 37 (2010).

137. Mark Mazzetti, *C.I.A. Employees Face New Inquiry Amid Clashes on Detention Program*, N.Y. TIMES, Mar. 5, 2014, http://www.nytimes.com/2014/03/05/us/new-inquiry-into-cia-employees-amid-clashes-over-interrogation-program.html?_r=0. Feinstein indicated that "CIA personnel had conducted a 'search'—that was John Brennan's word—of the committee computers…of the 'stand-alone' and 'walled-off' committee network drive containing the committee's own internal work product and communications." Senator Dianne Feinstein, *Statement on Intel Committee's CIA Detention, Interrogation Report*, Mar. 11, 2014, http://www.feinstein.senate.gov/public/index.cfm/press-releases?ID=db84e844-01bb-4eb6-b318-31486374a895. Asked to respond to the allegation that the CIA monitored Intelligence Committee computers, President Obama replied, "I'm going to try to make sure I don't spill anything on my tie." Jonathan S. Landay, Ali Watkins, & Marisa Taylor, *Senate Staffers Slipped Secret CIA documents from Agency's Headquarters*, WATCHING WASHINGTON AND THE WORLD: McCLATCHY DC, Mar. 5, 2014, http://www.mcclatchydc.com/2014/03/05/220273/senate-staffers-slipped-secret.html. Later, the President said that "that's not something that is an appropriate role for me and the White House to wade into at this point," Jennifer Epstein,

Barack Obama Weighs in on Senate-CIA Flap, POLITICO, Mar. 12, 2014, http://www.politico.com/story/2014/03/barack-obama-senate-cia-104597.html. Senator Mark Udall suggested that Obama knew of the CIA's action. Spencer Ackerman, *Obama Knew CIA Secretly Monitored Intelligence Committee, Senator Claims*, THE GUARDIAN, Mar. 5, 2014, http://www.theguardian.com/world/2014/mar/05/obama-cia-senate-intelligence-committee-torture. Senator Martin Heinrich, a member of the panel, expressed puzzlement about who was overseeing whom. "The Senate Intelligence Committee oversees the CIA, not the other way around," he said. Dan Froomkin, *The Inverse of Oversight: CIA Spies on Congress*, THE INTERCEPT, Mar. 5, 2014, https://firstlook.org/theintercept/2014/03/05/congress-intelligence-community-whos-overseeing/.

138. Senator Dianne Feinstein, *Statement on Intel Committee's CIA Detention, Interrogation Report*, Mar. 11, 2014, http://www.feinstein.senate.gov/public/index.cfm/press-releases?ID=db84e844-01bb-4eb6-b318-31486374a895. The White House reportedly knew in advance before the complaint was filed but did nothing to stop it. *White House Says CIA Gave "Heads Up" It Was Filing DOJ Complaint against Senate Aides*, ASSOCIATED PRESS (2014), Mar. 13, 2014, http://www.foxnews.com/politics/2014/03/12/white-house-says-cia-gave-heads-up-it-was-filing-doj-complaint-against-senate/.

139. Jennifer Kibbe, *Congressional Oversight of Intelligence: Is the Solution Part of the Problem?*, 25 INTELLIGENCE AND NATIONAL SECURITY 24, 26 (2010).

140. The *Washington Post* summarized the oversight charade:

> Unlike typical congressional hearings that feature testimony from various sides of a debate, the briefings in 2010 and 2011 on the telephone surveillance program were by definition one-sided affairs, with lawmakers hearing only from government officials

steeped in the legal and national security arguments for aggressive spying.

Additional obstacles stemmed from the classified nature of documents, which lawmakers may read only in specific, secure offices; rules require them to leave their notes behind and restrict their ability to discuss the issues with colleagues, outside experts or their own staff.

While Senate Intelligence Committee members can each designate a full-time staffer for the committee who has full access, House members must rely on the existing committee staff, many of whom used to work for the spy agencies they are tasked with overseeing.

Wallsten, *supra* note 58.

141. James Risen & Charlie Savage, *On Eve of Critical Vote, N.S.A. Director Lobbies House*, N.Y. TIMES, July 23, 2013, http://www.nytimes.com/2013/07/24/us/politics/nsa-director-lobbies-house-on-eve-of-critical-vote.html?gwh=BC248B30A3974D6BC63DC282F371EDDC, [http://perma.cc/0ydYMwAhiLv]. Representative F. James Sensenbrenner Jr., one of the principal authors of the PATRIOT Act, said "his handiwork was never meant to create a program that allows the government to demand the phone records of every American." Jonathan Weisman, *House Defeats Effort to Rein In N.S.A. Data Gathering*, N.Y. TIMES, July 24, 2013, http://www.nytimes.com/2013/07/25/us/politics/house-defeats-effort-to-rein-in-nsa-data-gathering.html?pagewanted=all&gwh=3CE3A2AA5DEA0D4C53701D1500D32D48, [http://perma.cc/02vBXQiJrm].

142. Jennifer Kibbe, *Congressional Oversight of Intelligence: Is the Solution Part of the Problem?*, 25 INTELLIGENCE AND NATIONAL SECURITY 24, 27 (2010).

143. RIZZO, *supra* note 6, at 1, 9.

144. *Id.* at 9–10. That only changed when the destruction of the tapes was reported—years later—by the *New York Times. Id.*

145. *Quoted in* LOCH K. JOHNSON, A SEASON OF INQUIRY: THE SENATE INTELLIGENCE INVESTIGATION 263 (1985).

146. Loch Johnson, *Ostriches, Cheerleaders, Skeptics, and Guardians: Role Selection by Congressional Intelligence Overseers,* 28 SAIS REVIEW OF INTERNATIONAL AFFAIRS 93, 98 (2008) ("Some have taken the approach of 'ostriches,' content to bury their heads in the sand and continue the earlier era of trust, when lawmakers deferred to the decisions of the executive branch within the domains of intelligence and defense.").

147. *Id.* at 98.

148. BRIT SNYDER, THE AGENCY AND THE HILL: CIA'S RELATIONSHIP WITH CONGRESS, 1946–2004, at 86 (2008).

149. Accordingly, the press learn little about what the agencies are doing; when it was revealed, for example, that the NSA was involved in intercepting the communications of the leaders of U.S. allies, Feinstein acknowledged that she and her committee knew nothing about it. Josh Gerstein, *Feinstein: Senate Intelligence Panel in Dark on Surveillance of Allies,* POLITICO, Oct. 28, 2013, http:// www.politico.com/blogs/under-the-radar/2013/10/ feinstein-senate-intelligence-panel-in-dark-on-surveillance-176123.html.

150. Johnson, *supra* note 146, at 93, 99–100.

151. Jennifer Kibbe, *Congressional Oversight of Intelligence: Is the Solution Part of the Problem?,* 25 INTELLIGENCE AND NATIONAL SECURITY 24, 35 (2010).

152. *Id.* at 36.

153. *Id.* at 24, 36.

154. *Id.* at 38.

155. Such relationships are a matter of public record and have been widely reported in the press. *See generally* Michael J. Glennon, *Liaison and the Law: Foreign Intelligence*

Agencies' Activities in the United States, 25 HARVARD JOURNAL OF INTERNATIONAL LAW 1 (1984).

156. 1 U.S.C. 112b (requiring that international agreements be transmitted to Congress within sixty days of the agreement's entry into force).

157. Letter from Frank C. Carlucci, Deputy Director of the CIA, to John Sparkman, Chairman, Senate Foreign Relations Committee (July 7, 1978), *reprinted in* 1 MICHAEL J. GLENNON & THOMAS M. FRANCK, UNITED STATES FOREIGN RELATIONS LAW 185–8 (1980).

158. I was present at the 1978 meeting in which Deputy Director Carlucci orally conveyed the administration's veto threat to Senator George McGovern, who had introduced the amendment. McGovern at the time was chairman of the Committee's Subcommittee on International Operations, which oversaw the State Department. An off-the-record understanding was reached at the meeting that intelligence liaison agreements would not be required to be transmitted, even agreements with significant foreign policy or national security implications; the President then signed the legislation. The effects of the understanding were far-reaching. In February 2014, for example, Western and Arab intelligence leaders met in Washington to decide upon what additional steps, if any, would be taken to support the Syrian rebels. One of the items under discussion was whether to supply the Syrian opposition with shoulder-fired anti-aircraft missiles. David Ignatius, *On Syria, a Spymasters' Conclave*, WASH. POST, Feb. 19, 2014, http://www.washingtonpost.com/opinions/david-ignatius-regional-spymasters-make-tactical-changes-to-bolster-syrian-moderates/2014/02/18/5d69596c-98f0-11e3-b931-0204122c514b_story.html. "In the wrong hands, shoulder-fired antiaircraft missiles pose a major threat to passenger air travel, the commercial aviation industry and possibly military aircraft around the world," Andrew J. Shapiro, an

assistant secretary of state who oversees the effort said in 2012. "Not only could a successful attack against an aircraft cause a devastating loss of life, but it could also cause significant economic damage." (A senior Obama administration official said in September 2012 that U.S. intelligence estimated that 100 to 1,000 MANPADS (man-portable air-defense systems) were still unaccounted for in Libya, despite U.S. efforts to destroy them. Intelligence officials believe that some of the MANPADS have been smuggled across Libya's borders.) Abigail Hausloherner, *Libya Militia Leader: Heat-seeking Missiles, Other Weapons Stolen during Firefight*, WASH. POST, Sept. 24, 2012, http://www.washingtonpost.com/world/asia_pacific/libya-militia-leader-heat-seeking-missiles-other-weapons-stolen-during-firefight/2012/09/24/8ab6f992-0675-11e2-afff-d6c7f20a83bf_story.html. Yet because of the understanding reached in 1978, any agreement to provide such weapons to Syrian rebels would not be required to be reported. The so-called "Five Eyes" agreement, which was once (erroneously) thought to prevent parties from spying on one another, also was not required to be transmitted. A major international contretemps was caused by the revelation of U.S. surveillance of European allies' leaders and populations. *See* James Glanz, *United States Can Spy on Britons Despite Pact, N.S.A. Memo Says*, N.Y. TIMES, Nov. 20, 2013, http://www.nytimes.com/2013/11/21/us/united-states-can-spy-on-britons-despite-pact-nsa-memo-says.html?_r=0; James Ball, *US and UK Struck Secret Deal to Allow NSA to "Unmask" Britons' Personal Data*, THE GUARDIAN, Nov. 20, 2013, http://www.theguardian.com/world/2013/nov/20/us-uk-secret-deal-surveillance-personal-data.

159. The resolution establishing the Senate Select Committee on Intelligence provided that "[n]othing in this resolution shall be construed as amending, limiting, or otherwise changing the authority of any standing committee of the

Senate to obtain full and prompt access to the product of the intelligence activities of any department or agency of the Government relevant to a matter otherwise within the jurisdiction of such committee." Sec. 3(d), S. Res. 400, 94th Cong., 2nd Sess. (1976), http://www.intelligence. senate.gov/pdfs/11214.pdf.

160. Amy Zegart & Julie Quinn, *Congressional Intelligence Oversight: The Electoral Disconnection*, 25 INTELLIGENCE AND NATIONAL SECURITY 744 (2010).

161. HOUSE PERMANENT SELECT COMMITTEE ON INTELLIGENCE, IC21: THE INTELLIGENCE COMMUNITY IN THE 21ST CENTURY (1996).

162. Zegart & Quinn, *supra* note 160, at 760.

163. *Id.*

164. *Id.* at 747.

165. Loch K. Johnson, *Ostriches, Cheerleaders, Skeptics, and Guardians: Role Selection by Congressional Intelligence Overseers*, 28 SAIS REVIEW OF INTERNATIONAL AFFAIRS 93, 106 (2008). *See generally* LOCH K. JOHNSON, SECRET AGENCIES: U.S. INTELLIGENCE IN A HOSTILE WORLD (1996).

166. James Bamford, *Five Myths about the National Security Agency*, WASH. POST, June 21, 2013, http:// articles.washingtonpost.com/2013-06-21/ opinions/40114085_1_national-security-agency-foreign- intelligence-surveillance-court-guardian, [http://perma. cc/0D75bvM5Et6].

167. *Hearings on H.R. 1013, H.R. 1317, and Other Proposals Which Address the Issue of Affording Prior Notice of Covert Actions to the Congress*, Subcommittee on Legislation, U.S. House Permanent Select Committee on Intelligence, 100th Cong., 1st sess, Apr.–June 1987 at 36 (statement of Stansfield Turner).

168. FINAL REPORT OF THE NATIONAL COMMISSION ON TERRORIST ATTACKS UPON THE UNITED STATES, THE 9/11 COMMISSION REPORT 420 (2004). *See* Heidi

Kitrosser, *Congressional Oversight of National Security Activities: Improving Information Funnels*, 29 CARDOZO L. REV. 1049, 1060 (2008); *see generally* Anne Joseph O'Connell, *The Architecture of Smart Intelligence: Structuring and Overseeing Agencies in the Post-9/11 World*, 94 CAL. L. REV. 1655 (2006).

169. *See* BOB WOODWARD, VEIL: THE SECRET WARS OF THE CIA, 1981–1987, at 324 (1987).

170. *See id.* at 486.

171. *See* Wallsten, *supra* note 58.

172. *See* WOODWARD, *supra* note 169, at 421.

173. For the most prominent works, *see* ARTHUR M. SCHLESINGER JR., THE IMPERIAL PRESIDENCY (1973); SAVAGE, *supra* note 20; ANDREW RUDALEVIGE, THE NEW IMPERIAL PRESIDENCY: RENEWING PRESIDENTIAL POWER AFTER WATERGATE (2006). For insightful, recent consideration of these issues, *see* THE PRESIDENCY IN THE TWENTY-FIRST CENTURY (Charles W. Dunn ed., 2011).

174. There is, however, precedent for outright disobedience. During the October War, President Nixon ordered the Pentagon to "get [the resupply aircraft] in the air now"— but experienced "total[] exasperation" at the military's unwillingness to carry out his decision. RICHARD NIXON, THE MEMOIRS OF RICHARD NIXON 927 (1978). "It is a relatively simple matter, in the absence of an oversight mechanism, for a disgruntled department head to simply ignore a decision by the president, or to establish so many obstacles to implementation that it is rendered meaningless." CHRISTOPHER C. SHOEMAKER, THE NSC STAFF: COUNSELING THE COUNCIL 30 (1991).

175. Former Marine Corps General Jim Jones, Obama's first National Security Advisor, "has emphasized the 'bottom up' approach to decision-making that both he and Obama favor...in which issues are first discussed in working groups, then brought to the 'deputies committee' of representatives from Cabinet departments."

Karen DeYoung, *National Security Adviser Jones Says He's "Outsider" in Frenetic White House*, WASH. POST, May 7, 2009, http://www.washingtonpost.com/wp-dyn/content/article/2009/05/06/AR2009050604134.html?hpid=topnews&sid=ST2009050702253, [http://perma.cc/0gwxVfzV3vG].

176. Dean Acheson, *Thoughts About Thought in High Places*, N.Y. TIMES MAGAZINE, Oct. 11, 1959.

177. *See, e.g.,* BOB WOODWARD, OBAMA'S WARS 314 (2010).

178. C. WRIGHT MILLS, THE POWER ELITE 286 (1956).

179. "[A] veritable political technocracy of White House aides has developed," Hugh Heclo has written, "helping the president in the short run and in the long run entangling the presidency in an extensive network of policy activists interested in particular issues." Hugh Heclo, *Introduction: The Presidential Illusion, in* THE ILLUSION OF PRESIDENTIAL GOVERNMENT 11 (Hugh Heclo & Lester M. Salamon eds., 1981).

180. "I'm tired of negotiating with the military," Obama told Gates. ROBERT M. GATES, DUTY: MEMOIRS OF A SECRETARY AT WAR 382 (2014). Gates objects that the President and his staff were "seeking total control and trying to centralize all power...." *Id.* at 301. It seems to have eluded Gates and other Trumanites that it is, after all, the President in whom military power *is* centralized—by the commander-in-chief clause of the U.S. Constitution.

181. *See* Hugh Heclo, *The Changing Presidential Office, in* THE MANAGERIAL PRESIDENCY (James P. Pfiffner ed., 1999).

182. Theodore Sorensen, *You Get to Walk to Work*, N.Y. TIMES MAGAZINE, Mar. 19, 1967.

183. DOUGLAS, *supra* note 100, at 304–05. Kennedy developed a growing lack of confidence in the judgment of the military leadership. "Kennedy distrusted America's military establishment as being too enamored of nuclear weapons and readiness to use them." ROBERT DALLEK, CAMELOT'S COURT: INSIDE THE KENNEDY WHITE HOUSE

68 (2013). Kennedy had barely settled into the Oval Office in January 1961 when the Chief of Naval Operations, Arleigh Burke, proposed to attack "the Soviet Union from hell to breakfast." Kennedy quashed the speech; Burke proceeded to leak the story to the *New York Times. Id.* at 71. Later, Kennedy's National Security Advisor, McGeorge Bundy, called on behalf of the President and asked the Joint Chiefs of Staff for a copy of the Joint Strategic Capabilities Plan. The general on the other end of the line replied: "We never release that." *Id.* at 74.

184. Carl Marcy, the legendary chief of staff of the Senate Foreign Relations Committee during the chairmanship of Senator Fulbright, said he became increasingly concerned about the role of the Agency in foreign policy in the 1960s:

> It was during that period that I first began to be aware of the extent to which CIA employees had infiltrated the career foreign service of the United States. . . . At one time, we did get figures on the number of CIA employees, as contrasted with the number of State Department–paid employees, in several embassies overseas. I remember being quite shocked at the time by the fact that in several of the embassies there were nearly as many CIA people on the payroll as there were foreign service people, although they were all listed as foreign service officers. . . . So I was worried about the infiltration of the foreign service by the CIA.

SENATE HISTORICAL OFFICE, UNITED STATES SENATE, ORAL HISTORY INTERVIEWS, SEPT.–NOV. 1983: CARL MARCY, CHIEF OF STAFF, FOREIGN RELATIONS COMMITTEE, 1955–1973, at 203–204.

185. Mark Mazzetti & Scott Shane, *Senate and C.I.A. Spar over Secret Report on Interrogation Program,* N.Y. TIMES, July 19, 2013, http://www.nytimes.com/2013/07/20/

us/politics/senate-and-cia-spar-over-secret-report-on-interrogation-program.html?pagewanted=all&gwh=8A 66075C7CF7F589C9F0023B795D679B, [http://perma. cc/0pAbVwjDQgJ].

186. MARK MAZZETTI, THE WAY OF THE KNIFE: THE CIA, A SECRET ARMY, AND A WAR AT THE ENDS OF THE EARTH 228 (2013).

187. Timothy B. Lee, *Why a More Transparent NSA Would Be Good for Barack Obama*, WASH. POST, July 3, 2013, http://www.washingtonpost.com/blogs/wonkblog/wp/2013/07/03/why-a-more-transparent-nsa-would-be-good-for-barack-obama/, [http://perma.cc/03Dsz7syik7].

188. *Id.*

189. RIZZO, *supra* note 6, at 13.

190. *Id.*

191. *See, e.g.*, 9/11 COMMISSION REPORT, *supra* note 168, at 206 ("[T]he CIA, at the NSC's request, had developed draft legal authorities—a presidential finding—to undertake a large-scale program of covert assistance to the Taliban's foes.... [T]he [Deputies Committee] agreed to revise the al Qaeda presidential directive, then being finalized for presidential approval.").

192. *See, e.g.*, DANIEL KLAIDMAN, KILL OR CAPTURE: THE WAR ON TERROR AND THE SOUL OF THE OBAMA PRESIDENCY 45–46 (2012) (describing how the Obama administration's initial decision to continue using the Bush administration's legal arguments with regard to the state secrets doctrine was made by the Justice Department and that "Obama only learned about it after the fact, from the front page of the *New York Times*.").

193. Compare this with Gibbon's description of the imperial government of Augustus, "an absolute monarchy disguised by the forms of a commonwealth. The masters of the Roman world surrounded their throne with darkness, concealed their irresistible strength, and humbly professed themselves the accountable ministers of the

senate, whose supreme decrees they dictated and obeyed." EDWARD GIBBON, THE DECLINE AND FALL OF THE ROMAN EMPIRE 38 (D. M. Low abridgement, 1960).

194. In the same sense, "authority *formally* resides 'in the people,' but the power of initiation is in fact held by small circles of men. That is why the standard strategy of manipulation is to make it appear that the people, or at least a large group of them, 'really made the decision.'" MILLS, *supra* note 178, at 317.

195. BAGEHOT, *supra* note 2, at 159.

196. For reasons such as this, Bagehot believed that classic presidential government is "incompatible with a skilled bureaucracy." *Id.* at 201. In classic presidential government, the President manages the execution of the law; initially, with no bureaucratic counterweight, it worked. "When Thomas Jefferson settled down in the White House in 1802," Bruce Ackerman has noted, "the executive establishment residing in Washington, DC, consisted of 132 federal officials of all ranks. (One was Jefferson's personal secretary, who served as his entire staff.)" BRUCE ACKERMAN, THE DECLINE AND FALL OF THE AMERICAN REPUBLIC 43 (2010).

197. David Frum, *Who Decided? Peter Baker's "Days of Fire,"* N.Y. TIMES, Oct. 18, 2013 (quoting from PETER BAKER, DAYS OF FIRE: BUSH AND CHENEY IN THE WHITE HOUSE (2013)).

198. *See* SEYMOUR M. HERSH, CHAIN OF COMMAND: THE ROAD FROM 9/11 TO ABU GHRAIB 122 (2004) (describing a "staged" assault on an supposedly enemy-held airfield that produced "exciting television footage"—but that was in fact "clear of Taliban forces").

199. William Saletan, *The Myth of Bin Laden: The False Story of His Life Meets the False Story of His Death,* SLATE, May 4, 2011, http://www.slate.com/articles/health_and_science/human_nature/2011/05/the_myth_of_bin_laden.html, [http://perma.cc/0Mn6SzRjx8S].

200. David D. Kirkpatrick, *Jessica Lynch Criticizes U.S. Accounts of Her Ordeal*, N.Y. TIMES, Nov. 7, 2003, http://www.nytimes.com/2003/11/07/national/07LYNC.html, [http://perma.cc/0vgrwEhbLJL].

201. The Defense Department did not cooperate in the making of *Dr. Strangelove or: How I Learned to Stop Worrying and Love the Bomb* (Columbia Pictures, 1964), the classic satire in which a deranged Air Force general launches a sneak attack against the Soviet Union. *Inside the Making of Dr. Strangelove* (Columbia Tristar Home Video Inc., 2000), http://www.youtube.com/watch?v=iJ6BiRtGTAk. In contrast, in the production of *Top Gun* (Paramount Pictures, 1986), "the Pentagon worked hand-in-hand with the filmmakers, reportedly charging Paramount Pictures just $1.8 million for the use of its warplanes and aircraft carriers." Navy enlistment spiked when the movie was released and the Navy set up recruitment tables at theaters where it played. David Sirota, *25 Years Later, How "Top Gun" Made America Love War*, WASH. POST, Aug. 26, 2011, http://articles.washingtonpost.com/2011-08-26/opinions/35271385_1_pentagon-brass-military-budget-top-gun, [http://perma.cc/96SN-SD8V]. Paramount permitted the Pentagon to review the script and suggest changes. *Id.* The CIA reviewed the script of *Zero Dark Thirty* (Columbia Pictures, 2012) and successfully pushed for the removal of certain scenes that might have cast the agency in a negative light. Ben Child, *CIA Requested Zero Dark Thirty Rewrites, Memo Reveals*, THE GUARDIAN, May 7, 2013, http://www.theguardian.com/film/2013/may/07/zero-dark-thirty-cia-memo, [http://perma.cc/9Z35-NL65]. Behind-the-scenes participation by the military and intelligence services in Hollywood movie-making has been going on for decades. *See* JEAN-MICHEL VALANTIN, HOLLYWOOD, THE PENTAGON AND WASHINGTON: THE MOVIES AND NATIONAL SECURITY FROM WORLD WAR II TO THE PRESENT DAY (2005). *See*

also David L. Robb, Operation Hollywood: How the Pentagon Shapes and Censors the Movies (2004); J. William Fulbright, The Pentagon Propaganda Machine (1971).

202. *2 Years after Soldier's Death, Family's Battle Is with Army,* N.Y. Times, Mar. 21, 2006, http://www.nytimes.com/2006/03/21/politics/21tillman.html?pagewanted=all, [http://perma.cc/0W9RcrkfWUb].

203. U.S. Dep't of State, 3 FAM 4800, Department Awards Program (2012); Medals of the CIA, Central Intelligence Agency, https://www.cia.gov/library/publications/additional-publications/the-work-of-a-nation/items-of-interest/medals-of-the-cia.html, [http://perma.cc/05YpcPJNqWQ] (last updated June 18, 2013).

204. "More informed argument about policy choices," as Hugh Heclo put it, "may produce more incomprehensibility." Hugh Heclo, *Issue Networks and the Executive Establishment, in* The New American Political System 121 (Anthony King ed., 1978).

205. In a recent poll, some 76% of the public professed confidence in the military—compared with 36% for the presidency, 34% for the Supreme Court, and 10% for Congress. Ed O'Keefe, *Confidence in Congress Drops to Historic Low,* Wash. Post, June 13, 2013, http://www.washingtonpost.com/blogs/the-fix/wp/2013/06/13/confidence-in-congress-drops-to-historic-low/, [http://perma.cc/0LRxSUWePsu].

206. Vali Nasr, The Dispensable Nation: American Foreign Policy in Retreat 180 (2013).

207. Michael D. Shear, *Petraeus Quits; Evidence of Affair Was Found by F.B.I.,* N.Y. Times, Nov. 9, 2012, http://www.nytimes.com/2012/11/10/us/citing-affair-petraeus-resigns-as-cia-director.html?pagewanted=all&_r=0, [http://perma.cc/0cV5ws5KKsX]; *see* Kimberly Dozier, *CIA Deputy Director Michael Morell Retires,* Associated Press (Yahoo News), June 12, 2013, http://

news.yahoo.com/cia-deputy-director-michael-morell-retires-211017834.html, [http://perma.cc/0ksgQABtNF4] (noting Morell's defense of "harsh" interrogation techniques).

208. *Denis C. Blair Biography*, THE ASPEN INSTITUTE, http://www.aspeninstitute.org/policy-work/homeland-security/ahsg/members/blair, [http://perma.cc/0JxwutP7NVj] (last visited Oct. 20, 2013).

209. Peter Bergen, *John Brennan, Obama's Counterterrorist*, CNN, Feb. 7, 2013, http://www.cnn.com/2013/02/06/opinion/bergen-brennan-counterterrorist/index.html, [http://perma.cc/04FqazPLoPs].

210. *See* note 3, pages 129–130.

211. THOMAS POWERS, INTELLIGENCE WARS: AMERICAN SECRET HISTORY FROM HITLER TO AL QAEDA 342–45 (2004).

212. *Id.* at 342.

213. *Id.*

214. *Id.* at 343.

215. *Id.*

216. *Id.*

217. *Id.* Gates's harsh assessment of Congress in his memoir, *Duty*, may not be unrelated. *See* Carl Hulse, *Years Before His Bipartisan Luster, a Rough Reception for Gates*, N.Y. TIMES, Jan. 17, 2014, http://www.nytimes.com/2014/01/18/us/politics/years-before-his-bipartisan-halo-rough-reception-for-gates.html?_r=0.

218. This was related to me by a person present at the briefings.

219. *Id.* at 343. Two of Gates's colleagues and friends in the CIA testified that he had pressured CIA analysts to exaggerate Soviet involvement in the plot to kill Pope John Paul II, and that he had suppressed and ignored signs of Soviet strategic retreat. *Id.* at 346.

220. LAURENCE E. WALSH, FINAL REPORT OF THE INDEPENDENT COUNSEL FOR IRAN/CONTRA MATTERS, Vol. I, Ch. 16

(1993), *available at* http://www.fas.org/irp/offdocs/
walsh/, [http://perma.law.harvard.edu/0kNXzcfwMi1].

221. Rowan Scarborough, *Gates' Tenure Successful,
Contradictory,* WASH. TIMES, June 26, 2011, http://www.
washingtontimes.com/news/2011/jun/26/gates-leaves-
legacy-of-major-achievements-contradi/?page=all,
[http://perma.cc/G7DA-UP8L].

222. Obama did in fact overrule Gates's objections to use of
force against Libya. NASR, *supra* note 206, at 180.

223. WOODWARD, *supra* note 169, at 319–20.

224. *Id.* at 313. Gates describes Donilon as having character-
ized General Mike Mullen (Chairman of the Joint Chiefs
of Staff) and the military as "insubordinate" and "in
revolt." GATES, *supra* note 180, at 377.

225. Eric Schmitt, *Challenging the Military; In Promising to
End Ban on Homosexuals, Clinton Is Confronting a Wall of
Tradition,* N.Y. TIMES, Nov. 12, 1992, http://www.nytimes.
com/1992/11/12/us/transition-analysis-challenging-
military-promising-end-ban-homosexuals-clinton.html,
[http://perma.law.harvard.edu/0vVjC19sxFe].

226. Paul F. Horvitz, *"Don't Ask, Don't Tell, Don't Pursue" Is
White House's Compromise Solution: New U.S. Military Policy
Tolerates Homosexuals,* N.Y. TIMES, July 20, 1993, http://
www.nytimes.com/1993/07/20/news/20iht-gay_1.html,
[http://perma.law.harvard.edu/0eE1wrcChws/].

227. A wholesale rejection of existing policies would, in addition, create severe management problems. Frequent or
significant reversals by management are dispiriting, particularly when managers are seen as having lesser expertise. "Though [the decision maker] has the authority,"
Kissinger has observed, "he cannot overrule [his staff]
too frequently without impairing its efficiency; and he
may, in any event, lack the knowledge to do so." HENRY
A. KISSINGER, AMERICAN FOREIGN POLICY: THREE ESSAYS
BY HENRY A. KISSINGER 20 (1969). The successful pursuit

of this objective during the early days of the Kennedy administration effectively circumscribed the latitude of presidential decision-making. "In the wake of the failure in the Bay of Pigs, Kennedy realized that he was hostage to the information and analysis that was provided to him by cabinet agencies." DAVID J. ROTHKOPF, RUNNING THE WORLD: THE INSIDE STORY OF THE NATIONAL SECURITY COUNCIL AND THE ARCHITECTS OF AMERICAN POWER 90 (2004).

228. DAVID E. SANGER, CONFRONT AND CONCEAL: OBAMA'S SECRET WARS AND SURPRISING USE OF AMERICAN POWER 27 (2013).

229. NASR, *supra* note 206, at 22–23.

230. *Id.* at 23–24.

231. *Id.* at 24.

232. WOODWARD, *supra* note 167, at 103.

233. *Id.* at 278. "It was a vintage White House trick, one that offered the illusion of choice. But even though everyone recognized this for the stunt it was, the Kissinger model remained popular." *Id.* at 104.

234. *Id.* at 280.

235. GATES, *supra* note 180, at 586. But, Gates added, the military did not "consciously intend" to do so. *Id.*

236. Richard Kohn, *The Erosion of Civilian Control of the Military in the United States Today*, NAVAL WAR COLLEGE REVIEW 9, at 9 (Summer 2002). *See also* PETER FEAVER, ARMED SERVANTS: AGENCY, OVERSIGHT, AND CIVIL-MILITARY RELATIONS (2003); MICHAEL DESCH, CIVILIAN CONTROL OF THE MILITARY: THE CHANGING SECURITY ENVIRONMENT (1999); Russell Weigley, *The American Military and the Principle of Civilian Control from McClellan to Powell*, 57 JOURNAL OF MILITARY HISTORY 27 (Oct. 1993).

237. BAGEHOT, *supra* note 2, at 176.

238. *Id.*

239. *See* Graham Allison, *How It Went Down*, TIME, May 7, 2012, *available at* http://content.time.com/time/magazine/

article/0,9171,2113156,00.html ("The most experienced member of his national-security team, Defense Secretary Robert Gates, opposed the raid, restating his view that putting commandos on the ground risked their being captured or killed. Vice President Joe Biden also felt that the risks of acting rather than waiting outweighed the benefits. The military leader in the loop from the outset and the most intensely engaged officer in this decision-making process, Joint Chiefs of Staff [JCS] Vice Chairman James Cartwright, preferred an air strike to boots on the ground.").

240. *See, e.g.,* Senator Fulbright's contributions to the Cuban Missile Crisis debate at the White House, Oct. 21, 1962. Audio and transcript available via David Coleman, *The Fourteenth Day: J. William Fulbright: Vietnam Dove/Cuban Hawk,* http://jfk14thday.com/fulbright-cuban-missile-crisis/, [http://perma.law.harvard.edu/0CBfxjn2HrF/].

241. As James Carroll has put it, "impersonal forces" (such as the Pentagon's culture) "can have an overriding impact on the range of any one person's possible choices, or on the efficacy with which choices are made." JAMES CARROLL, HOUSE OF WAR: THE PENTAGON AND THE DISASTROUS RISE OF AMERICAN POWER 302 (2006).

242. Theodore Sorensen, *Political Perspective: Who Speaks for the National Interest?,* in THE TETHERED PRESIDENCY 7 (Thomas M. Franck ed., 1981).

243. Peter Baker, *Moves to Curb Spying Help Drive the Clemency Argument for Snowden,* N.Y. TIMES, Jan. 4, 2014, http://www.nytimes.com/2014/01/05/us/moves-to-curb-spying-help-drive-the-clemency-argument-for-snowden.html.

244. S. REP. NO. 94-755, bk. III, at 736 (1976).

245. The Church Committee reported that "from the early 1960s until 1973, NSA targeted the international communications of certain American citizens by placing their names on a 'watch list.' Intercepted messages were

disseminated to the FBI, CIA, Secret Service, Bureau of Narcotics and Dangerous Drugs[], and the Department of Defense." The communications in question were "sent with the expectation that they were private...." Warrants were not secured. S. REP. NO. 94-755, bk. III, at 735 (1976). *See* JAMES A. BAMFORD, BODY OF SECRETS 428–29 (2002 ed.); JAMES A. BAMFORD, THE PUZZLE PALACE 323–24 (1983 ed.). "No evidence was found, however, of any significant foreign support or control of domestic dissidents." S. REP. NO. 94-755, bk. III, at 743 (1976).

246. The interception program was codenamed Operation SHAMROCK. S. REP. NO. 94-755, bk. III, at 740 (1976). "In no case did NSA obtain a search warrant prior to obtaining a telegram." S. REP. NO. 94-755, bk. III, at 765 (1976).

247. BAMFORD, PUZZLE PALACE, *supra* note 245, at 379 (quoting Senator Frank Church's interview on *Meet the Press*, NBC (Oct. 29, 1975)).

248. *Intelligence Activities—The National Security Agency and Fourth Amendment Rights*, 94th Cong. (1975) (statement of Senator Church, Chairman, Select Committee to Study Governmental Operations with Respect to Intelligence Activities).

249. BAMFORD, PUZZLE PALACE, *supra* note 245, at 379.

250. Matthew M. Aid & William Burr, *Secret Cold War Documents Reveal NSA Spied on Senators*, FOREIGN POLICY, Sept. 25, 2013, http://www.foreignpolicy.com/articles/2013/09/25/it_happened_here_NSA_spied_on_senators_1970s?page=full, [http://perma.law.harvard.edu/0b51cK8aL21/].

251. Foreign Intelligence Surveillance Act of 1978, Pub. L. No. 95-511, 92 Stat. 1783 (codified as amended at 50 U.S.C. § 1801 *et seq.* (2006)).

252. S. REP. NO. 95-604(1), at 2–4 (1977).

253. *See* pages 45–46.

254. 50 U.S.C. § 1803 (2006).

255. JANE MAYER, THE DARK SIDE: THE INSIDE STORY ON HOW THE WAR ON TERROR TURNED INTO A WAR ON AMERICAN IDEALS 69 (2008). As early as 1999 the NSA had "been pushing... to obtain the rule change allowing the analysis of Americans' phone and e-mail data." James Risen & Laura Poitras, N.S.A. Gathers Data on Social Connections of U.S. Citizens, N.Y. TIMES, Sept. 28, 2013, http://www.nytimes.com/2013/09/29/us/nsa-examines-social-networks-of-us-citizens.html?pagewanted=all, [http://perma.cc/0PML8vH3CjJ].

256. SAVAGE, supra note 20, at 128–29.

257. Charlie Savage & James Risen, New Leak Suggests Ashcroft Confrontation Was over N.S.A. Program, N.Y. TIMES, June 27, 2013, http://www.nytimes.com/2013/06/28/us/nsa-report-says-internet-metadata-were-focus-of-visit-to-ashcroft.html?pagewanted=all&_r=0&gwh=396ED0A77EED57D930844BB4BE5D6293, [http://www.perma.cc/0ASRXkXENWa].

258. SAVAGE, supra note 20, at 130.

259. Id.

260. Id.

261. Id. at 131. Yoo may later have disclosed the memorandum's core rationale. "I think there's a law greater than FISA," Yoo said, "which is the Constitution, and part of the Constitution is the president's commander-in-chief power. Congress can't take away the president's power in running a war." Id. That logic applied, Yoo presumably believed, to FISA's provision asserting the exclusivity of the procedure it established, which apparently had thitherto been uniformly honored by the administrations of Presidents Carter, Bush, Reagan, and Clinton. The NSA was denied access to Yoo's opinion but its own lawyers concluded that the NSA's recommended program was lawful; this was apparently conveyed orally, with no written legal opinion, to the NSA director, Michael V. Hayden. The NSA lawyers "came back with a real comfort level that this was

within the President's [Article II] authorities." Nomination of General Michael V. Hayden, USAF, to be Director of the Central Intelligence Agency, Hearing Before the Senate Select Committee on Intelligence, 109th Cong., 2d Sess. 54 (May 18, 2006).

262. Savage & Risen, *supra* note 257.

263. *Id.*

264. *NSA Inspector General Report on Email and Internet Data Collection under Stellar Wind—Full Document*, THE GUARDIAN, June 27, 2013, at 38–39, http://www.the-guardian.com/world/interactive/2013/jun/27/nsa-inspector-general-report-document-data-collection, [http://www.perma.cc/05pqoY3TDqq].

265. Glenn Greenwald & Spencer Ackerman, *NSA Collected U.S. Email Records in Bulk for More than Two Years under Obama*, THE GUARDIAN, June 27, 2013, http://www.theguardian. com/world/2013/jun/27/nsa-data-mining-authorised-obama, [http://perma.law.harvard.edu/0vz5A7poNbW/]. Kollar-Kotelly had been appointed as chief judge by Chief Justice William Rehnquist. Prior to her appointment, she had served as an attorney in the criminal division of the Justice Department during the Nixon administration, during the period in which Rehnquist headed OLC.

266. Savage & Risen, *supra* note 257.

267. *See* page 67.

268. Savage & Risen, *supra* note 257.

269. *Id.*

270. Greenwald & Ackerman, *supra* note 265.

271. James Risen & Eric Lichtblau, *Bush Lets U.S. Spy on Callers without Courts*, N.Y. TIMES, Dec. 16, 2005, http://www. nytimes.com/2005/12/16/politics/16program.html?pag ewanted=all&gwh=295DB8429C337294BBCB852A95CF 37B6, [http://www.perma.cc/0ceFidjgdX].

272. Margaret Sullivan, *Sources with Secrets Find New Outlets for Sharing*, N.Y. TIMES, June 15, 2013, http:// www.nytimes.com/2013/06/16/public-editor/

sources-with-secrets-find-new-outlets-for-sharing.
html?pagewanted=all, [http://perma.cc/0GHhR8zyqGb].

273. SAVAGE, *supra* note 20, at 262. As a replacement, Chief Justice Roberts appointed the federal district judge who had earlier ruled in favor of Vice President Cheney in a dispute concerning access to records by the General Accounting Office. *Id.*

274. *See supra* notes 36–37.

275. *See supra* notes 34–35.

276. *Id.* (the so-called "library records" provision, as it had earlier been called).

277. 50 U.S.C. § 1861 (2012).

278. *See supra* notes 34–35.

279. Charlie Savage & Edward Wyatt, *U.S. Is Secretly Collecting Records of Verizon Calls*, N.Y. TIMES, June 5, 2013, http://www.nytimes.com/2013/06/06/us/us-secretly-collecting-logs-of-business-calls.html, [http://perma.cc/0wBnEhW5ugq].

280. Timothy B. Lee, *Here's Everything We've Learned about How the NSA's Secret Programs Work*, WASH. POST, June 25, 2013, http://www.washingtonpost.com/blogs/wonkblog/wp/2013/06/25/heres-everything-weve-learned-about-how-the-nsas-secret-programs-work/, [http://perma.cc/0a1GcCbc42G]; Glenn Greenwald & Ewen MacAskill, *NSA Prism Program Taps in to User Data of Apple, Google and Others*, THE GUARDIAN, June 6, 2013, http://www.theguardian.com/world/2013/jun/06/us-tech-giants-nsa-data, [http://perma.cc/094q6gJSWvs].

281. 50 U.S.C. § 1881a (2012).

282. Glenn Greenwald, *NSA Collecting Phone Records of Millions of Verizon Customers Daily*, THE GUARDIAN, June 5, 2013, http://www.guardian.co.uk/world/2013/jun/06/nsa-phone-records-verizon-court-order, [http://perma.cc/0rS1CTFkxLR].

283. Scott Shane & Jonathan Weisman, *Earlier Denials Put Intelligence Chief in Awkward Position*, N.Y. TIMES, June

11, 2013, http://www.nytimes.com/2013/06/12/us/nsa-disclosures-put-awkward-light-on-official-statements. html, [http://perma.cc/0BkVDW6HEyu].

284. Marc Ambinder, *U.S. Responds to NSA Disclosures*, THE WEEK, June 6, 2013, http://theweek.com/article/index/245243/us-responds-to-nsa-disclosures, [http://perma.cc/04cJmWxVNpN].

285. *See id.*

286. James Risen & Charlie Savage, *On Eve of Critical Vote, N.S.A. Director Lobbies House*, N.Y. TIMES, July 23, 2013, at A3, *available at* http://www.nytimes.com/2013/07/24/us/politics/nsa-director-lobbies-house-on-eve-of-critical-vote.html, [http://perma.law.harvard.edu/05UfQ2zexSE/] (quoting Senator Wyden).

287. Charlie Savage & Edward Wyatt, *U.S. Is Secretly Collecting Records of Verizon Calls*, N.Y. TIMES, June 5, 2013, http://www.nytimes.com/2013/06/06/us/us-secretly-collecting-logs-of-business-calls.html, [http://perma.law.harvard.edu/0XwUvKmBN1N].

288. Glenn Greenwald, *NSA Taps in to User Data of Facebook, Google and Others, Secret Files Reveal*, THE GUARDIAN, June 7, 2013, http://www.guardian.co.uk/world/2013/jun/06/us-tech-giants-nsa-data, [http://perma.law.harvard.edu/0uXV7jfDwJZ/].

289. Editorial, *President Obama's Dragnet*, N.Y. TIMES, June 7, 2007, at A26, *available at* http://www.nytimes.com/2013/06/07/opinion/president-obamas-dragnet.html?partner=rssnyt&emc=rss&_r=0, [http://perma.law.harvard.edu/0S9WTbThGAo/].   Feinstein's indifference was not unusual. Asked by CBS's Norah O'Donnell whether the Obama administration's surveillance went further than the George W. Bush administration's, House Majority Leader Eric Cantor said that "these are questions we don't know the answers to." Dana Milbank, *Edward Snowden's NSA Leaks Are Backlash of Too Much Secrecy*, WASH. POST, June 11, 2013, http://

articles.washingtonpost.com/2013-06-10/opinions/ 39869013_1_james-clapper-leaks-eric-cantor, [http:// perma.law.harvard.edu/0SPh1ujqqbF/].

290. Editorial, *President Obama's Dragnet*, N.Y. TIMES, June 12, 2013, http://www.nytimes.com/2013/06/07/opinion/ president-obamas-dragnet.html?pagewanted=all&_r=0.

291. *Id.*

292. *See* Greg Miller, *Democrat Dianne Feinstein Proves an Obstacle to Obama's Push for Changes at Spy Agencies*, WASH. POST, Jan. 25, 2014, http://www.washingtonpost.com/ world/national-security/democrat-dianne-feinstein-proves-an-obstacle-to-obamas-push-for-changes-at-spy-agencies/2014/01/25/34f61118-8532-11e3-9dd4-e7278db80d86_story.html (describing Feinstein's support for intelligence agencies' opposition to proposed restrictions).

293. WOODWARD, *supra* note 169, at 319–22.

294. James Bamford, *Five Myths about the National Security Agency*, WASH. POST, June 21, 2013, http://articles. washingtonpost.com/2013-06-21/opinions/40114085_ 1_national-security-agency-foreign-intelligence-surveillance-court-guardian, [http://perma.law.harvard. edu/0yuetxdswu9/].

295. Jonathan Weisman & David E. Sanger, *White House Plays Down Data Program*, N.Y. TIMES, June 8, 2007, at A14, *available at* http://www.nytimes.com/2013/06/09/us/politics/ officials-say-congress-was-fully-briefed-on-surveillance. html, [http://perma.law.harvard.edu/0qmeom2SYDX/].

296. *Id.*

297. Connor Simpson, *The Majority of Senate Skipped a Classified PRISM Briefing*, THE ATLANTIC WIRE, June 15, 2013, http:// www.theatlanticwire.com/national/2013/06/majority-senate-skipped-classified-prism-briefing/66273/, [http:// perma.law.harvard.edu/0xmnaub3kvK/].

298. 9/11 COMMISSION REPORT, *supra* note 168, at 420.

299. *Id.*

300. *Liberty's Lost Decade*, THE ECONOMIST, Aug. 3, 2013, at 11, *available at* http://www.economist.com/news/leaders/21582525-war-terror-haunts-america-still-it-should-recover-some-its-most-cherished.

301. Glenn Kessler, *James Clapper's "Least Untruthful" Statement to the Senate*, WASH. POST, June 12, 2013, http://www.washingtonpost.com/blogs/fact-checker/post/james-clappers-least-untruthful-statement-to-the-senate/2013/06/11/e50677a8-d2d8-11e2-a73e-826d299ff459_blog.html, [http://perma.law.harvard.edu/0rMrGXeoYj7/].

302. *Id. See* NBC News Exclusive: Transcript of Andrea Mitchell's Interview with Director of National Intelligence James Clapper, June 9, 2013, http://www.nbcumv.com/mediavillage/networks/nbcnews/pressreleases?pr=contents/press-releases/2013/06/09/nbcnewsexclusiv1370799482417.xml.

303. Letter of James R. Clapper, Director of National Intelligence, to Senator Dianne Feinstein, Chairman, Senate Select Committee on Intelligence, June 21, 2013, http://www.dni.gov/files/documents/2013-06-21%20DNI%20Ltr%20to%20Sen.%20Feinstein.pdf.

304. 18 U.S.C. § 1001 (2012) ("[W]hoever, in any matter within the jurisdiction of the executive, legislative, or judicial branch of the Government of the United States, knowingly and willingly...makes any materially false, fictitious, or fraudulent statement or representation...shall be fined [or] imprisoned not more than 5 years...."). *See generally* Nick Kravitz & Margaret Netisham, *False Statements and False Claims*, 50 A. CRIM. L. REV. 953 (Fall 1013); Michael Gomez, *Re-examining the False Statements Accountability Act*, 37 HOUS. L. REV. 515 (Summer 2000).

305. Justin Amash, a Republican member of the House of Representatives, said that Mr. Clapper had "lied under oath." Geoff Dyer, *U.S. Intelligence Chief under Scrutiny*, FINANCIAL TIMES, June 14, 2013, http://www.ft.com/

cms/s/0/2fbd05da-d44d-11e2-8639-00144feab7de.
html#axzz2iqCkT9Dd, [http://perma.law.harvard.edu/
0NQaCMaiqnX/].

306. Obama allowed on January 21, 2014, that Clapper "should
have been more careful" in his testimony. Jake Tapper &
Chelsea J. Carter, *CNN Exclusive: President Obama Says
He's Not Recalibrating Ambitions*, Jan. 21, 2014, http://
www.cnn.com/2014/01/31/politics/obama-interview/.

307. The question arises whether President Obama was in
fact aware of major elements of the NSA's surveillance
programs. *See* Timothy B. Lee, *Did President Obama
Know about the NSA's Privacy Problems?*, WASH. POST,
Aug. 16, 2013, http://www.washingtonpost.com/blogs/
the-switch/wp/2013/08/16/did-president-obama-know-
about-the-nsas-privacy-problems/, [http://perma.law.
harvard.edu/0jUMkjGfoBx/]. The President's National
Security Advisor, Susan Rice, reportedly told her German
counterpart that Obama knew nothing about the monitoring of Chancellor Angela Merkel's cell phone—which
the NSA began during the Bush administration. David
E. Sanger, *In Spy Uproar, "Everyone Does It" Just Won't
Do*, N.Y. TIMES, Oct. 25, 2013, http://www.nytimes.
com/2013/10/26/world/europe/in-spy-uproar-everyone-
does-it-just-wont-do.html?hp&_r=0, [http://perma.law.
harvard.edu/0vhkjcvUfg6/]. "But certainly the National
Security Council and senior people across the intelligence community knew exactly what was going on,
and to suggest otherwise is ridiculous," a senior official
said. Ken Dilanian & Janet Stobart, *Intelligence Staffs
Feel Like Scapegoats*, L.A. TIMES, Oct. 29, 2013, http://
articles.latimes.com/2013/oct/29/world/la-fg-spying-
phones-20131029. (Some U.S. surveillance activities,
explained Secretary of State John Kerry, had occurred
"on autopilot." Dan Roberts & Spencer Ackerman, *US
Surveillance Has Gone Too Far, John Kerry Admits*, THE
GUARDIAN, Nov. 1, 2013, http://www.theguardian.

com/world/2013/oct/31/john-kerry-some-surveillance-gone-too-far/print, [http://perma.law.harvard.edu/0pw6cBkxJVq/].)

308. *See* pages 68–70. *See also* Charlie Savage, Edward Wyatt, & Peter Baker, *U.S. Confirms that It Gathers Online Data Overseas*, N.Y. Times, June 6, 2013, at A1, *available at* http://www.nytimes.com/2013/06/07/us/nsa-verizon-calls.html?ref=opinion, [http://perma.law.harvard.edu/0ojAbY6rfsR/].

309. *Obama Defends NSA's Surveillance of Phone, Web and Credit Card Use*, PBS Newshour, June 7, 2013, http://www.pbs.org/newshour/bb/government_programs/jan-june13/surveillance1_06-07.html, [http://perma.law.harvard.edu/09xbpeX8hEa/].

310. Criminal Complaint against Edward Snowden, No. 487, June 14, 2013 (E.D. Va.), *available at* http://www2.gwu.edu/~nsarchiv/NSAEBB/NSAEBB436/docs/EBB-094.pdf.

311. "[N]obody is listening to your telephone calls. That's not what this program is about. As was indicated, what the intelligence community is doing is looking at phone numbers and durations of calls. They are not looking at people's names, and they're not looking at content." Statement by the President, Fairmont Hotel, San Jose, California, June 7, 2013, http://www.whitehouse.gov/the-press-office/2013/06/07/statement-president.

312. "Metadata absolutely tells you everything about somebody's life," said Stewart Baker. "If you have enough metadata you don't really need content.... [It's] sort of embarrassing how predictable we are as human beings." Alan Rusbridger, *The Snowden Leaks and the Public*, N.Y. Rev. of Books, Nov. 21, 2013, http://www.nybooks.com/articles/archives/2013/nov/21/snowden-leaks-and-public/?pagination=false.

313. Andrea Peterson, *Remember When Obama Said the NSA Wasn't "Actually Abusing" Its Powers? He Was Wrong.*, Wash. Post, Aug. 15, 2013, http://www.washingtonpost.

com/blogs/the-switch/wp/2013/08/15/remember-when-obama-said-the-nsa-wasnt-actually-abusing-its-powers-he-was-wrong/,[http://perma.law.harvard.edu/0oA1vLv2th3/].

314. *Id.* Whether abuse had occurred would not, in any event, have been immediately evident from NSA files, since the NSA is not an enforcement agency; it merely provides information to "customers" such as the Federal Bureau of Investigation (FBI), Immigration and Customs Enforcement (ICE), and the Transportation Security Administration (TSA). NSA records thus would not necessarily indicate whether a person on whom it had collected and disseminated information had been deported, added to a "no fly" list, or subjected to other forms of surveillance. *See* JEFFREY KAHN, MS. SHIPLEY'S GHOST: THE RIGHT TO TRAVEL AND TERRORIST WATCH LISTS (2013); Charlie Savage & Laura Poitras, *How a Court Secretly Evolved, Extending U.S. Spies' Reach*, N.Y. TIMES, Mar. 11, 2014, http://www.nytimes.com/2014/03/12/us/how-a-courts-secret-evolution-extended-spies-reach.html ("The number of Americans whose unfiltered personal information has been shared among agencies is not clear."). The FISA court found, however, that the NSA did engage in unauthorized disseminations but the court did not identify the recipients. In an opinion apparently written in June 2009, the presiding judge of the Foreign Intelligence Surveillance Court, Reggie Walton, wrote that "the NSA likely has disseminated US person information derived from the [email and Internet bulk] metadata outside NSA without a prior determination from the NSA official designated in the court's orders that the information is related to counter-terrorism information and is necessary to understand the counter-terrorism information or assess its importance." Spencer Ackerman, *Fisa Court Documents Reveal Extent of NSA Disregard for Privacy Restrictions: Incensed Fisa Court Judges Questioned NSA's Truthfulness after Repeated Breaches of Rules Meant*

to *Protect Americans' Privacy*, THE GUARDIAN, Nov. 19, 2013, http://www.theguardian.com/world/2013/nov/19/ fisa-court-documents-nsa-violations-privacy.

315. Scott Shane, *Court Upbraided N.S.A. on Its Use of Call-Log Data*, N.Y. TIMES, Sept. 10, 2013, at A14, *available at* http:// www.nytimes.com/2013/09/11/us/court-upbraided-nsa- on-its-use-of-call-log-data.html?pagewanted=all, [http:// perma.law.harvard.edu/0VuDT5YZtwB/]. The Justice Department's Office of Professional Responsibility never investigated the FISC judges' complaints, though one FISC judge had suggested that NSA officials could be held in contempt of court. Brad Heath, *Justice Dept. Watchdog Never Probed Judges' NSA Concerns*, USA TODAY, Sept. 19, 2013, http://www.usatoday.com/story/ news/nation/2013/09/19/nsa-surveillance-justice-opr- investigation/2805867/, [http://perma.law.harvard.edu/ 0T8nCbWwPXe/].

316. Memorandum Opinion, FISA Ct., Oct. 3, 2011, at 16 n.14, *available at* https://www.eff.org/files/filenode/ fisc_opinion_-_unconstitutional_surveillance_0.pdf; *see* Charlie Savage & Scott Shane, *Secret Court Rebuked N.S.A. on Surveillance*, N.Y. TIMES, Aug. 21, 2013, at A1, *available at* http://www.nytimes.com/2013/08/22/ us/2011-ruling-found-an-nsa-program-unconstitu- tional.html?pagewanted=all, [http://perma.law.harvard. edu/0b8rEbzAeLt/].

317. Greg Miller, *Misinformation on Classified NSA Programs Includes Statements by Senior U.S. Officials*, WASH. POST, June 30, 2013, http://articles.washingtonpost.com/2013- 06-30/world/40292346_1_programs-clapper-jr-remark, [http://perma.law.harvard.edu/0AJoRguAHH9/]. Its action came on the same day that NSA's general counsel cautioned the public against believing all that was being said about NSA surveillance. "A lie can get half way around the world before the truth gets its boots on," said Robert Litt, alluding to Mark Twain. "Unfortunately, there's been

a lot of misinformation that's come out about these programs." *Id.*

318. Risen & Savage, *supra* note 286. Fox News reported that NSA Director General Keith Alexander told it—falsely—that the agency does not "hold data on U.S. citizens." *NSA Reportedly Collecting Phone Records of Millions, Though Officials Had Denied Holding "Data" on Americans*, Fox News, June 6, 2013, http://www.foxnews.com/politics/2013/06/06/nsa-collecting-phone-records-for-millions-verizon-customers-report-says/, [http://perma.law.harvard.edu/0KXsDQzFrQ5/].

319. Ellen Nakashima, *Newly Declassified Documents on Phone Records Program Released*, Wash. Post, July 31, 2013, http://www.washingtonpost.com/world/national-security/governments-secret-order-to-verizon-to-be-unveiled-at-senate-hearing/2013/07/31/233fdd3a-f9cf-11e2-a369-d1954abcb7e3_story.html, [http://perma.law.harvard.edu/0FcUyeG1ueG/].

320. *See* Editorial, *Absent on Presidential Power*, Wall St. J., July 28, 2013, http://online.wsj.com/article/SB10001424127887323610704578630102919888438.html, [http://perma.law.harvard.edu/0rYbgNgaBr3/].

321. Jonathan Weisman, *House Defeats Effort to Rein In N.S.A. Data Gathering*, N.Y. Times, July 25, 2013, http://www.nytimes.com/2013/07/25/us/politics/house-defeats-effort-to-rein-in-nsa-data-gathering.html?_r=0, [http://perma.law.harvard.edu/02GcWvB9G5Z/].

322. *Id.*

323. Ed O'Keefe, *Proposal to Restrict NSA Phone-tracking Program Defeated*, Wash. Post, July 25, 2013, http://articles.washingtonpost.com/2013-07-24/politics/40862333_1_obama-administration-proposal-americans, [http://perma.law.harvard.edu/0u9PDxh5Ukf/]. Rogers, who had served as an FBI agent before his election to Congress, was hardly alone among congressional overseers who had moved on from earlier careers among the overseen.

Another recent example was Porter Goss, who had been a CIA officer before resigning to enter politics and who came to chair the House Permanent Select Committee on Intelligence—and who then became CIA director. Rizzo, *supra* note 6, at 14.

CHAPTER 5

1. *See* pages 3–4.
2. *See* GRAHAM ALLISON & PHILIP ZELIKOW, ESSENCE OF DECISION: EXPLAINING THE CUBAN MISSILE CRISIS (2d ed. 1999).
3. "We have no eternal allies, and we have no perpetual enemies. Our interests are eternal and perpetual, and those interests it is our duty to follow." Lord Palmerston, remarked in the House of Commons, March 1, 1848, HANSARD'S PARLIAMENTARY DEBATES, 3rd series, vol. 97, col. 122 (defending his foreign policy).
4. *See* ALLISON & ZELIKOW, *supra* note 2, at 18.
5. *See, e.g.,* John Harsanyi, *Some Social Implications of a New Approach to Game Theory, in* STRATEGIC INTERACTION AND CONFLICT: ORIGINAL PAPERS AND DISCUSSION 1, 139 (Kathleen Archibald ed., 1966) (emphasis added) ("[I]f a person acts rationally, his behavior can be *fully explained* in terms of the goals he is trying to achieve."). Elements of this approach inhere in the "alternative competing hypothesis" approach, discussed at pages 88–91. A classic example is Hans Morgenthau's claim that World War I "had its origin exclusively in the fear of a disturbance of the European balance of power," and that that same catalytic fear drove Germany, Austria, Russia, Serbia, and France all to war in 1914. HANS MORGENTHAU, POLITICS AMONG NATIONS 154, 192 (1960).
6. *See, e.g.,* Jack Goldsmith, *Obama Passes the Buck: The President's Empty Rhetoric on Counterterrorism,* FOREIGN AFFAIRS, May 23, 2013, http://www.foreignaffairs.com/articles/139403/jack-goldsmith/obama-passes-the-buck?page=2 (the reason

that President Obama does not end the war against al Qaeda and its associates "is the same reason that Obama codified and bureaucratized his stealth war guidelines and robustly defended drone warfare: the threat from al Qaeda affiliates persists, and the United States, as Obama said, will continue to use military force to "finish the work of defeating" them.). Elsewhere, however, Goldsmith has recognized that multiple factors account for the continuity of U.S. national security policy. *See* Jack Goldsmith, Power and Restraint: The Accountable Presidency after 9/11, at 29 (2012).

7. *See* Howard Simon, *The Dialogue of Psychology with Human Nature*, 79 American Political Science Review 293, 301 (1985).

8. Allison & Zelikow, *supra* note 2, at 388. "[M]ost events of special interest, like missiles in Cuba," they acknowledge, "have so many unique features, they invite unique explanations." *Id*. at 388–89.

9. "Political scientists, historians, and reporters are often completely unaware of events or experiences unseen by the public eye that influence important decisions." Robert M. Gates, Duty: Memoirs of a Secretary at War 307 (2014).

10. *Quoted in* James Gleick, Chaos: Making a New Science 23 (1987).

11. Fernand Braudel, On History 26 (Sarah Mathews trans., 1980).

12. Shailagh Murray & Paul Kane, *Obama Rejects Truth Panel*, Wash. Post, Apr. 24, 2009, http://www.washingtonpost.com/wp-dyn/content/article/2009/04/23/AR2009042304314.html.

13. Thomas Powers, Intelligence Wars: American Secret History from Hitler to Al Qaeda 287 (2004).

14. Daniel Kahneman, Thinking Fast and Slow 10 (2011). I thank my colleague Bill Martel for helpful insights on these matters.

15. *Id*. at 14.

16. *Id*. at 8.

17. *See* Daniel Kahneman & Amos Tversky, *Judgment under Uncertainty: Heuristics and Biases*, 185 SCIENCE 1124 (1974).
18. KAHNEMAN, *supra* note 14, at 24. For an account of the effects of such distortions on policymaking within the British government *see* ANTHONY KING & IVOR CREWE, THE BLUNDERS OF OUR GOVERNMENTS (2013).
19. Cass R. Sunstein, *Terrorism and Probability Neglect*, 26 JOURNAL OF RISK AND UNCERTAINTY 121 (2003).
20. *Id.*
21. *Fatality Analysis Reporting System*, National Highway Traffic Safety Administration (2011).
22. Sunstein, *supra* note 19, at 122.
23. W. Kip Viscusi, *Alarmist Decisions with Divergent Risk Information*, ECONOMIC JOURNAL 1669 (1997).
24. John Mueller, *Six Rather Unusual Propositions about Terrorism*, 17 TERRORISM AND POLITICAL VIOLENCE 487 (2007) (quoting Leif Wenar).
25. The reason "we had gotten into trouble in both Iraq and Afghanistan" was that "most of the assumptions that underpinned early military planning had proven wrong, and no necessary adjustments had been made." GATES, *supra* note 9, at 116.
26. *See* ALEXANDER GEORGE, BRIDGING THE GAP: THEORY AND PRACTICE IN FOREIGN POLICY 19–29 (1993); EDITH STOKEY & RICHARD ZECKHAUSER, A PRIMER FOR POLICY ANALYSIS 5–6 (1978). "[T]he choice is not simply between liberty and security, but between effective security measures and counterproductive ones." DAVID COLE & JULES LOBEL, LESS SAFE, LESS FREE: WHY AMERICA IS LOSING THE WAR ON TERROR 17 (2007).
27. For an overview of the model, *see* ALLISON & ZELIKOW, *supra* note 2, at 255–321.
28. *Id.* at 294–95.
29. Jonathan Bendor & Thomas H. Hammond, *Rethinking Allison's Models*, 86 AMERICAN POLITICAL SCIENCE REVIEW 310, 318 (1992).

30. ALLISON & ZELIKOW, *supra* note 2, at 388.
31. These characteristics have been developed and refined over the years under the towering influence of the seminal bureaucracy theorist, Max Weber. Weber, a German, wrote twenty-five years after Bagehot, though there is no evidence that Weber was influenced directly by Bagehot's ideas. Their conceptual vocabularies differ. But the parallels between the thought of the two with respect to the core issue of institutional evolution are striking. *See, e.g.,* MAX WEBER, THE THEORY OF SOCIAL AND ECONOMIC ORGANIZATION (1947); MAX WEBER, ECONOMY AND SOCIETY (1922).
32. *See generally* Weber, *id.*; HERBERT A. SIMON, ADMINISTRATIVE BEHAVIOR (4th ed. 2013); GEERT HOFSTEDE, GERT JAN HOFSTEDE, & MICHAEL MINKOV, CULTURES AND ORGANIZATIONS: SOFTWARE OF THE MIND (3rd ed. 2010); ROBERT A. BARON & JERALD GREENBERG, BEHAVIOR IN ORGANIZATIONS (9th ed. (2008); EUGENE WITTKOPT, CHRISTOPHER M. JONES JR., & CHARLES W. KEGLEY, AMERICAN FOREIGN POLICY: PATTERN AND PROCESS (5th ed. 2008); ALLISON & ZELIKOW, *supra* note 2, at 143–96; CHARLES T. GOODSELL, THE CASE FOR BUREAUCRACY (3rd ed. 1994); RICHARD N. HAAS, THE POWER TO PERSUADE (1994); JAMES G. MARCH & HERBERT A. SIMON, ORGANIZATIONS (2nd ed. 1993); WALTER W. POWELL & PAUL J. DiMAGGIO, THE NEW INSTITUTIONALISM IN ORGANIZATIONAL ANALYSIS (1991); JAMES Q. WILSON, BUREAUCRACY: WHAT GOVERNMENT AGENCIES DO AND WHY THEY DO IT (1989); CHARLES PERROW, COMPLEX ORGANIZATIONS: A CRITICAL STUDY (1986); JONATHAN B. BENFOR, PARALLEL SYSTEMS: REDUNDANCY IN GOVERNMENT (1985); EDWARD O. LAUMANN & DAVID KNOKE, THE ORGANIZATIONAL STATE: SOCIAL CHOICE IN NATIONAL POLICY DOMAINS (1987); ALEXANDER GEORGE, SOME POSSIBLE (AND POSSIBLY DANGEROUS) MALFUNCTIONS OF THE ADVISORY PROCESS (1980).

33. For an illustration of these principles in practice, *see* Charles E. Neu, *The Rise of the National Security Bureaucracy, in* THE NEW AMERICAN STATE: BUREAUCRACIES AND POLICIES SINCE WORLD WAR II (Louis Galambos ed., 1987); RICHARD J. BARNET, THE ROOTS OF WAR: THE MEN AND INSTITUTIONS BEHIND U.S. FOREIGN POLICY (1972).

34. *See* Terry M. Noe, *The Politics of Bureaucratic Structure, in* CAN THE GOVERNMENT GOVERN? (John Chubb & Paul Peterson eds., 1989).

35. *See* JAMES G. MARCH & JOHAN P. OLSEN, AMBIGUITY AND CHOICE IN ORGANIZATIONS (1976).

36. The greater the number of clearances required before a program can take effect, the lower the probability of agreement, and the higher the probability of policy continuance. *See* JEFFREY L. PRESSMAN & ADAM WILDAVSKY, IMPLEMENTATION 107 (3rd ed. 1984).

37. Commenting on the "gargantuan, labyrinthine bureaucracy" of the Pentagon, Gates observed that the "very size and structure of the department assured ponderousness, if not paralysis, because so many different organizations had to be involved in even the smallest decisions." GATES, *supra* note 9, at 116.

38. "Any new approach," Gates concluded, "anything different from what they had always done ... was anathema to most officials in Defense...." *Id.* at 138.

39. ALLISON & ZELIKOW, *supra* note 2, at 146.

40. Harold A. Simon, *Rational Choice and the Structure of the Environment*, 63 PSYCHOLOGICAL REVIEW 129 (1956).

41. *See* ALLISON & ZELIKOW, *supra* note 2, at 180.

42. "[B]udgets and programs are locked in for years at a time, and all the bureaucratic wiles of each military department are dedicated to keeping those programs intact and funded." GATES, *supra* note 9, at 117.

43. HANS GERTH & C. WRIGHT MILLS, FROM MAX WEBER: ESSAYS IN SOCIOLOGY 180 (1946).

44. *Quoted in* J. P. MAYER, MAX WEBER AND GERMAN POLITICS 126–27 (2nd ed. 1956).

45. *See* MICHAEL LIPSKY, STREET LEVEL BUREAUCRACY (1980).

46. *See* ALLISON & ZELIKOW, *supra* note 2, at 404.

47. *See* pages 11–28.

48. For an excellent overview of the characteristics and operation of networks in various contexts, *see* MARK E. NEWMAN, NETWORKS: AN INTRODUCTION (2010).

49. Elliot Abrams, *The Prince of the White House: Eleven Rules for How Barack Obama, or Any U.S. President, Can Have His Way on National Security*, FOREIGN POLICY, Mar./Apr. 2013, *available at* http://www.foreignpolicy.com/articles/2013/03/04/the_prince_of_the_white_house.

50. ALLISON & ZELIKOW, *supra* note 2, at 165.

51. For the influence of contextual factors on the structure and formation of different types of networks, *see* MATTHEW O. JACKSON, SOCIAL AND ECONOMIC NETWORKS (2008).

52. "Particular professions may be prominent, but the true experts in the networks are those who are issue-skilled (that is, well informed about the ins and outs of a particular policy debate)." Hugh Heclo, *Issue Networks and the Executive Establishment*, *in* THE NEW AMERICAN POLITICAL SYSTEM 103 (Anthony King ed., 1978).

53. *Id.*

54. "For a host of policy initiatives undertaken in the last twenty years it is all but impossible to identify clearly who the dominant actors are." Heclo, *supra* note 52, at 102.

55. JOHN RIZZO, COMPANY MAN: THIRTY YEARS OF CONTROVERSY AND CRISIS IN THE CIA 140 (2014).

56. IRVING JANIS, GROUPTHINK (2nd ed. 1982).

57. GLENN L. CARLE, THE INTERROGATOR: AN EDUCATION 288 (2011).

58. James Stavridis, *The Dark Side of Globalization*, WASH. POST, May 31, 2013, at http://www.washingtonpost.com/opinions/how-terrorists-can-exploit-globalization/

2013/05/31/a91b8f64-c93a-11e2-9245-773c0123c027_
story.html.

59. *See* RICHARDS J. HEUER JR., PSYCHOLOGY OF INTELLIGENCE
ANALYSIS (1999), https://www.cia.gov/library/center-
for-the-study-of-intelligence/csi-publications/books-
and-monographs/psychology-of-intelligence-analysis/
index.html.

60. In fact, in one iteration of his approach, Jonathan Bendor
and Thomas Hamond noted, Graham Allison combined the
government politics and organizational behavioral models
into an overarching bureaucratic politics model. Jonathan
Bendor & Thomas H. Hammond, *Rethinking Allison's Models*,
86 AMERICAN POLITICAL SCIENCE REVIEW 310, 304 (1992).

61. Werner Heisenberg, *Über den Anschaulichen Inhalt der
Quantentheoretischen Kinematik und Mechanik [The Actual
Content of Quantum Theoretical Kinematics and Mechanics]*,
43, no. 3–4, ZEITSCHRIFT FÜR PHYSIK 197 (1927) (trans-
lated by Julia Brooks).

62. KAHNEMAN, *supra* note 14, at 200.

63. When all is said and done, perhaps the most lucid and suc-
cinct account of Trumanite behavior lies not in sociopsy-
chological theory but in ornithology—bird-watching. Craig
Reynolds has theorized that birds adhere to three simple
precepts: first, don't crowd your neighbors (separation);
second, steer toward the average heading of your neighbors
(alignment); and third, steer toward the average position
of your neighbors (cohesion). C. W. Reynolds, *Flocks, Herds,
and Schools: A Distributed Behavioral Model*, 21 COMPUTER
GRAPHICS 25 (Conference Proceedings, SIGGRAPH '87,
1987). Members of the Trumanite network maintain separate though often only nominal allegiance to distinct organizations that respect each other's autonomy while at the
same time competing for authority (rather like states in
the international realm). They align themselves in steering
toward other organizations' efforts to maintain the continuing direction of existing national security policy. And

they cohere in the "average position" of their Trumanite neighbors in resisting Madisonian encroachments—while perpetuating the impression of Madisonian control.

CHAPTER 6

1. WALTER BAGEHOT, THE ENGLISH CONSTITUTION 251 (Cornell University Press 1963) (1867).
2. *Id.*
3. *Id.*
4. A recent case in point concerned the interception of foreign leaders' communications, of which both the President and the Chairman of the Senate Intelligence Committee denied knowledge. *See* Scott Wilson & Anne Gearan, *Obama Didn't Know about Surveillance of U.S.-allied World Leaders until Summer, Officials Say*, WASH. POST, Oct. 30, 2013, http://www.washingtonpost.com/politics/obama-didnt-know-about-surveillance-of-us-allied-world-leaders-until-summer-officials-say/2013/10/28/0cbacefa-4009-11e3-a751-f032898f2dbc_story.html, [http://perma.law.harvard.edu/0Udk99ndnJm/]. Some U.S. surveillance activities, explained Secretary of State John Kerry, had occurred "on autopilot." Dan Roberts & Spencer Ackerman, *US Surveillance Has Gone Too Far, John Kerry Admits*, THE GUARDIAN, Nov. 1, 2013, http://www.theguardian.com/world/2013/oct/31/john-kerry-some-surveillance-gone-too-far/print, [http://perma.law.harvard.edu/0pw6cBkxJVq/].
5. Elizabeth Mendes & Joy Wilke, *Americans' Confidence in Congress Falls to Lowest on Record*, GALLUP POLITICS (June 13, 2013), http://www.gallup.com/poll/163052/americans-confidence-congress-falls-lowest-record.aspx, [http://perma.law.harvard.edu/0VG9MijqFLu/].
6. BAGEHOT, *supra* note 1, at 100.
7. *Id.* at 138.
8. *Foreign Affairs'* 2012 circulation was 161,450. *Foreign Affairs Circulation Up Nearly 10%*, FOREIGN AFFAIRS, Aug. 2, 2012, http://www.foreignaffairs.com/discussions/news-

and-events/foreign-affairs-circulation-up-nearly-10,
[http://perma.law.harvard.edu/0L3R2VrcsnF/].

9. *People Magazine's* 2013 circulation was 3,542,185.
Magazine Circulation Slides in 1st Half of 2013, HUFFINGTON
POST (AP), Aug. 6, 2013, http://www.huffingtonpost.
com/2013/08/06/magazine-sales-2013_n_3715153.html,
[http://perma.law.harvard.edu/0GHwAiAD6Up/].

10. "In 1958," the *Washington Post* reported, "more than
70 percent of Americans said they trusted the government. Today, that number hovers in the mid-20s." Ezra
Klein, *The NSA vs. Democracy*, WASH. POST, June 28,
2013, http://www.washingtonpost.com/blogs/wonkblog/
wp/2013/06/28/the-nsa-vs-democracy/, [http://perma.cc/
TKH8-R4VY].

11. OLIVER WENDELL HOLMES JR., REMARKS AT A TAVERN
CLUB DINNER for DR. S. WEIR MITCHELL (Mar. 4, 1900),
reprinted in THE ESSENTIAL HOLMES: SELECTIONS FROM
THE LETTERS, SPEECHES, JUDICIAL OPINIONS, AND OTHER
WRITINGS OF OLIVER WENDELL HOLMES, JR. 48–49
(Richard A. Posner ed., 1992).

12. To cite one example, when *Rolling Stone* published a profile
of the Boston bomber Dzhokhar Tsarnaev that featured his
picture on the cover, Boston's mayor and Massachusetts'
governor criticized the magazine, and leading chain
stores refused to sell the issue. Noam Cohen, *CVS and
Walgreens Ban an Issue of Rolling Stone*, N.Y. TIMES, July
17, 2013, http://www.nytimes.com/2013/07/18/busi-
ness/media/cvs-and-walgreens-ban-an-issue-of-rolling-
stone.html?gwh=4E80411E28C233B49C1C6DACD0AC
588A, [http://perma.law.harvard.edu/0B7ZX13MLDz].
The photograph was the same one that had been printed
on the first page of the Sunday *New York Times* following
the bombing, along with a profile of Tsarnaev. *Morning
Edition*, NATIONAL PUBLIC RADIO, July 18, 2013. *Rolling
Stone's* account described Tsarnaev as a "monster." Janet
Reitman, *Jahar's World*, ROLLING STONE, July 17, 2013,

available at http://www.rollingstone.com/culture/news/
jahars-world-20130717, [http://perma.law.harvard.edu/
0NF1Si8QCpH].

13. Theodore Sorensen, *Political Perspective: Who Speaks for
the National Interest?, in* THE TETHERED PRESIDENCY 13
(Thomas M. Franck ed., 1981).

14. "Never was so much owed by so many to so few." Winston
Churchill, Speech at the House of Commons: The Few (Aug.
20, 1940).

15. *See* pages 22–24.

16. John Rizzo, the CIA's former general counsel, reports
that "virtually every serious journalist" working on classified national security stories customarily calls the CIA's
public affairs office to give the Agency an opportunity to
vet details in a proposed news story. When an "irrespon-
sible and sneaky" *New York Times* reporter, James Risen,
declined to do so, Risen and his boss were "summoned"
to the White House. The *Times* "ultimately agreed to spike
the story." JOHN RIZZO, COMPANY MAN: THIRTY YEARS
OF CONTROVERSY AND CRISIS IN THE CIA 229 (2014). The
Obama White House, similarly, tried to kill David Sanger's
Times story on Stuxnet; this time the *Times* refused to capit-
ulate. ROBERT M. GATES, DUTY: MEMOIRS OF A SECRETARY
AT WAR 328–29 (2014).

A reporter new to the White House assignment—and to
the meaning of "off the record"—let slip something that,
not surprisingly, was not widely reported. Catherine Anaya
recounted an off-the-record coffee with Press Secretary Jay
Carney.

> And then he also mentioned that a lot of times, unless
> it's something breaking, the questions that the report-
> ers actually ask—the correspondents—they are
> provided to him in advance. So then he knows what
> he's going to be answering and sometimes those cor-
> respondents and reporters also have those answers

printed in front of them, because of course it helps when they're producing their reports for later on. So that was very interesting.

The White House promptly denied it. Daniel Halper, *Reporter: WH Press Secretary Gets Questions from Reporters Before Press Briefing*, THE WEEKLY STANDARD, Mar. 20, 2014, http://m.weeklystandard.com/blogs/reporter-wh-press-secretary-gets-questions-reporters-press-brief-ing_785607.html.

17. Eric Alterman, *Think Again: Why Didn't the Iraq War Kill "The Liberal Media"?*, CENTER FOR AMERICAN PROGRESS (Apr. 4, 2013), http://www.americanprogress.org/issues/media/news/2013/04/04/59288/why-didnt-the-iraq-war-kill-the-liberal-media/, [http://perma.law.harvard.edu/ 0pY4zq8VYFx].

18. *Id.*

19. Eugene J. McCarthy, U.S. Senator (1968), EIGEN'S POLITICAL & HISTORICAL QUOTATIONS, http://politicalquotes.org/node/39560, [http://perma.law.harvard.edu/04fS3UAZxTE].

20. For an argument along these lines, *see* JACK GOLDSMITH, POWER AND CONSTRAINT: THE ACCOUNTABLE PRESIDENCY AFTER 9/11, at 57 (2012) ("The press's many revelations about the government's conduct of the war were at the foundation of all of the mechanisms of presidential accountability after 9/11. They informed the public and shaped its opinions, and spurred activists, courts, and Congress to action in changing the government's course.").

21. "The autonomy of [public] discussions is an important element in the idea of public opinion as a democratic legitimation," Mills noted. C. WRIGHT MILLS, THE POWER ELITE 299 (1956).

22. *Id.* at 266. But "the problem is the degree to which the public has genuine autonomy from instituted authority." *Id.* at 303.

23. *See* pages 22 and 43.

24. *See* MILLS, *supra* note 21, at 299, 303, 305.

25. For an argument along these lines, *see* ERIC A. POSNER & ADRIAN VERMEULE, THE EXECUTIVE UNBOUND: AFTER THE MADISONIAN REPUBLIC (2010).

26. *See id.*

27. This was the solution of Crossman, writing in 1963. BAGEHOT, *supra* note 1, at 56.

28. Lest this scenario be dismissed as fanciful, consider the reaction of one in a position to appreciate the pressures generated by such events. General Tommy Franks headed the U.S. Central Command at the time of the September 11 attacks. In a 2003 interview, Franks reflected on what would happen in the event of another significant terrorist attack. "[T]he Constitution will likely be discarded in favor of a military form of government," he said. The result would be that "the Western world, the free world, loses what it cherishes most, and that is freedom and liberty we've seen for a couple of hundred years. . . ." Marvin R. Shanken, *General Tommy Franks: Marvin R. Shanken conducts an exclusive interview with America's top general in the war on terrorism*, CIGAR AFICIANADO, Nov./Dec. 2003, http://www. cigaraficionado.com/webfeatures/show/id/6180.

29. Joy Wilke & Frank Newport, *Fewer Americans Than Ever Trust Gov't to Handle Problems*, GALLUP POLITICS, Sept. 22, 2013, *available at* http://www.gallup.com/poll/164393/ fewer-americans-ever-trust-gov-handle-problems.aspx, [http://perma.law.harvard.edu/0HPh1ECRDPL].

30. Zeke J. Miller, *TIME POLL: Support for Snowden—and His Prosecution*, TIME, June 13, 2013, *available at* http:// swampland.time.com/2013/06/13/new-time-poll-support-for-the-leaker-and-his-prosecution/, [http:// perma.law.harvard.edu/0ndPYmXw2hP].

31. John Bacon & William M. Welch, *Security Clearances Held by Millions of Americans*, USA TODAY, June 10, 2013, http://www.usatoday.com/story/news/2013/06/09/

government-security-clearance/2406243/, [http://perma. law.harvard.edu/0t3EVpNVYQD].

32. Jonathan Weisman, *I.R.S. Apologizes to Tea Party Groups over Audits of Applications for Tax Exemption*, N.Y. TIMES, May 10, 2013, http://www.nytimes.com/2013/05/11/ us/politics/irs-apologizes-to-conservative-groups-over-application-audits.html?pagewanted=all, [http://perma. law.harvard.edu/0WJfsh2fyc].

33. *See* GEOFFREY R. STONE: PERILOUS TIMES: FREE SPEECH IN WARTIME: FROM THE SEDITION ACT OF 1798 TO THE WAR ON TERRORISM (2005).

34. *See* CHRISTOPHER FINAN: FROM THE PALMER RAIDS TO THE PATRIOT ACT: A HISTORY OF THE FIGHT FOR FREE SPEECH IN AMERICA (2008).

35. *See* MARTHA MINOW: BETWEEN VENGEANCE AND FORGIVENESS: FACING HISTORY AFTER GENOCIDE AND MASS VIOLENCE (1999).

36. For a comprehensive account, *see* ANDREW RUDALEVIGE, THE NEW IMPERIAL PRESIDENCY: RENEWING PRESIDENTIAL POWER AFTER WATERGATE 57–100 (2006).

37. *See* LOUIS FISHER, THE CONSTITUTION AND 9/11: RECURRING THREATS TO AMERICA'S FREEDOMS 188–210 (2008); DAVID COLE & JULES LOBEL, LESS SAFE, LESS FREE: WHY AMERICA IS LOSING THE WAR ON TERROR 107–28 (2007).

38. One response to the potential re-emergence of such threats is the maintenance of governmental "watch lists." The "vast and secret world of terrorism watch lists," the *New York Times* reported,

> currently contains almost 900,000 names scattered among as many as a dozen lists. The no-fly list, which consisted of 16 names before Sept. 11, 2001, had approximately 21,000 names as of early 2012. . . . The government doesn't reveal listing criteria or the evidence it relies on to put people on the lists. For those who believe they have been improperly added, removal

is a long, obscure process that requires appealing to the authorities responsible for creating the list in the first place.

Editorial, *The Black Hole of Terrorism Watch Lists*, N.Y. TIMES, Dec. 15, 2013, http://www.nytimes.com/2013/12/16/opinion/the-black-hole-of-terrorism-watch-lists.html#h[TgdAlo,1]. *See also* Anya Bernstein, *The Hidden Costs of Terrorism Watch Lists*, 61 BUFFALO L. REV. 461 (2013), http://www.buffalolawreview.org/past_issues/61_3/Bernstein.pdf.

39. MACKUBIN THOMAS OWENS, US CIVIL-MILITARY RELATIONS AFTER 9-11: RENEGOTIATING THE CIVIL-MILITARY BARGAIN 80 (2011).

40. *See* pages 13–14.

41. In a 2013 speech to the University of New Hampshire, Justice Souter suggested that the greatest threat to America's republican form of government will come not from foreign invasion or a military coup but from what he described as "the pervasive civic ignorance" of Americans today. He continued:

> What I worry about is that when problems are not addressed, people will not know who is responsible. And when the problems get bad enough—another serious terrorist attack, another financial meltdown—some one person will come forward and say, "Give me total power, and I will solve this problem." That is how the Roman republic fell.... That is how democracy dies. And if something is not done to improve the level of civic knowledge, that is what you should worry about at night.

Margaret Warner, *David Souter Gets Rock Star Welcome, Offers Constitution Day Warning*, The Rundown, PBS NEWSHOUR, Sept. 17, 2012, http://www.pbs.org/newshour/rundown/conversation-justice-david-souter/.

42. *See* page vi.

43. THE FEDERALIST No. 51 (James Madison).

44. *See, e.g.,* James G. Carr, *A Better Secret Court,* N.Y. TIMES, July 22, 2013, http://www.nytimes.com/2013/07/23/opinion/a-better-secret-court.html?gwh=CBAFAFA2402FF2971D6B6B8812015EF6, [http://perma.law.harvard.edu/0XR6SHkae8Z]; Editorial board, *Reforming the FISA Court,* WASH. POST, July 23, 2013, http://articles.washingtonpost.com/2013-07-23/opinions/40859606_1_fisc-fisa-court-appointed-judges, [http://perma.law.harvard.edu/0VDEFpeV4hR]; Editorial board, *More Independence for the FISA Court,* N.Y. TIMES, July 27, 2013, http://www.nytimes.com/2013/07/29/opinion/more-independence-for-the-fisa-court.html?gwh=3FBECEFF516E9AD223A555467197B941, [http://perma.law.harvard.edu/0Zga1CvYLPr].

45. *See, e.g.,* MICHAEL J. GLENNON, CONSTITUTIONAL DIPLOMACY (1990).

46. When British Foreign Secretary Robin Cook told U.S. Secretary of State Madeleine Albright that he had "problems with our lawyers" about attacking Yugoslavia without U.N. Security Council approval, she responded: "Get new lawyers." James P. Rubin, *Countdown to a Very Personal War,* THE FINANCIAL TIMES, Sept. 30/Oct. 1, 2000, at ix.

47. North Atlantic Treaty, Apr. 4, 1949, 63 Stat. 2241, T.I.A.S. No. 1964, 34 UNTS 243.

48. *See generally* MICHAEL J. GLENNON, THE FOG OF LAW: PRAGMATISM, SECURITY, AND INTERNATIONAL LAW (2010); MICHAEL J. GLENNON, LIMITS OF LAW, PREROGATIVES OF POWER: INTERVENTION AFTER KOSOVO (2001).

49. United Nations, Security Council Resolution 1973, S/RES/1973 (17 March 2011).

50. *Obama's Remarks on Libya,* N.Y. TIMES, Mar. 28, 2011, http://www.nytimes.com/2011/03/29/us/politics/29prexy-text.html?pagewanted=all.

51. *Id.*

52. *Id.*
53. *Id.*
54. Barack Obama, David Cameron, & Nicholas Sarkozy, *Libya's Pathway to Peace,* N.Y. TIMES, Apr. 14, 2011, http://www.nytimes.com/2011/04/15/opinion/15iht-edlibya15.html.
55. *Id.* The trust of the Russians and Chinese has not been enhanced. Patrick Goodenough, *Russia, China Accuse West of Exceeding UN Resolution, Making Libyan Crisis Worse,* CNSNEWS.COM, Mar. 29, 2011, http://m.cnsnews.com/news/article/russia-china-accuse-west-exceeding-un-resolution-making-libyan-crisis-worse; Patrick Goodenough, *Russia, Angry About Libya, Won't Support Resolution on Syria,* CNSNEWS.COM, May 19, 2011, http://m.cnsnews.com/news/article/russia-angry-about-libya-won-t-support-resolution-syria.
56. *See, e.g.,* C. J. Chivers & Eric Schmitt, *In Strikes on Libya by NATO, an Unspoken Civilian Toll,* N.Y. TIMES, Dec. 17, 2011, http://www.nytimes.com/2011/12/18/world/africa/scores-of-unintended-casualties-in-nato-war-in-libya.html?pagewanted=all.
57. *My Life as a Writer,* Interview with Philip Roth, Sunday Book Review, N.Y. TIMES, Mar. 2, 2014, http://tinyurl.com/l4ewokf.
58. For an effort to inject greater vitality into public deliberation on electoral issues, *see, e.g.,* BRUCE ACKERMAN & JAMES S. FISHKIN, DELIBERATION DAY (2005); Bruce Ackerman, *Reviving Democratic Citizenship,* 41 POLITICS AND SOCIETY 309 (2013).
59. BRUCE ACKERMAN, THE DECLINE AND FALL OF THE AMERICAN REPUBLIC 144–45, 146, 177 (2010).
60. *See generally* Neal Kumar Katyal, *Internal Separation of Powers: Checking Today's Most Dangerous Branch from Within,* 115 YALE L.J. 2314 (2006).
61. Attorney General Alberto Gonzalez testified that President Bush personally intervened to halt the investigation. Neil A. Lewis, *Bush Blocked Ethics Inquiry, Official*

Says, N.Y. Times, July 19, 2006, http://www.nytimes. com/2006/07/19/washington/19gonzales.html?gwh=C7 6D59ACF61333DCF2934A12DD9A162E, [http://perma. cc/0RXnDpbGviT].

62. Charlie Savage & Michael S. Schmidt, *The F.B.I. Deemed Agents Faultless in 150 Shootings*, N.Y. Times, June 18, 2013, http:// www.nytimes.com/2013/06/19/us/in-150-shootings- the-fbi-deemed-agents-faultless.html?_ r=0&pagewanted=print, [http://perma.cc/X4TP-Y7BE]. In most of the shootings, the FBI's internal investigation was the only official inquiry. *Id.*

63. *See, e.g.*, Ryan M. Check & Afsheen John Radsan, *One Lantern in the Darkest Night: The CIA's Inspector General*, 4 J. Nat'l Security L. & Pol'y 247, 284–87 (2010) (describing how the CIA's Office of Inspector General "has generally produced better results when addressing discrete, isolated problems," but "[w]hen the largest problems surfaced, the statutory OIG did not add significant remedial value"); *id.* at 287–88 ("[W]hen it was Dana Priest who broke *The Washington Post* story about secret CIA prisons—prisons that OIG had not investigated before the story—it leads to the conclusion that intelligence insiders deem Ms. Priest (or Mr. Risen, or Mr. Lichtblau, or Mr. Pincus, or any other investigative reporter) a more effective agent of change than OIG. And not only did the whistleblower choose Ms. Priest either instead of, or in addition to, OIG, he or she did so despite the risk of being disciplined, discharged, or even arrested for disclosing secrets to a reporter.").

64. Jared A. Favole, *Inspector-General Vacancies at Agencies Are Criticized*, Wall St. J., June 19, 2013, http://online.wsj. com/article/SB10001424127887323300004578555491906 170344.html, [http://perma.cc/QP2R-WY6B].

65. Spencer Ackerman, *Pentagon Watchdog "Not Aware" of NSA Bulk Phone Data Collection*, The Guardian, Mar. 18, 2014, http://www.theguardian.com/world/2014/mar/18/pen- tagon-watchdog-nsa-bulk-phone-collection (admission by

deputy Department of Defense inspector general that his office was "not aware" of the programs before the Snowden disclosures and still was not investigating it).

66. For an authoritative account, see SEYMOUR M. HERSH, CHAIN OF COMMAND: THE ROAD FROM 9/11 TO ABU GHRAIB (2004).

67. In September 2013, ten senators asked the intelligence community's inspector general, Charles McCulloch III, to investigate the NSA's programs to collect phone call logs and Internet data. Over a month later McCulloch declined, writing that the requested inquiry would "implicate existing oversight efforts" and that "we are not resourced to conduct the requested review." Tony Rom, *Intel IG Rebuffs Hill on Surveillance Probe*, POLITICO, Nov. 6, 2013, http://www.politico.com/blogs/under-the-radar/2013/11/intel-ig-rebuffs-hill-on-surveillance-probe-176929.html.

68. *See* Seymour M. Hersh, *Huge CIA Operation Reported in U.S. Against Antiwar Forces, Other Dissidents in Nixon Years*, N.Y. TIMES, Dec. 22, 1974, at 1, *available at* http://www.nytimes.com/packages/pdf/politics/19741222_hersh.pdf, [http://perma.law.harvard.edu/04dZrUMehPL]; Seymour M. Hersh, *Underground for the C.I.A. in New York*, N.Y. TIMES, Dec. 29, 1974, http://select.nytimes.com/gst/abstract.html?res=FA0C11FD355F107A93CBAB1789D95 F408785F9, [http://livepage.apple.comperma.law.harvard. edu/0qNKSzFYoGP].

69. Exec. Order No. 11,828, 40 Fed. Reg. 1219 (1975).

70. *See Members of Panel in Study on C.I.A.*, June 11, 1975, at 21, *available at* ProQuest Historical Newspapers.

71. WILLIAM COLBY, HONORABLE MEN: MY LIFE IN THE CIA 400 (1978).

72. *Id.*

73. SELECT COMM. TO STUDY GOVERNMENTAL OPERATIONS, INTERIM REPORT: ALLEGED ASSASSINATION PLOTS INVOLVING FOREIGN LEADERS, S. REP. NO. 94-465, at 2 (1975) ("Although the Rockefeller Commission initiated an

inquiry into reported assassination plots, the Commission declared it was unable, for a variety of reasons, to complete its inquiry."").

74. Referring to the NSA surveillance programs, President Obama said on June 7, 2013, that "my team evaluated them. We scrubbed them thoroughly. We actually expanded some of the oversight...." He concluded: "You can complain about Big Brother and how this is a potential program run amok, but when you actually look at the details, then I think we've struck the right balance." Statement by the President, Fairmont Hotel, San Jose, California, June 7, 2013, http://www.whitehouse.gov/the-press-office/2013/06/07/statement-president. Obama as a candidate had suggested that security and freedom are not in tension, criticizing President Bush's "false choice between the liberties we cherish and the security we provide." Peter Baker, *Obama's Path From Critic to Overseer of Spying*, N.Y. TIMES, Jan. 15, 2014, http://www.nytimes.com/2014/01/16/us/obamas-path-from-critic-to-defender-of-spying.html.

75. The media widely referred to the group as an independent, outside body, implying its detachment from insider influence. *See, e.g.*, *Would New NSA Oversight Recommendations Adversely Slow Down Intelligence?*, PBS NEWSHOUR, Dec. 18, 2013, http://www.pbs.org/newshour/bb/government_programs-july-dec13-surveillance_12-18/.

76. This ad hoc panel is not to be confused with the Privacy and Civil Liberties Oversight Board (PCLOB), an agency set up by Congress in 2004 in response to the recommendation of the 9/11 Commission. On January 23, 2014, it issued a report highly critical of the NSA's telephony data collection program, suggesting that the program is not authorized by section 215 of the PATRIOT Act (or by congressional action that delayed its termination); that the program violates the Electronic Communications Privacy Act; that the program is of doubtful constitutionality; that the program has

shown minimal value in safeguarding the nation from terrorism; and that the program poses grave risks to constitutionally protected individual rights. *See* Privacy and Civil Liberties Oversight Board, REPORT ON THE TELEPHONE RECORDS PROGRAM CONDUCTED UNDER SECTION 215 OF THE USA PATRIOT ACT AND ON THE OPERATIONS OF THE FOREIGN INTELLIGENCE SURVEILLANCE COURT, Jan. 23, 2014, http://www.pclob.gov/SiteAssets/Pages/default/ PCLOB-Report-on-the-Telephone-Records-Program. pdf. *See also* Charlie Savage, *Watchdog Report Says N.S.A. Program Is Illegal and Should End*, N.Y. TIMES, Jan. 23, 2014, http://www.nytimes.com/2014/01/23/us/politics/ watchdog-report-says-nsa-program-is-illegal-and-should-end.html. Obama announced his own proposed changes on January 17, a week before the PCLOB issued its report. Mark Landler & Charlie Savage, *Obama Outlines Calibrated Curbs on Phone Spying*, N.Y. TIMES, Jan. 17, 2014, http:// www.nytimes.com/2014/01/18/us/politics/obama-nsa. html.

77. The Associated Press described the members' backgrounds:

> Four of the five review panel members previously worked for Democratic administrations: Peter Swire, former Office of Management and Budget privacy director under President Bill Clinton; Michael Morell, Obama's former deputy CIA director; Richard Clarke, former counterterrorism coordinator under Clinton and later for President George W. Bush; and Cass Sunstein, Obama's former regulatory czar. A fifth panel member, Geoffrey Stone of the University of Chicago, leads a university committee looking to build Obama's presidential library in Chicago and was an informal adviser to Obama's 2008 presidential campaign.... Stone wrote in a July op-ed that the NSA surveillance program that collects the phone records of every American every day is constitutional.

Obama's Independent Spying Review Team Is Closely Tied to White House, Fox News, Sept. 22, 2013, http://www. foxnews.com/politics/2013/09/22/obama-independent-spying-review-team-is-closely-tied-to-white-house/?intcmp=latestnews, [http://perma.cc/UW7D-8HZU]. Sunstein and Stone both were colleagues of Obama on the faculty of the University of Chicago Law School. Am. Assn. of Law Schools, The AALS Directory of Law Teachers 2000–2001, at 1021, 1032 (2000). Sunstein is a "close friend" of President Obama. John M. Broder, *Powerful Shaper of U.S. Rules Quits, with Critics in Wake*, N.Y. Times, Aug. 3, 2012, http://www.nytimes.com/2012/08/04/ science/earth/cass-sunstein-to-leave-top-regulatory-post. html. He is married to Samantha Power, U.S. Ambassador to the United Nations and a former senior director on the staff of Obama's National Security Council.

78. *Id.*

79. *Id.*

80. The closest that it came was to assert that it "found no evidence of illegality or other abuse of authority *for the purpose of targeting domestic political activity." Id.* at 76 (emphasis added). Whether it found such evidence with respect to other purposes, or whether it even looked for such evidence, it did not say. Nor did it say whether it found such evidence with respect to the political activity of U.S. persons that occurs not domestically but abroad, which is under at least some circumstances still constitutionally protected. *See* Haig v. Agee, 453 U.S. 280 (1981). Apparently the panel did not look at the NSA's "customer" agencies, such as the FBI, ICE, or TSA, which is where such evidence would be found. The equivocation is important because, two sentences later, the panel acknowledges that "there have been serious and persistent instances of noncompliance in the Intelligence Community's implementation of its authorities." *Id.*

81. Liberty and Security in a Changing World: Report and Recommendations of The President's Review

GROUP ON INTELLIGENCE, AND COMMUNICATIONS TECH-
NOLOGIES, Dec. 12, 2013, http://www.whitehouse.gov/
sites/default/files/docs/2013-12-12_rg_final_report.pdf.

82. *See, e.g.*, Recommendation 31 (recommending "measures
that will increase *confidence* in the security of online communications" [emphasis added]). *Id.* at 37.

83. *Id.* at 3.

84. One of the panel's recommendations was that telephony
metadata collected under section 215 of the Foreign
Intelligence Surveillance Act no longer be stored by the
government, but instead be held privately for the government to query when necessary. *Id.* at 17.

85. *See* page 49.

86. *See* page 68.

87. *See* page 12.

88. Ambitions may shift slightly as seniority increases; more
senior members of Congress who have risen in seniority
to chair a committee may be able to curry favor with the
executive in the hopes of securing high-level appointment.

89. *See, e.g.*, James Stavridis, *The Dark Side of Globalization*,
WASH. POST, May 31, 2013, http://www.washingtonpost.
com/opinions/how-terrorists-can-exploit-globalization/
2013/05/31/a91b8f64-c93a-11e2-9245-773c0123c027_
story.html, [http://perma.cc/HL4G-XMXT].

90. What Senator Fulbright wrote about the military applies
broadly to the Trumanite network:

> They are in the main patriotic, hard-working men,
> but their parochial talents have been given too much
> scope in our topsy-turvy world. There is little in the
> education, training, or experience of most soldiers to
> equip them with the balance of judgment needed to
> play the political role they now hold in our society.

> We live in a time "when subtlety of mind and meticulous ques-
> tions of right over might ought to command us," he wrote,
> roles of "mentors and opinion-molders" in such matters

"are not their proper business." J. WILLIAM FULBRIGHT, THE PENTAGON PROPAGANDA MACHINE 15–16 (1971). "[I]t's good to have men like Curt LeMay and Arleigh Burke commanding troops once you decide to go in," President Kennedy said to *Time*'s Hugh Sidey. "But these men aren't the only ones you should listen to when you decide whether to go in or not." ROBERT DALLEK, CAMELOT'S COURT: INSIDE THE KENNEDY WHITE HOUSE 75 (2013).

91. FINAL REPORT OF THE NATIONAL COMMISSION ON TERRORIST ATTACKS UPON THE UNITED STATES, THE 9/11 COMMISSION REPORT 403, 418 (2004).

92. For the argument that the United States' "harmonious system" has produced a "general consensus" that would make "the father of the Constitution...smile," *see* GOLDSMITH, *supra* note 20, at 210, 243.

93. Pew Center polling data in July 2013 indicated that the public is split over the wisdom of U.S. counterterrorism policies. "Nearly half of Americans (47%) say their greater concern about government anti-terrorism policies is that they have gone too far in restricting the average person's civil liberties; 35% say their greater concern is that they have not gone far enough to adequately protect the country." *Few See Adequate Limits on NSA Surveillance Program*, PEW RESEARCH CENTER FOR THE PEOPLE & THE PRESS (July 31, 2013), http://www.people-press.org/2013/07/26/few-see-adequate-limits-on-nsa-surveillance-program/, [http://perma.cc/8RUA-H55L].

94. LESLIE GELB & RICHARD BETTS, THE IRONY OF VIETNAM: THE SYSTEM WORKED (1979).

95. THE FEDERALIST No. 51 (James Madison).

96. *Id.*

97. "Obama, like all presidents, wanted harmony. If there was anything other than that, it would get out that there had been a knockdown, drag-out fight in the Situation Room and the president would look like he had lost control of his team." BOB WOODWARD, OBAMA'S WARS 289 (2010).

98. EDWARD S. CORWIN, THE PRESIDENT 1787–1984, at 201 (Randall Bland et al. eds., 5th ed. 1984).
99. Bagehot, *supra* note 1, at 68 n.1.
100. *See* pages 8–9.
101. *See supra* note 41.
102. THE FEDERALIST No. 51 (James Madison).
103. *Id.*
104. THE FEDERALIST No. 55 (James Madison).
105. *See* THE FEDERALIST No. 55 (James Madison); Cass Sunstein, *Beyond the Republican Revival*, 97 YALE L. J. 1539, 1561 (1988).
106. Madison's view was laid out in remarks to the Virginia Ratifying Convention:

> I go on this great republican principle, that the people will have virtue and intelligence to select men of virtue and wisdom. Is there no virtue among us? If there be not, we are in a wretched situation. No theoretical checks, no form of government, can render us secure. To suppose that any form of government will secure liberty or happiness without any virtue in the people, is a chimerical idea. If there be sufficient virtue and intelligence in the community, it will be exercised in the selection of these men; so that we do not depend on their virtue, or put confidence in our rulers, but in the people who are to choose them.

J. ELLIOT, THE DEBATES IN THE SEVERAL STATE CONVENTIONS ON THE ADOPTION OF THE FEDERAL CONSTITUTION VOL. III 536–37 (1836).
107. THE FEDERALIST No. 55 (James Madison).
108. BAGEHOT, *supra* note 1, at 245.
109. *Id.* at 215.
110. VISCOUNT JAMES BRYCE, THE AMERICAN COMMONWEALTH VOL. 1, at 357 (The MacMillan & Co. 1912) (1893).
111. THE FEDERALIST No. 48 (James Madison).
112. BAGEHOT, *supra* note 1, at 113, 142.

113. JOHN STUART MILL, REPRESENTATIVE GOVERNMENT 212–13 (1861).
114. LEARNED HAND, THE SPIRIT OF LIBERTY 190 (Irving Dilliard ed., 3d ed. 1960).
115. Bagehot was particularly taken with America's New England states in this regard. "[I]f they were a separate community," he wrote, they "would have an education, a political capacity and an intelligence such as the numerical majority of no people, equally numerous, ever possessed." BAGEHOT, *supra* note 1, at 245. "[T]he men of Massachusetts could, I believe, work *any* Constitution." *Id.* at 220.
116. *Id.* at 124.
117. JOSE ORTEGA Y GASSET, THE REVOLT OF THE MASSES (1932); *see also* Michael Walzer, *Civility and Civic Virtue in Contemporary America*, 41 SOCIAL RESEARCH 593 (1974).
118. Robert Dahl, *Participation and the Problem of Civic Understanding, in* RIGHTS AND THE COMMON GOOD: A COMMUNITARIAN PERSPECTIVE 261 (Amitai Entzioni ed., 1995).
119. *See generally* ANDREW PETERSON, CIVIC REPUBLICANISM AND CIVIC EDUCATION: THE EDUCATION OF CITIZENS (2011); MICHAEL SANDEL, DEMOCRACY'S DISCONTENT (1996); J. G. A. POCOCK, THE MACHIAVELLIAN MOMENT (1975); GORDON WOOD, THE CREATION OF THE AMERICAN CONSTITUTION 1776–1787, at 46–90, 430–67 (1969); BERNARD BAILYN, THE IDEOLOGICAL ORIGINS OF THE AMERICAN REVOLUTION (1967).
120. The terms "liberal" and "republican" are used here in the classic philosophical sense, not the contemporary political sense.
121. *See* Cass Sunstein, *Beyond the Republican Revival*, 97 YALE L. J. 1539, 1566 (1988).
122. *See generally* MICHAEL SANDEL, LIBERALISM AND ITS CRITICS (1984); Isaac Kramnick, *Republican Revisionism Revisited*, 87 AM. HIST. REV. 629 (1982).

123. For the classic statement of this view, *see* BERNARD MANDEVILLE, THE FABLE OF THE BEES: OR, PRIVATE VICES, PUBLIC BENEFITS (1714).

124. *See generally* ILYA SOMIN, DEMOCRACY AND POLITICAL IGNORANCE: WHY SMALLER GOVERNMENT IS SMARTER 20 (2013); Ilya Somin, *When Ignorance Isn't Bliss: How Political Ignorance Threatens Democracy*, 525 POL'Y ANALYSIS (2004).

125. *See* VOLTAIRE, CANDIDE, OR OPTIMISM (Burton Raffel trans., Yale Univ. Press 2005) (1759).

126. For one of the earliest discussions, *see* ANTHONY DOWNS, AN ECONOMIC THEORY OF DEMOCRACY (1957).

127. In this climate it can seriously be contended—in a respected publication such as *Foreign Policy*—that the Founding Fathers, if alive today, would eagerly sit at the NSA's keyboards, peer into its monitors, and piece together the lives of their fellow citizens. *See* Stephen F. Knott, *If George Washington Were Alive, He'd be Reading Your Email*, FOREIGN POLICY, Jan. 29, 2014, http://www. foreignpolicy.com/articles/2014/01/29/if_george_wash-ington_were_alive_he_d_be_reading_your_email_founding_fathers_nsa.

CHAPTER 7

1. WALTER BAGEHOT, THE ENGLISH CONSTITUTION 262 (Cornell University Press 1963) (1867).

2. *Id.* at 263.

3. *Id.* at 263.

4. Max Weber, *Politics as a Vocation, in* FROM MAX WEBER, ESSAYS IN SOCIOLOGY 77, 128 (Hans Gerth & Charles Mills eds. & trans., Galaxy Books 2009).

5. FRIEDRICH A. HAYEK, THE CONSTITUTION OF LIBERTY 262 (1960).

6. ERIC FROMM, ESCAPE FROM FREEDOM viii, 185–86, 206 (1941).

7. IRVING L. JANIS, GROUPTHINK 13 (2d ed. 1982).

8. *See generally* Michael Reisman, *Representation and Power in International Organization: The Operational Constitution and Its Critics*, 103 AM. J. INT'L L. 209 (2009).

9. C. WRIGHT MILLS, THE POWER ELITE 215, 223 (1956).

10. Moos was Eisenhower's chief speechwriter. *See, e.g.*, Walter Pincus, *Eisenhower's Farewell Speech Has Wise Words on Split Government and Militarism*, WASH. POST, Dec. 13, 2013, http://www.washingtonpost.com/wp-dyn/content/article/2010/12/13/AR2010121304986.html, [http://perma.law.harvard.edu/0KgZdfMLYLG]. For an account of the origins and impact of the speech *see* JAMES LEDBETTER, UNWARRANTED INFLUENCE: DWIGHT D. EISENHOWER AND THE MILITARY-INDUSTRIAL COMPLEX (2011).

11. President Dwight D. Eisenhower, Farewell Address (Jan. 17, 1961), *available at* http://www.ourdocuments.gov/doc.php?flash=true&doc=90&page=transcript, [http://perma.law.harvard.edu/0RBcuRkpTny]. "Eisenhower had been in the military long enough to become deeply suspicious of how it sought to manipulate his decisions. Obama discovered the same thing, six decades later...." DAVID E. SANGER, CONFRONT AND CONCEAL: OBAMA'S SECRET WARS AND SURPRISING USE OF AMERICAN POWER 420 (2013). Mark Mazzetti has described the transformation of the military-industrial complex into a "military-intelligence complex." MARK MAZZETTI, THE WAY OF THE KNIFE: THE CIA, A SECRET ARMY, AND A WAR AT THE ENDS OF THE EARTH 5 (2013).

12. Bagehot, *supra* note 1, at 196.

13. *Id.* at 135.

14. *Id.* at 190.

15. *See* ANDREW J. BACEVICH, WASHINGTON RULES: AMERICAS' PATH TO PERMANENT WAR 29 (2010).

16. ROBERT A. DAHL, ON DEMOCRACY 186 (1998).

17. JOHN ADAMS, THE POLITICAL WRITINGS OF JOHN ADAMS 361 (George W. Carey ed., 2000).

18. Max Boot, responding to concerns generated by the NSA surveillance leaks, has written that "[a]lmost all

dictatorships throughout history have arisen when a strongman has seized power by force from a weak and illegitimate regime." Max Boot, *What the Snowden Acolytes Won't Tell You*, WALL ST. J., July 2, 2013, http://online.wsj. com/article/SB100014241278873244361045785791500 65765928.html, [http://perma.cc/0bAMpZrxNCp].

19. de Tocqueville knew this. War, he wrote, "must automatically concentrate the direction of all men and the control of all things in the hands of the government. If that does not lead to despotism by sudden violence, it leads men gently in that direction by their habits." ALEXIS DE TOCQUEVILLE, 2 DEMOCRACY IN AMERICA 625 (Harper & Row 1965).

20. James Madison, Address at the Virginia Convention to Ratify the U.S. Constitution (June 6, 1788), CONST. SOC'Y, *available at* http://www.constitution.org/rc/rat_va_05. htm, [http://perma.law.harvard.edu/0SaCmRgdSDc].

21. DAHL, *supra* note 16, at 145.

22. Thomas Jefferson, Letter to William Charles Jarvis, Sept. 28, 1820, *in* THE WRITINGS OF THOMAS JEFFERSON 160, 161 (Paul L. Ford ed., 1899).

23. *See* BEVERLY H. BURRIS, TECHNOCRACY AT WORK 21 (1993).

24. BURRIS, *id.*, at 144–48.

25. BURRIS, *id.*, at 148–51.

26. *See generally* PAUL C. LIGHT, MONITORING GOVERNMENT: INSPECTORS GENERAL AND THE SEARCH FOR ACCOUNTABILITY (1993); HUGH HECLO, A GOVERNMENT OF STRANGERS: EXECUTIVE POLITICS IN WASHINGTON (1977).

27. *See, e.g.*, BURRIS, *supra* note 23; JACQUES ELLUL, JOHN WILKINSON, & ROBERT K. MERTON, THE TECHNOLOGICAL SOCIETY (1967).

28. *See* David M. Herszenhorn, *Congressional Leaders Stunned by Warnings*, N.Y. TIMES, Sept. 19, 2008, http:// www.nytimes.com/2008/09/20/washington/19cnd-cong. html?_r=1&,[http://perma.law.harvard.edu/06tEHM6sPch]; David M. Herszenhorn, *Administration Is Seeking $700 Billion for Wall Street*, N.Y. TIMES, Sept. 20, 2008, http://

www.nytimes.com/2008/09/21/business/21cong. html?pagewanted=all, [http://perma.law.harvard.edu/ 0uES5AUR9LZ]; *see* SIMON JOHNSON & JAMES KWAK, 13 BANKERS: THE WALL STREET TAKEOVER AND THE NEXT FINANCIAL MELTDOWN 207, 222, 231 (2010).
29. Michael J. Glennon, *Investigating Intelligence Activities: The Process of Getting Information for Congress, in* THE TETHERED PRESIDENCY: CONGRESSIONAL RESTRAINTS ON EXECUTIVE POWER 152 (Thomas M. Franck ed., 1981).
30. *See generally* Neil M. Richards, *The Dangers of Surveillance,* 126 HARV. L. REV. 1934, 1935 (2013).

INDEX

ABM (anti-ballistic missile
system), 1, 2, 9, 43,
130n38, 151n115
Abrams, Eliot, 211n49
Abu Ghraib, 103
Accountability, 7, 23, 116
ACH. *See* Alternative competing
hypotheses
Acheson, Dean, 11, 16, 33, 58,
137n6, 139n46, 184n176
Ackerman, Bruce, 187n196,
221nn58–59
ACLU v. Clapper, 169–170n97
Acree v. Republic of Iraq, 162n36
Adams, John, 115, 232n17
Afghanistan, 9, 17, 19, 25, 63, 64,
121n8, 121n10, 123n15,
124n20, 208n25
Air Force, U.S., 62
Al-Awlaqi, Anwar, 2, 123n16
Alexander, Keith, 72n318
Alien and Sedition Acts, 97
Alito, Samuel, 42
Allison, Graham, 73, 76, 80, 192–
193n239, 206n2, 206n4,
207n8, 209nn27–28,
210n39, 210n41, 211n46,
211n50, 212n60
Al Qaeda, 120n3, 170n104,
186n191
cost of 9/11 attacks by, 21

drone strikes on, 119n1
Alternative competing
hypotheses, 88–90, 206n5
and claims of unicausality, 89
and logical discreteness of,
88–89
summary and benefits of, 88
Amish, Justin, 200n305, 72
Anaya, Catherine, 215n16
Anti-ballistic missile system. *See*
ABM
AP (Associated Press), 3, 49, 89
Army, U.S. *See also* Intelligence
oversight; *Laird v. Tatum*;
Pentagon; Surveillance
surveillance of American
civilians, 40, 46
Ashcroft, John, 67, 171n105
Associated Press. *See* AP
Augustus, 186–187n193
AUMF (Authorization to Use
Military Force, 2001 law),
33, 50
Austria, 206n5
Authorization to Use Military
Force (AUMF, 2001 law),
33, 50
Autocracy, 7, 219n41

Bacevich, Andrew, 158n31,
232n15